The Book of the
KING ARTHUR
4-6-0s

By Richard Derry

Irwell Press

For Roger Burfitt, old school chum
and fellow devotee of the Arthurs

First published in the United Kingdom in 2008
by Irwell Press Limited, 59A, High Street, Clophill,
Bedfordshire MK45 4BE
Printed by Charlesworth Print, Wakefield

Contents

Acknowledgements

The Arthurs were either greater in number or ran for longer than any other Southern class of express locomotive and much has been written about this legendary (in more than one sense) class, with some efforts better than others. I can only proffer mine in the usual 'Book Of' spirit of adding a few bricks to the wall of knowledge while fixing a bit of mortar here and there. Newly polished nuggets are there in the works records, trawled from the Public Record Office (now the National Archives – hard to stop calling it the PRO) and the National Railway Museum, York. As usual I have relied on a number of authorities to grasp the wheel from my hands at critical points, avoiding a plunge over the cliff. Here my thanks must go principally to Eric Youldon, who with others corrected many slips and errors; what he does with all the banana skins collected from my path I will never know. Without him and the help of the following... I don't know. Jim Aston, Ian Sixsmith, Peter Swift, Robert Stevenson, Roger Merry-Price, George Reeve and Allan C. Baker.

Bibliography

S C Townroe *The Arthurs, Nelsons and Schools of the Southern* (Ian Allan); Gavin Bowie *Built at Eastleigh* Revised edition (Waterfront Publications); Brian Haresnape *Maunsell Locomotives* (Ian Allan); Brian Haresnape *Drummond Locomotives* (Ian Allan); D L Bradley *Locomotives of the LSWR Part Two* (RCTS); D L Bradley *An Illustrated History of LSWR Locomotives: The Drummond Classes* (Wild Swan); D L Bradley *An Illustrated History of LSWR Locomotives: The Urie Classes.* (Wild Swan); R Derry *The Book of the Schools 4-4-0s* (Irwell Press); R Derry *The Book of the Lord Nelson 4-6-0s* (Irwell Press); G J Gammell *Southern Region Engine Workings* (OPC); P Swift *Locomotives in Detail; Maunsell 4-6-0 King Arthur Class* (Ian Allan); C Hawkins and G Reeve *An Historical Survey of Southern Sheds* (OPC); P B Hands *BR Steam Shed Allocation. Part Nine: Southern Region Sheds, What Happened to Steam: The Southern 4-6-0s* (Defiant Publications).
Railway Observer; Trains Illustrated; Steam Classic; Railway Magazine; Railway Engineer; Railway Gazette; various Ian Allan ABCs.
National Railway Museum, York. Southern Railway 'Wx183' (Engine Record Cards); National Archives, Kew (formerly Public Record Office) BR 9215 (Engine Record Cards); BR Southern Region Form BR9637: Return of Locomotives undergoing or awaiting repairs at Locomotive Works: week endings for Ashford, Brighton and Eastleigh.

This is how I remember 30782 SIR BRIAN, in run-down BR green, a livery that suited the class; a touch of priming has left its mark on the smokebox. Now it has its smokebox number plate and the shed code underneath reads 71B (Bournemouth). So the period is between June 1951, when the loco made its last transfer, and withdrawal in September 1962. A 'regular', it was no wonder I saw it work a good few times through Oatlands Cutting. At one time in 1959 Bournemouth shed had a small run of Arthurs, 30780-30783.

Introduction

At last I have been able to complete this final 'Book of' the Southern Railway/Region named passenger steam locomotives, the legendary King Arthurs. So far as spotting them was concerned, there was no chance of a 'full bag' as all twenty of the Urie-built engines had been withdrawn before I started my serious days of lineside loitering and tramping round sheds; indeed inroads had already started into the Maunsell examples and especially lamentable was the withdrawal of 30454 QUEEN GUINEVERE on 18 October 1958, to be cut up the following month. Indeed only thirty-two of the class got that blue if sometimes not straight and slightly smudged underlining in my Ian Allan ABC. I like to imagine, at least, that I saw more of them in the early years, watching the trains go by under 'Haines Bridge', a road bridge near our home in Weybridge, Surrey. First of all I was there in my pram in 1949 courtesy of big sister, Jean and then along with a good number of friends known locally as the 'Haines Bridge mob'. So I will never know how many Arthurs I really saw.

Bradley likes to refer to the Urie engines as the N15 class and the Maunsell-built ones as the 'King Arthurs' or 'Maunsell N15s'; these latter also included 'the Scotchmen'; that is, those examples built at North British rather than Eastleigh. Coming upon the N15s right at the end of their working lives one tended to see a lot of only a few individuals; in our neck of the woods this was especially true of 30451 SIR LAMORAK (son of 30738) which had received a General at Eastleigh as late as January 1961, eighteen months before withdrawal. The King Arthur legend had an effect on our young lives and to have engines bearing the relevant names especially 30453 KING ARTHUR, pass below us in Oatlands Cutting (which Haines Bridge overlooked) was the stuff of romance. We felt a bit privileged and superior to others elsewhere who had to make do with lesser fare.

With the class being depleted rapidly it was a challenge to see as many of them as we could, but that of course went for the Schools and Lord Nelsons too. Then suddenly at the end of 1962 they were *all* gone – all three classes that is, which was very unsettling at our tender age. Eastleigh disposed of the majority of the Arthurs very quickly though thankfully 30777 (777) survives today as part of the National Collection.

A very powerful express locomotive capable of performing the heavy work demanded...

In the previous 'Books of...' the Southern Railway/Region passenger engines the designers were Maunsell and Bulleid and of course we are back with the former in this volume. But here we have something relatively unusual in British locomotive lore, a class brought into existence by one designer which his successor was happy to 'upgrade', to use a modern term. CMEs were usually autocratic figures and men supremely confident in their own powers; they tended to be a bit new broomish when they finally gained office, throwing out the old and bringing in their own. The first class of Arthurs, the LSWR N15s, were the work of Robert Urie, the final Chief Mechanical Engineer of the London and South Western Railway (1912-1922). He had succeeded Dugald Drummond who died in office, working under him as Works Manager at Nine Elms and following him down to Eastleigh when the LSWR moved its main works south.

Urie certainly had a challenge on his hands for Drummond's later designs were not popular; famously inspiring terror in all around him he held there

Nine Elms shed on 19th September 1925 with an original Urie engine 746 (built June 1922) in front of a Maunsell engine, 774 SIR GAHERIS (built June 1925). The chimney difference is of course striking, the Urie stovepipe (with capuchin) compared with the standard lipped version on the second Arthur. 746 also has the all-round 'loop' hand rail over the smokebox; 774 has a straight hand rail but no 'single loop' (as was usual with a Maunsell smoke-box door). No steampipe visible on the Urie instead an inspection cover; no cab side number or nameplate, observe also how short the smokebox hinge straps are. For all we hear about how tidy sheds were years ago there is a great deal of ash left lying around. Photograph H.C. Casserley, courtesy R.M. Casserley.

739, later KING LEODEGRANCE, father of 454, when first fitted for oil burning in response to yet another coal strike, in June 1921, in Eastleigh Works yard with the oil tank dangerously out of gauge, you'd think, looking at those rogue pipes. Doubtless some further fitting work is in the offing. Based at Nine Elms it worked trains to Bournemouth and Salisbury before bursting into flames there; it was converted back to coal burning in the August.

Further experiments in oil firing took place after World War Two and 740 MERLIN is on shed at Eastleigh on 11th September 1948 having been converted to oil in December 1946. This time the conversion was by Government order, to save the coal the country was exporting in order to stay solvent in those desperate days. As it turned out we couldn't afford the oil either so, in somewhat sad state, 740 is waiting to re-enter the works for conversion back to coal firing, which will be complete by the end of October 1948. Note also electric lighting and the generator set to the rear of the smoke deflector. 740 sports a Maunsell boiler with a multi-plug firebox. Photograph H.C. Casserley, courtesy R.M. Casserley.

752 LINETTE (daughter of 780) was another oil conversion, from September 1947. She is in Malachite Green livery received during its previous visit to Eastleigh. The Lemaître exhaust had been fitted during the first of its visits in 1941 to Eastleigh. Conversion back to coal burning was during visit ending 25th September 1948. Note somewhat hopeful cabling running under the hand rail for the electric lights. Note upright smoke deflector.

were no bad engines of his, only bad enginemen. Drummond's attempts at producing 4-6-0s resulted in poor reputations and poor performances and it's a safe bet he never heard the old one about 'LSWR' on his 'water-cart' tenders standing for 'Lazy Swines Won't Run'. No one would have had the suicidal courage to tell him!

In the standard works on LSWR locomotives by the late D.L. Bradley and in other accounts it has been noted that Drummond's 4-4-0s were eminently successful, and he is fondly remembered for his LSWR T9 4-4-0s. His reputation is somewhat tarnished by the lack of success of his later 4-6-0s but as Haresnape reminds us, when it came to the transition from 4-4-0 to 4-6-0, with the need to work heavier trains, none of the Victorian locomotive engineers around this period, except Churchward, achieved great distinction when forced into the same position. Drummond's last design was the D15 4-4-0; ten were constructed at Eastleigh in 1912 and proved a relative success.

The irascible Drummond nevertheless earned the respect of those around him, including Robert Urie who had worked with him at St. Rollox in Glasgow before following him south in 1897. Urie moved first to address the LSWR need for reliable six coupled mixed traffic locomotives to work the ever increasing traffic. Taking office he found himself

with five Drummond 4-6-0 classes in service though these totalled only twenty-six individual locos. Two outstanding orders existed according to Swift (*Locomotives in Detail; King Arthurs*), one for five 4-6-0s and, oddly, five four cylinder 0-8-0s, though both designs incorporated 'the shallow grates and troublesome four cylinder configurations which had plagued the 4-6-0s'. Urie cancelled these orders and replaced them with one order for a less complicated two cylinder 4-6-0 classified H15. Two outside cylinders and Walschaerts valve gear established the pattern for future design: the first H15 came out in 1914 with some surviving until 1961.

The Great War and the consequent munitions work interrupted new building at Eastleigh but Urie was looking to the future and on 27 January 1916 he placed plans before the Locomotive Committee and obtained permission to construct ten express and five heavy goods 4-6-0s 'when circumstances permitted'. Drawings were assembled over the next two years but Government permission was needed to start construction and as the fortunes of War in France changed for the better this was duly forthcoming. Thus a locomotive legend was born, a class that was to last forty years and beyond with the first of the N15 order appearing at the end of August, 1918 before the Great

War ended. This was 736 with the last, 745, arriving in November 1919. The new locomotives received approving coverage in the railway technical press of the time: *To a large extent the details of the engines are duplicates of the mixed traffic which Mr.Urie designed and built in 1914. It will be noticed that the boilers have a conical ring which is placed at the front end, but that the clothing is parallel.*

With the new engines Urie introduced his own design of superheater'. *The Railway Engineer* of October 1918 noted that *The engines are fitted with Mr.Urie's 'Eastleigh' Superheater, the Detroit four-feed hydrostatic lubricator having bull's eye glasses, the Vacuum Brake Co.'s 25/20 Dreadnought Ejector, Greshams No.11 Hot Water Injectors, an exhaust steam tubular water heater on tender, Siemens' electric pyrometer for measuring the temperature of the superheated steam in cylinder steam chest, a steam boiler tube cleaner which is connected to a steam cock on the side of smokebox and the standard vacuum brake and train-heating fittings.*

The new locomotives, *The Railway Gazette* noted in October 1918, ranked as the 'heaviest of their type in the UK when complete with tenders' though the journal immediately explained that this was mainly accounted for by the tender, which was 'necessarily heavier than that ordinarily employed on the majority of railways'. The LSWR famously lacked water troughs. The cylinders, 22 inches

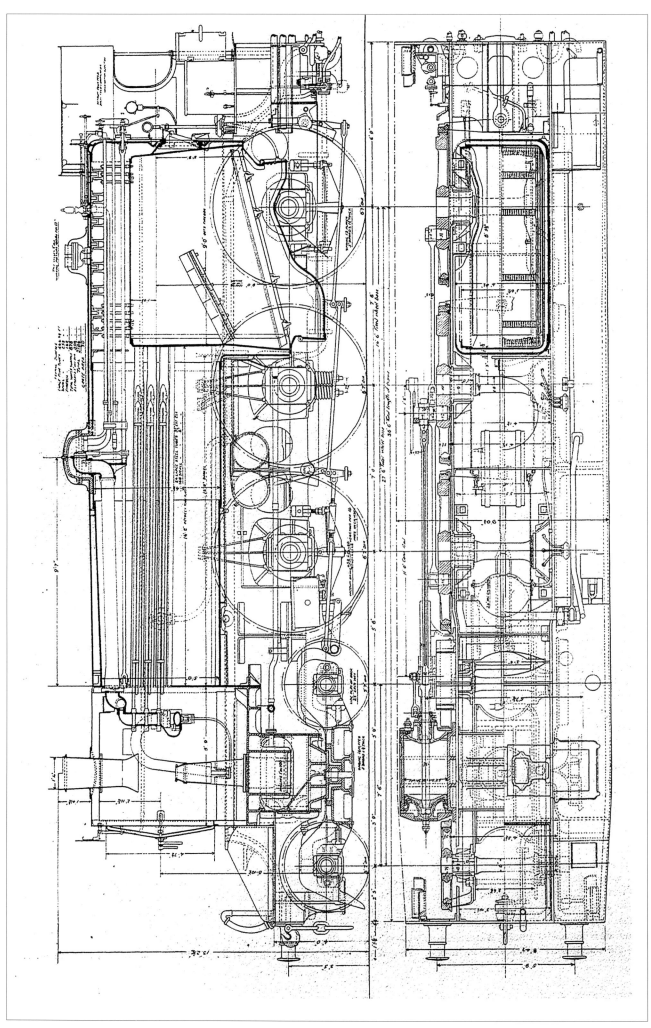

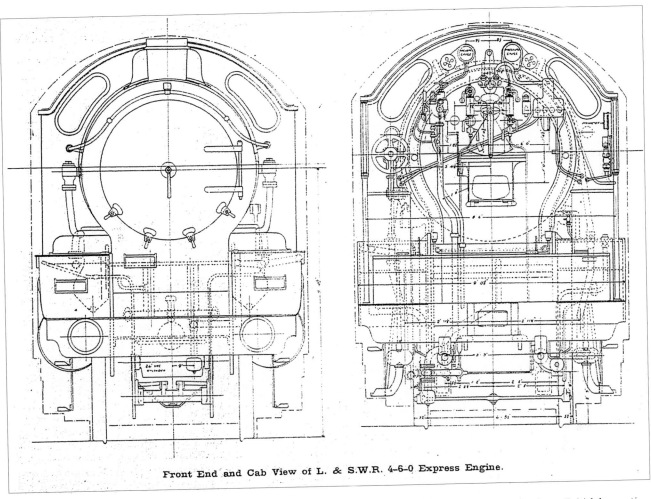

Front End and Cab View of L. & S.W.R. 4-6-0 Express Engine.

DECEMBER 13, 1918.   THE RAILWAY GAZETTE.

An objection—and it is in some degree a legitimate one—often urged against the use of outside cylinders, and especially those of large size, is that the distance between the cylinder centres is too great to allow of steady running and equalised driving effort. The tendency on the part of outside cylinder engines is to set up what is known as a " shouldering " action when the locomotive is running at anything more than the lowest speeds. This is caused by the alternate thrusts of the pistons on each side of the engine, and certainly it is, in some cases, very noticeable. It makes the engine uncomfortable to ride upon, and is not good either for the track or the structure of the locomotive itself, and therefore in the opinion of many locomotive engineers it is preferable to increase the number of cylinders and by so doing reduce the impulses imparted to the wheels and axles by individual pistons, whilst at the same time nothing is lost in the way of aggregate power development for the reason that the larger number of cylinders (individually smaller in themselves) suffice to provide the necessary tractive power for the work to be performed. It will be noticed that in this particular design the distance between the cylinder centres is 6 ft. 7¾ in. Had the cylinders been placed within the frames it would have been at the most 2 ft. 4 in., or a little more than one-third of what it at present is. The " shouldering " action referred to is a matter which cannot and should not be allowed to determine locomotive design, and speaking from experience on the footplates of locomotives with very large outside cylinders, we should certainly not think of condemning a form of construction because it included them. We have had experience of high speed locomotives with 22-in. by 28-in. cylinders, and, so far from their being unsteady or noticeably inclined to lift from the track, they were among the most comfortable from the riding point of view that we have ever travelled upon, and it would therefore seem that, given correct design in other respects, the plan of employing large outside cylinders with compulsorily wide centerings is not in itself the error that some would have us believe.

Considerable experience has been gained on the London & South-Western Railway with powerful outside-cylindered 4-6-0 type locomotives, and as in this latest design Mr. Urie perpetuates the practice, it is evident that he, at least, entertains no outstanding objection to the plan.

diameter and 28 inches stroke 'had to be mounted outside the frame and the use of two cylinders only, outside the frames, reduces big-end and axlebox troubles to a minimum and dispenses altogether with the possibility of crank axle failure'. Two of the new LSWR locomotives had already been completed and placed in service when *The Railway Gazette* deliberated in December 1918 and the pair were indeed *found to ride in excellent fashion and perform all that is required of them with ease. The tractive power of the cylinders, 24,700 lb. at 80 per cent pressure is well balanced by the 56 tons of adhesion weight.* Urie had come up with a new, striking, chimney in which *...the ordinary 'bell' top or cap is practically dispensed with. We have inspected the new chimney at Eastleigh, and to our thinking it is one of the neatest designs used on a British locomotive.* They were to be replaced by Maunsell at the end of the 1920s, to improve steaming.

From new seven of the class went to Nine Elms to work to Salisbury and Bournemouth while the other three went to Salisbury shed, which was a home for the class right up to their demise, to work east to Waterloo and west to Exeter. Another ten were ordered, 746 to 755, and delivered from Eastleigh from June 1922 to March 1923. The actual order numbers were:-

   N15: 736-740
   P15: 741-745
   L16: 746-750
   N16: 751-755

Allocation from new for 746-755 was five to Nine Elms; four to Exmouth Junction and one to Salisbury.

Urie retired in 1922 leaving his old company with three distinctive classes of 4-6-0s. The third, not yet mentioned, was the goods class S15 and very successful they were, both Urie and the later Maunsell versions. The LSWR was the largest company incorporated in the Southern Railway of which Richard Maunsell became CME. An Irishman, he had experience of English, Indian and Irish Railways before becoming CME of the South Eastern and Chatham Railway. When Maunsell took over at Eastleigh he found an outstanding order for the rebuilding of fifteen Drummond four cylinder 4-6-0s, 330-334 and 448-457, as two cylinder H15s. However,

30772 SIR PERCIVALE looking rather tired. The 5P power classification is over the middle number and 772 is chalked on the smoke deflector so this had presumably been 'off' recently. A good illustration of how the hand rail attached to the top of the smoke deflector; at the other end of the rail are those two prominent washout plugs, reminiscent of LSWR practice.

the Western section of the Southern was already replete with mixed traffic locomotives and so the second, Maunsell, group of King Arthurs came about. These were 448-457, 'rebuilt' from Drummond's G14 and P14 class of 1908-11. They were hardly 'rebuilds' in truth, utilising little more than the water cart tenders. They had the Urie coned boilers (with Maunsell superheaters) with pressure increased from 180 to 200lb. The lipped chimney was almost the most obvious difference, for even the distinctive Urie cab roof was retained. Of more note were the conventional outside steam pipes between smokebox and cylinders; the earlier Urie ones had no conventional steam pipes, only panels or plates, about six inches deep, over the top of

the cylinders. This 1925 batch of Arthurs also had a crosshead driven vacuum pump on the left-hand side; the long travel valves, increased boiler power and slightly smaller cylinders were not really visible differences though the unique eight wheeled Drummond water cart tender certainly was.

Order numbers were:

B17: 453-457
C17: 448-452

The original allocations were: 448 and 449 to Exmouth Junction, 450-452 to Nine Elms and 453-457 to Salisbury. These ten, 448-457, remained faithful to the Western section for life, never moving away from former LSW sheds.

In 1924 the powers that be determined that more passenger locomotives were required for the whole of the Southern Railway and not just the Western section. Ashford, Brighton and Eastleigh Works were fully occupied, such that there was no capacity for new construction, so tenders were sought from outside contractors in December 1924. The North British Locomotive Co. won the contract, an initial order for twenty more King Arthurs quoting £7,780 for each. In January 1925 the

order was increased to thirty. Numbered 763-792 they were delivered between May and October 1925, to be forever known as the 'Scotch Arthurs' – at least in the literature. Townroe in his *Arthurs, Nelsons and Schools* does not mention the phrase and he was never shy of an anecdote. Certainly the term, though in fact common, was never used in our lineside or platform end circles, though these, admittedly, were somewhat low in the hierarchy of such things.

Meanwhile Maunsell had decided that though the Urie Arthurs were good enough in themselves, some modification might be in order to realise their full potential. No.742, reputed to be the poorest of this group, was fitted with a smokebox personnel shelter and indicating equipment to run a series of trials between Waterloo and Salisbury in the summer of 1924. The result saw King Arthur style chimneys replace the Urie stovepipes, the area of the steam and exhaust ports was increased, exhaust clearance adjusted slightly and blastpipe diameter reduced a little, in the 'instinctive' manner (in part at least) that such alterations were conducted. By the end of the 1920s all these alterations

6

had been carried out on the Uries, 736-755, as they passed through works.

There was a gap in numbering between these Maunsell Arthurs and the Urie ones because the series 756-762 was occupied by the former Plymouth and Devonport engines and the narrow gauge locomotives running on the Lynton and Barnstaple Railway in Devon. The NBL locos did not perform quite as well as 448-457 but the outside contractors had under quoted when tendering and, it seems 'corners were cut' to save expense. Matters were serious enough for the General Manager to demand a report; certainly the deficiencies were significant. The camber on the brick arches of 763-782 were different to that specified, it turned out, and materials and dimensions varied from the drawings so that tender axleboxes ran hot. The engines suffered hot axle boxes which meant all the engines had to be lifted to have them 'forcibly removed', adjusted as necessary and refitted. All thirty boilers required some degree of caulking, re-riveting and attention to the tubes. Among other errant features the firebox staying did not follow the Eastleigh specification. It was not until they received general

repairs (763, 765-767, 772 and 783 got fresh boilers) between 1927-1929 that they could be said to have attained their full potential it was normal practice on the Southern for locomotives requiring general overhauls to receive boilers which had already been refurbished. This enabled the duration of the overhaul to be reduced.

1925-1926 saw the final order when a further batch of Arthurs were constructed at Eastleigh under works order E121. These were 793-807, ordered in May 1925; coupled to 3,500 gallon tenders they were intended for the Central section. In March 1926 a final ten, 808-817 with 4,000 gallon tenders, were ordered for the Central section but these were never built; only 793-806 were completed, with 807 cancelled, to be replaced by 850 LORD NELSON. See *The Book of the Lord Nelson 4-6-0s* (Irwell Press, 2005); the proposed Arthurs 808-817 too were cancelled, replaced by Lord Nelsons 851-860.

Completion of this final batch of King Arthurs saw the highest numbered 806 appear in January 1927. The 3,500 gallon tenders of Ashford design had higher drawgear and some alterations had to be made to the framing below the cab

to suit. Pictures of the time show this last batch, the Eastleigh Arthurs, fitted with piston tail rods as had other Maunsell designs but no other 4-6-0s. All were removed in the next few years.

Naming
The naming of the class after characters and places from the Arthurian legends was an inspired suggestion by John Elliot, the SR public relations officer. Thomas Malory's *Le Morte D'Arthur* the source for most of them and the story is well told in Townroe's *Arthurs, Nelsons and Schools of the Southern* (Ian Allan, 1973). The Urie series carried names of places and persons associated with the legends; 448-457 were named after some of the more famous Knights of the Round Table (save 453 and 454) with the remainder, 763-806, after more Knights. These were English and French, some of them quite obscure, especially if your main sources were the Saturday Morning Pictures. The plates were fitted just above the running plate, directly over the middle driving wheel and all save 453 had the subsidiary KING ARTHUR CLASS centrally below. When the original twenty Urie Arthurs were withdrawn in the 1950s twenty of

DIMENSIONS

The dimensions of locos are always of interest of course but even more so, probably, in the case of the King Arthurs. The engines were unusual in being two rather different, though closely related designs, one a development of the other, and the work of two different Engineers. There was nothing particularly out of the ordinary in this, but instead of forming separate or sub-classes they were 'assimilated' into a single group, forever differentiated by the names of 'their' CME. Meaningless to the professionals no doubt (principal visual difference was the cab) but beloved of the enthusiast now, so long after events; here are the main dimensions for comparison.

Urie Arthurs 736-755
Two outside cylinders 22" stroke x 28" diameter
Bogie wheels 3' 7" in diameter
Driving wheels 6' 7" in diameter
Wheelbase 7' 6" + 5' 6" + 7' + 7' 6" Total 27' 6"
Boiler diameter 5' 1⅜" to 5' 5¾"
Boiler length 13' 9"
Tubeplates 14' 2"
Firebox length 9'
Heating surfaces
Small tubes 167 x 2" = 1,252 sq ft
Large tubes 24 x 5¼" = 464 sq ft
Firebox = 162 sq ft
Total evaporative = 1,878 sq ft
Superheater = 308 sq ft
Overall total = 2,186 sq ft
Grate area 30sq ft
Boiler pressure 180lbs psi

Weights in working order
LSWR 1920
Bogie wheels = 21t 18cwt
Leading drivers = 18t 14cwt
Middle drivers = 19t
Rear drivers = 18t 5cwt
Tender = 57t 1cwt
Total = 134t 18cwt

Southern Railway in 1930
Bogie wheels = 22t
Leading drivers = 19t 7cwt
Middle drivers = 19t 10cwt
Rear drivers = 19t 10cwt
Tender = 57t 1cwt
Total =137t 8cwt

Building costs
736-740 £6,740
741-745 £7,765
746-750 £8,237
751-752 £7,116
753-755 £7,354

Maunsell's 'Improved N15s' 448-457
Two outside cylinders 20½" diameter x 28" stroke
Bogie wheels 3' 7" in diameter
Driving wheels 6' 7" diameter
Wheelbase 7' 6" + 5' 6" + 7' + 7' 6" = 27' 6"
Boiler diameter 5' 1⅜" to 5' 5¾"
Boiler length 13' 9"
Tubeplate 14' 2"
Firebox length 9'
Heating surfaces
Small tubes 167 x 2" = 1,252 sq ft
Large tubes 24 x 5¼" = 464 sq ft
Firebox = 162 sq ft
Total evaporative = 1,878 sq ft
Superheater = 337 sq ft
Overall total = 2,215 sq ft
Working pressure 200 lbs psi
Grate area 30 sq ft

Weights in working order

	448-452	453-457
Bogie wheels	20t 19 cwt	20t 15cwt
Leading drivers	20t	19t 16cwt
Middle drivers	20t	19t 17cwt
Rear drivers	20t	19t 10cwt
Loco total	80t 19cwt	79t 18cwt
Tender	49t 3cwt	49t 3cwt
Total	130t 2cwt	129t 1cwt

Cost of 448-457 £6,320 each

NBL 'Scotch Arthurs' 763-792
'N' pattern cabs; Ashford smokebox doors and Urie 5,000 gallon double bogie tenders affected the weight.
Weights in working order
Bogie wheels = 21t 3cwt
Leading drivers = 20t
Middle drivers = 20t
Rear drivers = 20t
Loco total = 81t 3cwt
Tender = 57t 11cwt
Total = 138t 14cwt
Cost of 763-792 variously said to be £7,780 each, or £10,085 each

Final batch of Eastleigh Arthurs 793-806
Tail-rods were fitted to these Arthurs though they were removed at the first general repair. The Ashford pattern 3,500 gallon tenders meant that the drawgear/frames at the rear end of 793-806 had to be adjusted while being built.Weights in working order:
Bogie wheels = 21t 5cwt
Leading drivers 20t 4cwt
Middle drivers 20t 4cwt
Loco total 81t 17cwt
Tender 41t 5cwt
Overall total 123t 2cwt
Cost of 793-806 £6,300 each

the new BR Standard class 5 4-6-0s based on the Southern Region, 73080-73089 and 73110-73119, carried their names but not in the same order; the first, 73080 for instance, was MERLIN, while the plates (straight, as before) did not carry the subsidiary words.

Some Life and Some Times

As main line engines of course they worked over all the important routes of the SR and in the Second World War some even went on loan to the LNER, providing for some bulging eyes on Tyneside. The Urie and Maunsell designs are dealt with as separate groups until the formation of British Railways in 1948. There were twenty Urie Arthurs, constructed between 1918 and 1923, numbered 736-755 and they were all built at Eastleigh Works, the last passenger class constructed for the LSWR. The first one, 736, was run in on the main line from Bournemouth to Eastleigh in September 1918; it undertook various trials and was then based at Nine Elms. The final engine from the first order of ten, 745, entered traffic in November 1919; it had taken over a year to produce the first ten, for the work was constantly interrupted by the lack of metals such as copper. Once completed the shed allocation was:

Nine Elms 736,738-743
Salisbury 737,744 and 745.
At Nine Elms, Bradley has recorded, there were four jobs to Salisbury and two to Bournemouth whilst Salisbury had two to Exeter and one to Waterloo. The second batch of Urie Arthurs were delivered between June 1922 and February 1923 and the initial allocations were:

Nine Elms 746-748,751,752
Exmouth Junction 749,753-755
Salisbury 750.

Poor steaming at first marred performances and some suffered frame fractures, including 736,742,743, 745 and 747. Once in office Maunsell had to remedy these deficiencies and as we have seen he had the poorest performer, 742, fitted out for tests between Waterloo and Salisbury. The alterations consequent upon this (replacing the valve gear was one of the options but the Locomotive Committee blanched at the expense)eventually saw the class gain the reputation the design deserved and a locomotive legend developed. By June 1928 the Urie engines were allocated as:

Nine Elms 738,741,742,745,748,750,752,753,755
Bournemouth 736,743
Salisbury 739,749,751,754
Exmouth Junction 737,740,744,746,747.

Early in 1929 737 and 753 were transferred to Eastleigh where they were used on that shed's Bournemouth-Waterloo turns. An excellent source of contemporary comment is of course *The Railway Magazine*, in particular the series *British Locomotive Practice and Performance* by first Cecil J. Allen and later O.S. Nock. I must thank the editor at the time of writing, Mr N. Pigott for allowing me to quote from the magazine. In November 1928 755 THE RED KNIGHT featured, in a poor light unfortunately, its work contrasting badly with later members of the class; CJA experienced a 'grim struggle' up Honiton Bank with THE RED KNIGHT nearly 17 minutes down on the schedule.

The alterations to the front ends of the Urie engines were not regarded particularly as improvements by the Salisbury men and their brethren even further west, for a feeling grew that the capacity of the Uries on the banks was diminished. Yet the Arthurs were at the top of the tree, working regular first class expresses such as the Waterloo-Exeter restaurant car train. In contrast with 755, 749 ISEULT in the October 1931 *British Locomotive Practice and Performance* is reported to have 'put up an excellent performance with a 400 ton train from Salisbury to Waterloo' which included 37 mph up Porton Bank, a speed of 76.3 mph from Basingstoke to Winchfield and 79.4 mph from Brookwood to Byfleet. From Weybridge to Waterloo it had signal checks but covered the 90 minute journey in a net time of just under 87 minutes. The Urie engines, whatever their shortcomings were well used in the 1930s and all seemed to run high annual mileages, increasing from 70,000 to 85,000 between general repairs in 1936. By early 1929 all the Urie King Arthurs were fitted with the

Brighton's E794 SIR ECTOR DE MARIS during the Southern E suffix days at Stewarts Lane shed. Photograph Andrew Westlake Collection.

E771 SIR SAGRAMORE at the same spot in equally dazzling condition. Bogie tender, NBL plate on smoke box side and coupling hung correctly unlike above. Photograph Andrew Westlake Collection.

E456 SIR GALAHAD (you can just make out the E on the tender side) in original condition with Urie smokebox door, four lugs/dogs, central dart and all round hand rail, between Earlsfield and Clapham Junction. Lamp irons protruding from smokebox with second-hand eight wheel Drummond water cart tender complete with coal rails. The location is somewhere on the former LSWR main line near London (note conductor rail on all four running lines) before July 1931 when the engine lost its E prefix.

E745 TINTAGEL (this was the castle of King Mark of Cornwall) fitted with an indicator shelter for draughting trials, designed to improve the performance of the Urie Arthurs some time in the late 1920s; something art deco in the background seems to suggest West London to me. Indicator drive lever visible from crosshead. Photograph J E Simpson/Andrew Westlake collection.

E451 SIR LAMORAK at Nine Elms, fitted with indicator shelter for trial running out on the main line, to see if any improvements could be made to the front end of the first built group of Eastleigh Arthurs. Everybody happily posing for the camera. It sounds enticing at first sight but an indicator shelter was no place for the faint-hearted. Photograph Andrew Westlake collection.

standard SR cast iron chimneys in place of the stovepipes they had been fitted with. *The Railway Magazine* of August 1935 gave the allocation as:

Nine Elms
738,739,741,742,745,748,751,752
Bournemouth 736
Salisbury 749,750,754
Exmouth Junction
740,743,744,746,747
Eastleigh 737,753,755.

One of the regular workings at the time was the 12.40pm Waterloo to the West of England turn. By September 1939 the allocation was:
Nine Elms 736-742
Salisbury 745-748
Exmouth Junction 743,744
Eastleigh 749-755.

There were some transfers at the start of the War with 741 and 742 moving to Eastleigh; 755 went to Nine Elms in February 1940 and 740 to Eastleigh. By November 1940 Eastleigh's complement was 739,740,742,744,747-754 and they covered main line goods or van trains plus a Bournemouth West to Waterloo semi-fast and a slow train, Eastleigh-Bournemouth-Weymouth; 740 was known to have worked a Plymouth-

Brighton cross country train from Exeter. Urie/Maunsell 4-6-0s were not permitted to run west of Exeter, though they could run to Okehampton from about 1950.

THE RED KNIGHT, his aplomb recovered, received a multiple jet blast pipe and chimney arrangement and it was moved to Nine Elms where it was employed in the Lord Nelson link, where it proved a strong engine, building a good reputation. It was at this period of the War that nothing larger than a King Arthur was seen on the Eastern Section of the Southern Railway. On 4 November 1940 755 was at Blandford working a special train over the Somerset and Dorset route. Late in 1940 755 again proved itself as it took a 400 ton, 12 bogie train over the Alton line unassisted, according to the contemporary *Railway Magazine*. By 1941 736, 737, 741 and 752 had been fitted with the same equipment as 755 and though they did excellent work they seemed not quite up to the same standard.

In October 1942 the LNER asked the SR for the loan of ten 4-6-0s and a number of Nelsons were offered but the LNER rejected them as too complicated to maintain. It was only after pressure was brought to bear in the right places that ten of the Urie Arthurs were sent instead, beginning with 747 ELAINE and

749 ISEULT, consigned north on the GC in a freight train the next month, November. The ten sent to the North East were 739, 740, 742, 744, 747-751 and 754. They were based at Heaton shed in Newcastle and were mainly used on goods trains to Edinburgh, Leeds, Doncaster and so on. Sometimes they worked passenger trains on such lines as Leeds to Hull, to Scarborough and on the Darlington-Newcastle stretch of the East Coast main line. They found favour in Scotland, it is said, because of the Drummond cab layout. Various reports surfaced through 1943 before their presence duly became less anomalous; the Arthurs were seen at Hull on freights while 739 for instance worked a slow passenger train from Leeds to Harrogate. All ten were noted in Edinburgh, working the same loads as K3 2-6-0s. They were familiar at Starbeck shed on goods turns and any number of services, from sundry parcels to a heavy twenty coach Edinburgh-Kings Cross train from Berwick to Newcastle. In early 1944 *The Railway Magazine* reported that the ten had been returned to the Southern but in fact they had arrived back in July 1943, going to Eastleigh shed save for 744 which was allocated to Salisbury. Their time in the North East has, famously, gone almost unrecorded by photographers. By the

E452 SIR MELIAGRANCE in its first guise, smoke deflectors yet to come; snifting valves prominent on smokebox top, running number on buffer beam with 'o' in the 'No' underlined. These ten locos, 448-457, never wandered from the Western Section; the main reason was the Urie cab which was out of gauge for the Eastern Section. Double bogie Drummond tender, coal rails in this instance yet to be filled in.

Familiar portrait of an unbelievably sparkling E802 SIR DURNORE with cabside numberplate, snifting valve protruding from the smokebox. The condition of some of these Southern locos in this era can be breathtaking. Just look at the livery and the attention to detail. The lining out is immaculate and includes the cylinders, footsteps and even the tender frames. Running number applied to tender with E prefix as well as those cabside plates. Closer inspection shows the letter A, the SR power classification, visible on the running plate just behind the buffer beam. Smoke deflectors were fitted in September 1928. Piston tail rod visible. Smokebox door hand rail is long (later shortened).

30743 LYONESSE ex-works in June 1949 at Eastleigh shed. This was the last repaint of a Urie Arthur in Malachite Green. Blank tender and black deflector and wheels. The boiler is Maunsell 797. Photograph R.K. Blencowe.

A beautifully turned out 800 SIR MELEAUS DE LILE on 6th September 1949 leaving Cannon Street on the 5.40pm to Ashford. Nearly a year after nationalisation the engine is still in SR black but with green driving wheels. Apparently a shortage of the malachite green at Eastleigh led to four emerging thus. It was not until the autumn of 1949 that it got the BR green, numbering, and the removal of the snifting valves. At the time it was based at Hither Green which took great pride in 'their Arthur'; hence the sparkling condition seen here. The strange 'ghost' SOUTHERN is due to earlier lettering showing through. Photograph J.H. Aston.

E771 SIR SAGRAMORE on the Dover turntable, the castle in the background. The Arthur had been at Stewarts Lane from new in 1925. Fully lined Southern livery including the footsteps with the A power classification just behind the buffer beam. Running number on both tender and cabside and those awkward 'wing' lamp brackets on the side of the smokebox. The North British works plate (23217) sits just above the steampipe. This was later covered over when smoke deflectors were fitted and might have been discarded when a new smokebox was required. The loco later spent three separate periods at Dover shed (see The Record). Photograph Andrew Westlake collection.

Glorious scene at Waterloo station on 26th September 1936. On the left is H15 476, its Urie origins displayed by the conical smokebox door; Maunsell Arthur 785 SIR MADOR DE LA PORTE (of the door? better than 'plume de ma tante' I suppose). Very similar in appearance, the H15 has the hand rail on the top of the smokebox and the N15 the horizontal hand rail on the smokebox door. Both have the prominent snifting valves on the smokebox and the lamp irons re-arranged 'inwards'. The headcode on 785 (half tail lamp, half route indicator) indicates a Waterloo-Bournemouth express while the H15, on duty 38, appears to be on a Waterloo-Southampton Terminus train. At the time 785 was a Bournemouth engine while the H15 could have been at Nine Elms or Eastleigh. The scene is set off by the schoolboy observer with uniform - cap and socks but - hands in his pockets, what would the teachers have said? 'No' on the buffer beam has the 'dot under the dash', such a nice touch.

One of the higher numbered Arthurs, 801 SIR MELIOT DE LOGRES still in Southern livery and lettering, on 23rd April 1949 at the Ashford coal stage, the tender replenished. There's Malachite Green under that grime; at its next General (or 'A') overhaul in July 1949 it was renumbered and kept the same livery. BR Green was not applied until March 1951. Note hoods above cab spectacles, evidently fitted to all Arthurs during the middle 1930s. Photograph J.H. Aston.

spring of 1945 the Uries were disposed thus:
Nine Elms 755
Salisbury 744-746
Exmouth Junction 738, 753
Eastleigh 736, 737, 739-743, 747-752, 754.

One working in 1945 involved Salisbury or Eastleigh engines on a through train from Southampton to Newcastle via Basingstoke and Banbury via Oxford with the SR engines working as far as Woodford Halse and Hinton on the LNER. Among those noted were 739,744,746 and 754. Before the formation of British Railways in 1948 five of the class were involved in the famously abortive oil burning programme (740,745,748,749 and 752) which carried on into BR days but they were all converted back to coal before the end of 1948.
Allocation (BR numbers) 1/1/48:
Nine Elms 30738, 30742, 30753, 30755
Bournemouth 30736, 30743
Eastleigh 30737, 30739-30741, 30745, 30748-30752, 30754
Salisbury 30744, 30746
Exmouth Junction 30747.

The photographer Derek Cross was a fan of the class and felt that they 'worked 500 ton trains over that terrible saw tooth line west of Salisbury with consummate ease and when given the chance of the flatter stretches towards London they would run like the wind'.

The Maunsell Engines
The first Arthurs built under Maunsell were 448-457 (nominally rebuilds of a Drummond class) and 763-806, between 1925 and 1927. First sheds of the first batch were:

Exmouth Junction 448, 449
Nine Elms 450-452
Salisbury 453-457.

These ten engines spent their working lives on the Western Section where, it is safe to say, performance, especially west of Salisbury, was perfectly satisfactory. However the next lot, the 'Scotch' Arthurs 763-793, proved disappointing when first in service. After running in on the former LSWR main line 763-772 went to Stewarts Lane, mainly to work the Continental Boat trains, 773-782 were allocated to Nine Elms and replaced 737, 739, 740 and 747 which moved to Exmouth Junction and 754 which moved on to Salisbury. Bournemouth got 783-792 in replacement for H15s which had not performed too well on the Waterloo expresses. After rectification to various aspects of the design, as described earlier, these Arthurs came up to scratch; as Derek Cross put it 'they didn't slip going uphill and could run like hell coming down'. The final ones, 793-806, were ordered in 1925; in April 1926 793-795 went to Stewarts Lane for such workings as the Victoria-Ashford via Maidstone East semi fasts. 796-806 were at first based at Brighton (soon to be joined by 793-795) but for a few weeks local restrictions at the London end meant they could not work into London Bridge though they hauled morning and evening commuter trains from Victoria

30747 ELAINE, completed in July 1922 so it just qualifies to have had three owners (LSWR, SR and BR). Its Urie origins can especially be seen in the 'two halves' look of the cab roof (actually merely a stifferner) and handsome bogie tender. By now in its final form with BR running number and livery this loco spent its last five years working out of Eastleigh. Spare disc for next job or a job done, no.284, hanging on the tender front.

30449 SIR TORRE with steam heating gear and screw coupling hanging in the correct position, on the coaling line at Nine Elms on Saturday 8th September 1956 before working a train back to its home shed of Salisbury. In the line up are another good looking Q1, 33018 then of Feltham shed and, bringing up the rear, a diminutive M7, 30124. Photograph Brian Morrison.

765 SIR GARETH, NBL built in May 1925, Works no.23211, hard at work on what must have been a taxing job, the Down Continental, at Sydenham Hill in September 1927. Note the lower quadrant signal and the third rail which would eventually seal the demise of steam on the SR. What (literally) sticks out is the riveting at the top of the cabside and around the cab window. The loco still has those awkward 'wing' lamp brackets and the buffer beam has the 'No' with the 'o' underlined, with dot beneath. NBL applied 'Southern' yellow serif numerals while Eastleigh was still using 'LSWR' sans serif gilt ones.

and some off peak Victoria to Eastbourne trains. They were apparently well-liked by crews but the third rail came on the scene and a lot of their duties were lost. All of the Maunsell designed Arthurs had been fitted with smoke deflectors by February 1931, 796 SIR DODINAS LE SAVAGE being the last to get them.

In 1928 E795, E796, E799 and E802 were noted in the Eastbourne district; Easter Sunday of the same year saw E765 SIR GARETH work a morning Continental Boat train made up of fifteen vehicles and on the return journey E767 SIR VALENCE worked the same load. *British Locomotive Practice and Performance* in November 1928 frequently turned its attention to the engines on the Salisbury to Exeter route, such as 456 SIR GALAHAD with a minimum of 28mph at Honiton Tunnel – deemed 'an astounding feat'. Occasional visits to Reading were noted and in the spring of 1929 E804 SIR CADOR OF CORNWALL worked a Continental express to Newhaven, normally the preserve of the Brighton Atlantics. In March 1929 a two hour express was worked by E773 SIR LAVAINE in both directions between Waterloo and Bournemouth, *The Railway Magazine* announcing the 'very good news' of the reinstatement of two hour

expresses daily between Waterloo and Bournemouth in the summer. The last time this had been in the regular timetable was in 1914 before the start of the Great War.

1931 saw the Southern remove the untidy E prefix and on July 5th of the same year the 'Bournemouth Belle' was introduced leaving London at 10.30am and returning from Bournemouth at 4.50pm. The engine on the inaugural run was E780 SIR PERSANT and later the same year E797 SIR BLAMOR DE GANIS was noted on the down 'Southern Belle' near Patcham. *British Locomotive Practice and Performance* in October 1931 had a number of return Waterloo-Bournemouth runs. The Arthurs proved up to 'the high order of performance required by the present day Western Division of the Southern Railway'. Typical workings in 1932 included E806 SIR GALLERON on the 'Southern Belle', E768 SIR BALIN on a down Eastern Section Continental express, E795 SIR DINADAN on a down Eastbourne Pullman Car express and E769 SIR BALAN on the down 4pm Continental express.

In 1933 the arrival of the third rail on the Central Section meant several were on the move; allocations in January that year were:

Nine Elms 452, 773-782
Salisbury 450, 451, 453-457
Exmouth Junction 448, 449, 769
Bournemouth 783-792
Stewarts Lane 763-768, 770-772, 793-796
Ramsgate 797-806.

The Railway Magazine reported that 793-806 had also gone to Bricklayers Arms and in the year we had 797, 800, 802 and 804 on Cannon Street to Kent Coast trains, 803 on the 5.10pm Charing Cross to Folkestone, 457 worked the down 'Atlantic Coast Express' and noted on express trains at Reading were 763, 764, 766, 767, 771, 779 and 804.

British Locomotive Practice and Performance in December 1933 declared that the Arthurs on the Salisbury-Exeter route 'now show themselves capable of handling fourteen coach trains of 480 tons gross weight over this mountainous course in times which are considerably shorter than those scheduled'. Some transfers noted in May 1934 saw 770 and 771 move to Dover shed from Stewarts Lane which in turn gained 777 and 778 from Nine Elms; 770 and 771 returned to Stewarts Lane in the autumn and then moved back to Dover in 1935, staying there until 1940.

The August 1935 issue of *The Railway Magazine* listed the allocation as:

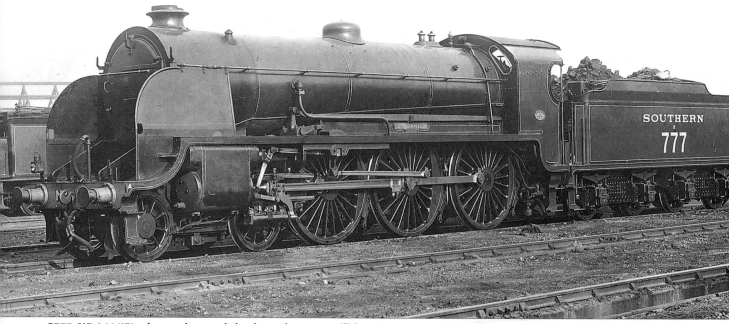

E777 SIR LAMIEL, the survivor and thank goodness we still have one to remind us of how stylish these engines were. To see them in action from my perch overlooking Oatlands Cutting in Surrey during the last days was a privilege. This is the loco prior to June 1932 when it had the E prefix removed, just visible on the tender directly above the middle 7. The loco still has the two lamp brackets sticking out from the smokebox, obscuring the view from the footplate. They had been raised when smpke deflectors were first fitted making the situation worse. Vacuum pump on cross-head prominent; all Maunsell N15s had these but they never appeared on the Uries.

In almost impossibly perfect condition, 30794 SIR ECTOR DE MARIS (father of 450) on 27th September 1952 after a Light Casual that finished on the 19th. The BR Green had first been applied in 1950. It was awaiting return to Stewarts Lane and did not become a Western Section engine until arrival at Basingstoke shed at the start of 1959. It survived until August 1960. Photograph L. Elsey.

There was always an air of neglect and scruffiness at Nine Elms and it suffered labour shortages that were endemic in London even more than the other sheds in the capital. 30765 SIR GARETH rests on one of the roads of the 'New Shed' on 22 April 1956; fine collection of fire irons in the tender; 5P power classification now in Gill sans to match the running number. The A under the number long gone. Photograph R.C. Riley, www.transporttreasury.co.uk

Nine Elms 773-776, 779-782
Stewarts Lane 763-768, 772, 778, 793-795, 799
Bournemouth 783-792
Salisbury 450-457
Exmouth Junction 448, 449, 769
Ramsgate 777, 796-798, 800-806
(Dover, with 770 and 771, was omitted).

Workings of the time included 456 SIR GALAHAD on the down ACE carrying reporting number 440; 457 SIR BEDIVERE on an Eastleigh-Salisbury goods train on the bank west of Dean and 763 SIR BORS DE GANIS on a Ramsgate-Victoria express. *British Locomotive Practice and Performance* in June 1936 tells of 'the most astonishing example of King Arthur ability on the Southern Railway yet to be seen in print', though it had actually taken place several years before. This concerned 777 SIR LAMIEL and was nothing less than a gain of seventeen and three quarters of a minute on a schedule of 90 minutes over the 83.8 miles from Salisbury to Waterloo. This run included a time of precisely 17 minutes from Basingstoke to Woking, an average of over 80 mph for the 23.4 miles distance.

The third rail reached Portsmouth in 1937 which released Schools 924-933; these moved to Bournemouth, replacing 783 and 786-792 on the Waterloo jobs. Allocation by now, July 1937, was:
Nine Elms 772-780
Salisbury 448-457
Exmouth Junction 786-792
Bournemouth 784, 785
Stewarts Lane 763-769, 781-783, 793, 794, 798, 799
Dover 770, 771
Ramsgate 795-797, 800-806.

Bournemouth retained two of the Arthurs as the GWR refused to accept Schools on through workings to Oxford. The superlatives kept coming in *British Locomotive Practice and Performance*; in June 1937 for instance CJA called two runs by the Arthurs on the up Bournemouth Ltd. 'the most remarkable ascent to Litchfield that I have ever yet seen on record with any type of locomotive'. However, unfortunately 'it could not be said that these runs are typical of working over the Bournemouth main line, which much evidence goes to prove as being very variable in quality'. At the other end of

the railway, so far as the difficult conditions of the Kent Coast work were concerned, the Arthurs had demonstrated 'complete mastery'. Late in 1937 786-792 moved to Exmouth Junction and 783 went on temporary loan from Bournemouth to Stewarts Lane. 449 SIR TORRE piloted by T9 4-4-0 727 covered 88 miles in 92 minutes on the up Atlantic Coast Express. In 1938 798 SIR HECTIMERE and 799 SIR IRONSIDE were lent by Ramsgate to Newhaven shed to work the regular and heavy summer formations of Newhaven boat expresses. On one July Sunday 798 had 13 corridor coaches and one extra van, 450 tons gross at least on an up train which according to the report was 'under easy steam'. It was an odd arrangement, for though 798 and 799 worked the Newhaven 'boats', the sharp curve into Newhaven shed prohibited the entrance of the 4-6-0s so they travelled to Brighton to turn and even spent the night on shed there.

In September 1938 *The Railway Magazine* reported an amusingly aberrant news item in *The News Chronicle*. Describing a boat train of sorts, according to the *Chron* conjured up 'a

Dear old 30451 SIR LAMORAK at home on Salisbury shed on 23rd April 1962, two months before withdrawal. During the first six months of 1962 every time I visited the lineside near home this engine seemed to appear, so it was working very regularly. Well, giving it a General in January 1961 BR understandably wanted its money's worth – and got it, I'd say. Its water cart was replaced Urie tender 3211 ex-N15X 32333 in February 1957. Photograph Gavin Morrison.

30782 SIR BRIAN, a simple name to remember for once compared with some of the French ones. In April 1947 it was one of the four repainted in black with green driving wheels and the following May was renumbered, which is the state it is in here. The numbers are in 'sunshine' including number on the front buffer beam. No smokebox number plate and SOUTHERN still on the tender. It was repainted BR green during a General at Eastleigh in October 1949 when it acquired its full BR identity. This was one of two King Arthurs that never saw Malachite Green; the other one was 800. Photograph J.H. Aston.

fine old vintage locomotive of the 'King Arthur' class weighing 115 tons, with 350 tons of Swiss Hotel financiers, high class travellers, babies, dogs, chefs and luncheons behind it'. *The Railway Magazine* calculated that 'assuming the average of 16 passengers to the ton and allowing several tons for the babies, dogs and luncheons we may assume that the passenger complement on this remarkable train was over 5,000 persons; the total weight baffles the imagination.'

Typical of the work of the King Arthurs before the War was 'The Granville' for many years, officially and unofficially, the principal afternoon down and mid-morning up Thanet expresses between Victoria and Margate, Broadstairs and Ramsgate; apparently the name derived from a famous Ramsgate hotel. The 74 miles non-stop to Margate was fraught with difficulties yet for many years it had been the preserve of 4-4-0s, the heaviest permitted engines. The new King Arthurs were something of a revolution, taking trains of new corridor stock of over 300 tons, proving masters of the task with that vital margin of power for summer weekends and specials.

Typical in the pre-war period were 452 SIR MELIAGRANCE on an SR banana train out of Southampton, 456 SIR GALAHAD on the Atlantic Coast Express at Milborne Port, 790 SIR VILLIARS on a Waterloo to Sidmouth and Exeter express, 779 SIR COLGREVANCE backing the empty stock of the Bournemouth Belle into the sidings at Bournemouth West and of course a host of related workings. In October 1939 there was a movement of engines, Nine Elms sending 772-774, 777-780, 784, 785 and 795 to Stewarts Lane and getting Lord Nelsons in return; this came about because of the outbreak of War and the consequent abandonment of the Dover and Folkestone Continental boat services. At the same time 764 and 767 moved to Dover and 798 and 799 to Ramsgate. Hither Green got 765, 768, 769, 794, 796, 801 and 806 to replace S15 4-6-0s which had been transferred to Feltham. After the fall of France in the summer of 1940 non-essential engines were moved away from the exposed sheds around the coast such as Dover and Ramsgate which were effectively abandoned for periods. The Maunsell Arthur allocation by June 1940 was:

Nine Elms 775-777, 781, 782
Salisbury 448-457
Exmouth Junction 786-792
Stewarts Lane 763-768, 770-774, 778, 780, 785, 793, 795, 799
Hither Green 769, 779, 783, 784, 794, 796-798, 801, 806
Ramsgate 800, 802-805.

The summer of 1941 saw 773, 779 and 781 at Bournemouth to cover the Schools on the London services and 772, 778, 793 and 795 moved to Eastleigh as cover for the Urie Arthurs lent to the LNER. The War of course meant restrictions both on reporting and on paper and this shortage saw thinned-down journals go bi-monthly, while locations described were often given false names. What was almost certainly Southall shed in an account in *Railways* for instance, became 'Cranford Junction'. Despite all this one or two positive references emerge; there were a 'rousing succession of maxima at Gillingham, Axminster, Honiton and 84mph at Broad Clyst' for 773 SIR LAVAINE for instance and 777 SIR LAMIEL succeeded in reducing a late start of 37 minutes from Salisbury to a late arrival of only 17 minutes at Waterloo. 'A fine achievement on this run was the 51mph attained from the Andover start, uphill three miles at 1 in 78 to milepost 62½.' The allocation by July 1943 was:

Nine Elms 766-768, 770, 771, 775, 776, 777, 780, 784, 785, 788
Salisbury 448-457, 773
Exmouth Junction 786, 787, 789-792
Bournemouth 772, 774, 781
Stewarts Lane 763-765, 769, 778, 779, 782-783, 793-796
Ashford 797-801
Hither Green 802-806.

743 LYONNESSE; King Arthur chimney fitted in 1925, smoke deflectors added in 1927 then in 1930, Maunsell superheater, Maunsell pattern cylinders and double exhaust ports. By now an Exmouth Junction engine, 743 is on Salisbury shed on 20th May 1935, perhaps waiting to work a Plymouth train as far as Exeter. Photograph H.C. Casserley, courtesy R.M. Casserley.

A lovely original Arthur, at Salisbury shed on 19th July 1924. A Urie engine with original features and still in LSWR livery, see initials on tender side. Photograph H.C. Casserley, courtesy R.M. Casserley.

What we were spared. 772 during the six years (1926-1932) it ran with the German style smoke deflectors. In fact it was a copy of the arrangement on the German 01 Pacifics. Though they worked well, thank heaven a better design was decided upon as these just did not suit the class.

A wartime edition of *The Railway Magazine* reported that on one Saturday 456 SIR GALAHAD worked the 5.55pm from Exeter into Yeovil Junction made up of 13 bogies, a large and small van plus three full milk wagons, equivalent to 16 bogies. The 1.25am from Waterloo had by now become a long and heavy train. 771 SIR SAGRAMORE was observed with it, a load of four corridors for Plymouth, a bogie van for Padstow, four corridors for Ilfracombe, a corridor composite for Torrington, a bogie van for Exeter, two corridors for Yeovil and three bogie vans for Salisbury, 16 bogies in all. It was handled 'in the best Arthurian tradition' and had additional and lengthy stops at Wimbledon, Woking and Andover; it did well to be only 18 minutes late at Salisbury where a Merchant Navy took over. By mid-1945 the allocation was:

Nine Elms 766, 770, 771, 775, 777
Salisbury 448-457, 773, 774, 784, 785
Exmouth Junction 786, 789-792
Bournemouth 772
Stewarts Lane 763-765, 776, 778-783, 787, 788, 793-799
Ashford 800-806
Dover 767-769.

767-769 had been moved to Dover to help work Army leave trains as the troops came back from fighting in Europe. Even though the big concrete shed sat by the foreshore, a tempting, vulnerable target, it had nevertheless passed the War more or less unscathed.

806 SIR GALLERON had been derailed by a flying bomb between Chatham and Sittingbourne but no Arthurs were lost to enemy action. In March 1947 the Polhill Tunnel was closed and 767 SIR VALENCE was noted on a Folkestone to Charing Cross working diverted over the Chislehurst loop.

The Arthurs, Urie and Maunsell, under BR

All King Arthurs were eventually repainted in the BR 'GW' dark green, had 30,000 added to their numbers along with the fitting of smokebox door numberplates and the removal of the snifting valves. Allocation for the complete class on 1 January 1948 (later BR numbers) was:

Nine Elms 30738, 30742, 30753, 30755, 30766, 30773, 30774, 30779, 30782, 30783, 30786, 30788, 30791, 30792
Eastleigh 30737, 30739-30741, 30745, 30754, 30777, 30784, 30785
Bournemouth 30736, 30743, 30772, 30787, 30789, 30790
Exmouth Junction 30747-30752
Salisbury 30448-30457, 30744, 30746
Stewarts Lane 30763-30765, 30775, 30776, 30778, 30780, 30781, 30793-30797
Bricklayers Arms 30798, 30799
Hither Green 30800
Ashford 30801-30806
Dover 30767-30771.

All were not repainted and renumbered straight away of course and in the winter of 1949 several were placed in store, a

practice which persisted annually until their final withdrawal. This winter saw them in store at Nine Elms, Eastleigh, Salisbury and Exmouth Junction and involved 30738, 30740-30743, 30750, 30751, 30754 and 30755, all Uries. In 1949 despite the new Bulleid Pacifics becoming available, the King Arthurs frequently predominated on Saturday main line workings east of Salisbury. It was at this time that another celebrated periodical, *Trains Illustrated*, came to prominence. Edition number 8 has an article about the Portsmouth Direct Line which described a lot of pre-war workings before the advent of the third rail; one of these involved the 9.32pm from Portsmouth with which Driver Payne on the 8½ miles from Rowland's Castle to Petersfield on one memorable night with 776 SIR GALAGARS took 10 minutes 48 seconds start to stop. 'He passed Buriton box in 8 minutes 6 seconds and down the falling grade to Petersfield he did a quarter mile at 74mph.'

By 1950 it was becoming rare for Arthurs to work the Continental Boat trains; up to fifteen had been in store because of the influx of the Bulleid light Pacifics. 30803 SIR HARRY LE FISE LAKE (then still an Ashford engine) was noted at Waterloo on, of all things, a breakdown train. A number were returned to traffic ready for the summer timetable and in the last fortnight of June 1950 30755, 30780 and 30787 of Nine Elms were noted at Exeter; the early Urie members were often handling principal

E791 SIR UWAINE in early Southern Railway days, still with the E prefix, rather small on the tender above the middle number; smoke deflectors fitted January 1928. So with the E prefix being removed in December 1931 we can date the period of the photo.

794 SIR ECTOR DE MARIS, apparently leaving Broadstairs. E prefix gone; six wheel tender for the Central Section although most of its life was spent on the Eastern Section. It did not arrive on the Western Section until 1959, bringing its six wheeled tender with it.

A near perfect profile of E794 SIR ECTOR DE MARIS with the footplate man painfully aware he is having his photo taken. Smoke deflectors were not added until May 1928, with the E prefix discarded in July 1932 and it wasn't just a case of painting it out on the tender for the 'E' was on the cabside plaque too. Once again the livery stands out and everything capable of lining seems to have been duly lined, including the footsteps and the splasher over the driving wheels. Even the power classification, the letter A can just be made out behind the front buffer beam above the front footsteps. Photograph Andrew Westlake Collection.

30450 SIR KAY at Yeovil Junction shed in BR days looks like its been in some sort of tussle – observe the distorted feed water pipe on the side – no one would dared modelling that! The two washout plugs this side are leaking badly, depositing the usual white salt staining down the side and making a mess behind the nameplate. Its water cart had been replaced by Urie tender 851 from 30737 in March 1956. Photograph J. Davenport, Initial Photographics.

Nine Elms on 30th May 1931 with the new coaler and the mortal remains of the old coal stage. E785 SIR MADOR DE LA PORTE (one of those strange names from Malory) is receiving some attention from the driver; wide variety of lamp irons, the old 'oven door handle' still on the smokebox door and that pleasant 'block' style of lettering on buffer beam. Although smoke deflectors were fitted in January 1928 those awkward lamp irons are still sticking out from the smokebox sides. Photograph H.C. Casserley, courtesy R.M. Casserley.

expresses to Bournemouth and the West Country but west of Salisbury they were mainly working stopping trains. In late August one was put on the Bournemouth Belle when the Pacific failed and 30780 SIR PERSANT took over the up working. On the introduction of the winter timetable in 1950 the SR put 142 steam locomotives into store including twenty-nine Arthurs, nearly half the class. It even stored seventeen of the much newer light Pacifics, though many were put back to work over the Christmas holiday period, when more people and goods travelled by train than they do today. Easter 1950 saw the Urie Arthurs allocated thus:

Nine Elms 30742, 30745, 30747, 30755
Feltham 30738
Eastleigh 30749, 30752
Bournemouth 30736, 30737, 30740, 30741, 30743, 30746, 30750, 30751, 30754
Salisbury 30739, 30744, 30748, 30753.

By the spring of 1951 these had been re-arranged so that consecutively numbered engines had been grouped together:

Bournemouth 30736-30743
Feltham 30744
Basingstoke 30745
Eastleigh 30746-30749

Nine Elms 30750-30755.
This was also done with the Maunsell engines so their allocation in 1951 was:

Nine Elms 30456, 30457, 30780, 30781
Salisbury 30448-30455
Bournemouth 30782, 30783
Eastleigh 30784-30790
Stewarts Lane 30763-30769, 30777-30779, 30791-30795
Bricklayers Arms 30799-30801
Dover 30770-30776, 30796-30798
Ashford 30802-30805
Hither Green 30806.

This apparently caused some resentment at Bournemouth, Dover and

Hither Green when their well maintained and clean engines were replaced by others not so well looked after. Hither Green lost 30800 to Bricklayers Arms and gained 30806 from Dover but once the shed cleaners had a go at it this one soon looked the part at the head of the shed's only passenger turn, the 5.40pm Cannon Street to Dover, with its tradition of a very smartly turned out King Arthur. The balancing working was the much less glamorous 12.50am goods. This was Duty no.182 run as below:

Hither Green 3.15pm light engine		
3.39pm	Ewer Street	5.34pm light engine
5.34pm	Cannon Street	5.47pm passenger train
7.47pm	Dover Priory	8.15pm light engine
8.23pm	Loco Yard	9.15pm light engine
	Dover Town	9.35pm goods train
10.55pm	Ashford Sidings	11.20pm light engine
11.23pm	Loco Yard	12.45am light engine
	Ashford Sidings	1.15am goods train
4.0am Hither Green Sidings light engine		
Hither Green Loco		

Hither Green men work the only 'King Arthur' duty and their only passenger train, the 5.47pm from Cannon Street to Dover Priory. Ashford men take over at 7.10pm and work back to Ashford Loco where they are relieved by Hither Green men at 11.55pm who return the engine to Hither Green Loco after working the 1.15am goods.
(From 'Southern Region Engine Workings', Ian Allan 1994, by C.J. Gammell).

Enormously dignified and almost impossibly clean and shiny, E804 SIR CADOR OF CORNWALL at somewhere on the tip of the tongue. It was built in December 1926 and got smoke deflectors in October 1928. Cabside numberplate, earlier style of lettering on buffer beam. Handle on smokebox door and all six 'LSW' irons converted by having a bar jammed in them. Firing irons stacked neatly in the tender, hooked on that pillar. Charming 'ghost' (it could be an 0-6-2T) behind in the days of long exposures.

KING ARTHUR himself, complete with proud footplateman at Salisbury shed on 30th July 1925. 453 remained at Salisbury shed all its working life. Photograph H.C. Casserley, courtesy R.M. Casserley.

Another of the Central Section locos 798 SIR HECTIMERE and another fitted with a six wheeled tender. They spent a part of their lives working out of Kentish sheds such as Ashford and Ramsgate. SIR HECTIMERE was one of the few to spend time at Hither Green. Again it did not reach the Western Section until late, June 1959, at Salisbury. This is Bricklayers Arms shed, on 25th March 1933; it illustrates a fourth place for the running number, high on the back of the tender above the vacuum pipe and below the extended lamp bracket. Photograph H.C. Casserley, courtesy R.M. Casserley.

Looking almost like a painting, brand new 453 KING ARTHUR in fully lined out Southern Livery at Waterloo for inspection. The nameplate was soon raised slightly to come flush with the top of the splasher. Coal rails on tender yet to be filled in; four 'clamps' on the smokebox door; 'wing' lamp brackets still in situ on smokebox door, prominent snifting valves.

453 KING ARTHUR at Salisbury on 28 April 1928 carrying its first set of smoke deflectors which were replaced by a standard set in July of the same year. Number plates carried on the cabside and the rear of the tender. Photograph H.C. Casserley, courtesy R.M. Casserley.

The Railway Magazine reported that twenty-six of the class had been returned to work to cover the Christmas in 1950 and *Trains Illustrated* told of unusual visitors to Guildford, including 30744, 30745, 30753, 30773 and 30777. 30745 TINTAGEL was fitted with electric lighting and Pacific type ladders at the rear of its tender, 30792 SIR HERVIS DE REVEL got multiple jet blast pipes and a large diameter chimney, 30788 SIR URRE OF THE MOUNT was fitted with a 'beefeater' spark arrester chimney but had its original one restored because the modified chimney affected its steaming adversely.

At the end of 1950 30451 SIR LAMORAK, a long-time Western Section engine normally banned from the Central Section, was under repair at Brighton Works. On 5 November 1951 30767 SIR VALENCE of Stewarts Lane worked a 'boat' from Southampton to London while on 26 September 30448 and 30453 had been noted at Guildford, where Arthurs were to become a fairly common sight, working in on special trains. On 2 December 1951 30770 SIR PRIANIUS was working tender first at Dover Marine station on the 1.30pm boat train from Victoria for the Ostend route to Brussels.

In the early spring of 1952 30777 SIR LAMIEL was in collision with a Brighton tank engine. It sustained minor damage

and was hauled dead tender first from Bricklayers Arms by 30930 RADLEY to Eastleigh. During November, KING ARTHUR was stranded away from home at Guildford shed because the rails in front of it were moved during the reconstruction of the shed.

On 24 January 1953 came the first withdrawal, 30754 THE GREEN KNIGHT; a number had once again been put into store the previous October. Another source gives the withdrawal of 30754 as 10 February but whatever the date the reason for withdrawal was cracked frames, the engine having a recorded mileage of 1,151,285. Other Urie Arthurs were luckier, 30738, 30741, 30743, 30748 and 30753 receiving heavy repairs and repaints so they could be used on the crowded summer Saturday schedules. 30754 was scrapped at Eastleigh Works. During a week in March 30455 SIR LAUNCELOT was noted shunting in the mornings at Ash station; on 30th of the same month 30795 SIR DINADAN worked a relief Newhaven boat train, a morning job from Victoria station. At this time the Merchant Navys were withdrawn for alterations and 30763 SIR BORS DE GANIS hauled a Brussels continental train which included ten corridors, two Pullmans and two vans. In complete contrast 30803 SIR HARRY LE FISE LAKE was at Ashford with a

coal train from Chislet colliery. On the South Western section on 2 August 1953 30786 SIR LIONEL banked WR 6991 ACTON BURNELL HALL on the 7pm train from Weymouth and the following SR train was hauled by 30787 SIR MENADEUKE. The 17th of the previous month had seen 30449 SIR TORRE on a typical King Arthur working of the period, a Salisbury to Waterloo semi-fast. On 22 November an unadvertised Sunday train, the 7.05pm Waterloo to Salisbury with 30752 LINETTE 'came to grief' at Woking with a faulty big end and was replaced by M7 0-4-4T 30246 from Guildford which in turn was replaced at Basingstoke by 30745 TINTAGEL. Arrival at Salisbury was 75 minutes down. The usual practice after the summer timetable ensued and seventeen of the class were placed in store. Allocation at 10 December 1953:

Nine Elms 30455-30457, 30744, 30750-30752, 30755, 30778-30781
Basingstoke 30745, 30749, 30753
Eastleigh 30746-30748, 30784-30790
Bournemouth 30736-30743, 30782, 30783
Salisbury 30448-30454
Stewarts Lane 30763-30774, 30791-30795
Bricklayers Arms 30799-30801
Ashford 30802-30805
Dover 30775-30777, 30797-30798
Hither Green 30806
Ramsgate 30796

736 EXCALIBUR specially posed, in two very different guises, rods set in the 'best' position for photography. The works grey does its job of 'etching' the detail; no nameplate as yet. The engine looks very different in Southern days, with the same bogie tender; by now named, full SR livery with large number on the tender and a small cabside badge. It carries an E prefix to the running number and an A behind the buffer beam. Stovepipe chimney. No snifting valves; these appeared on the Urie Arthurs when they were fitted with a Maunsell superheater, in the case of 736 EXCALIBUR, for instance, in September 1930. Slide bars are fluted type, as used on the first ten; the second ten had plain bars.

738 KING PELLINORE at Salisbury shed on 27 May 1929 and what a change in a few short years for here we have in full Southern livery, standard smoke deflectors, King Arthur chimney but still with 'wing' lamp irons. Photograph H.C. Casserley, courtesy R.M. Casserley.

Of the 73 members of the class working in the summer of 1954 42 were on the Western Section and the remainder on the Eastern Section with four at Ashford, four at Bricklayers Arms, six at Dover, two at Hither Green and fifteen working out of Stewarts Lane. On the Western Section they still worked through to the WR such as 30741 JOYOUS GARD photographed at Oxford on the 10.15 am (Saturday) Bradford through train to Bournemouth and Poole. They could still be seen west of Salisbury; on 12 June for instance 30751 ETARRE of Nine Elms worked to Exeter on the 3.05pm from Waterloo. At Whitsun, on 4 June 1954, a couple of double headers were at Waterloo; the 6.45pm to Basingstoke had 34020 SEATON piloting 30788 SIR URRE OF THE MOUNT and two hours later the 8.54pm to Salisbury had 34064 FIGHTER COMMAND piloting 30452 SIR MELIAGRANCE. A couple of foreign workings for the class saw 30790 SIR VILLIARS of Eastleigh working through to Leicester Central on a return holiday train from Portsmouth in October having run via Basingstoke, Banbury and Woodford Halse. At Leicester Central it ran light into a loop alongside V2 60862, Black Five 45219 and 6942 ESHTON HALL, a rare grouping indeed.

In April 1955 *British Locomotive Practice and Performance* compared 30768 SIR BALIN with a Bulleid Pacific, 34066 SPITFIRE on the 24.3 miles from Bromley South to Chatham via Swanley concluding that there was 'very little indeed to choose between (the two

runs)'. 34066 completed the 32 miles in 25mins 30secs while 30768 took just 25secs more; maximum on the descent from Sole Street was 75mph, not bad for a veteran. On 30 March one of the Nine Elms Urie Arthurs was noted west of Salisbury, 30752 LINETTE on the 12.36pm Salisbury to Exeter. In the June Stewarts Lane acquired the first of a planned twenty-five BR Standard Class 5 4-6-0s to replace its King Arthurs. The first arrivals were 73080-73082 and the idea was to move some of its Arthurs to Eastleigh, retaining the six wheel tender engines and the pride of the place, 30768 SIR BALIN. In the summer 30768 was in beautiful condition when it visited Dover; 30769 SIR BALAN by contrast was coated in grime when noted at the same spot. For a number of months the 3.35pm Victoria to Ramsgate and the 7.45pm return working from Ramsgate was the preserve of 30768 but even it was noted in store in the winter. 30448-30457 still worked on the Western Section and Salisbury had its very own, KING ARTHUR. In the spring of 1955 30451 SIR LAMORAK was noted shunting at Salisbury before working a westbound goods train. In 1955 more Urie Arthurs were withdrawn with 30743 and 30746 going in October and 30740 and 30752 in December. The first two were scrapped at Eastleigh Works and the other two at Brighton. For 30752 it was its first and last journey on the Central Section! Others, including 30738 30748 30750 30751 and 30755 received heavy repairs with the majority finding work

on the heavy summer Saturday schedules.

30740, in poor condition, stood in Guildford shed for many weeks before being sent to the Longmoor Military Railway where it was used for a televised sabotage demonstration. This was on 11 February 1956 on BBC's 'Saturday Night Out' but 30740 didn't really cooperate… 'its stately progress at slow speed down a low embankment was a slight anti-climax'. *The Railway Magazine* reported that it was then sent to Eastleigh for cutting up, though Bradley records this taking place at Brighton. According to the BR9637 forms it was in fact dealt with there, in the week ending 30 June 1956. In the same year came further withdrawals:

January 30744
February 30741, 30745
June 30737
October 30747
November 30736.

30737 and 30753 were also withdrawn in March but were reinstated even though they got as far as Brighton for scrapping! Still, the 'governor's last minute reprieve' came and 30753 MELISANDE, for instance, was observed working both ways on a through portion of the Sussex-Birkenhead train between Brighton and Redhill on 28 July 1956. It was also later noted light engine at Wimbledon, where it coupled up to a goods train, leaving for the west with 39 wagons and a brake. But 30737 KING UTHER

Nine Elms on 6 May 1922 and 740 still a full blown LSWR loco, as yet without name. Working all the top expresses, the Arthurs were the elite of their time and how 740 looks the part. See how clean it is, sleek boiler, those mighty cylinders; standard bogie tender attached. Photograph H.C. Casserley, courtesy R.M. Casserley.

Dover's 30776 SIR GALAGARS at what looks like Ashford shed about 1956. It has the shed plate 74C which remained thus despite an official change to 73H in 1958. As elaborated in *The Book of the Schools 4-4-0s*, the plates of the 74 District sheds which were supposed to change to codes in the 73 District were probably never even cast. The front buffers are losing a coat of white paint so had 30776 worked a special train recently, perhaps even a Royal? Anyway the last visit of SIR GALAGARS to Eastleigh Works for attention was September-October 1957, a General. Its next works visit was for scrapping in January 1959.

A stunning image at Nine Elms; it carried one of the shortest nameplates, SIR KAY and is here in Southern Railway guise complete with 'E' prefix, cab side number plate, crosshead vacuum pump, four 'lugs' (or 'clamps') on smokebox door and 'wing' lamp brackets on smokebox.

survived only until June 1956 while 30753 soldiered on into March 1957. On 23 June 1956 Basingstoke's 30771 SIR SAGRAMORE worked the 10.58am Exeter to Waterloo; during the autumn 30777 SIR LAMIEL was noted several times on the 1.05pm 'boat' from Dover and also on the 9.10am Dover Marine (9.20am from Dover Priory) to London via Chatham. On 9 September Stewarts Lane's 30793 SIR ONTZLAKE handled the noon departure from Victoria to Ramsgate. December 22nd 1956 saw 30450 SIR KAY of Salisbury shed working a mid-afternoon extra Waterloo to Bournemouth, the engine most likely borrowed by Nine Elms. At the start of 1957 the allocation for the surviving Uries was:

Eastleigh 30748
Bournemouth 30739, 30752, 30738
Nine Elms 30750
Basingstoke 30749, 30751, 30753, 30755.

Nine were left in service at the beginning of the year and all but 30738 KING PELLINORE had been withdrawn by the end of 1957, to be scrapped at Eastleigh Works. Withdrawal dates in 1957 were:

February 30742
March 30753
May 30739, 30755
June 30749, 30751
July 30750
September 30748.

The highest mileage was recorded by 30745 at 1,464,032. Finally 30738 was withdrawn in March 1958, to be scrapped the same month at Eastleigh

Works. So from this time on the term King Arthurs meant 'Maunsell Arthurs'. They would not be intact for long and all had gone as withdrawals accelerated in the early 1960s. A straw in the wind had been 30798 SIR HECTIMERE on 8 January 1958, working tender first on the 3.43pm Canterbury East to Dover instead of the usual 4-4-0. 30456 SIR GALAHAD was on the little-used Sturt Lane West curve at Farnham on 4 March with the 11.44am Camberley to Salisbury and the 5pm return specials for cadets from the Royal Military Academy, Sandhurst. The 31st of the month had 30789 SIR GUY on the 10.54am from Waterloo to Bournemouth. On 15 April 1958 30792 SIR HERVIS DE REVEL had a Dover-Victoria 'boat' via Maidstone East and on 24 April 30738 KING PELLINORE had charge of the 5.10pm Weymouth-Bournemouth made up of four coaches. Willesden saw 30778 SIR PELLEAS on 8 May, heading a return train from Southampton Docks bound for Leighton Buzzard. Allocation for June 1958 was:

Nine Elms 30457, 30763, 30774, 30778, 30779
Basingstoke 30455, 30456
Salisbury 30448-30454
Bournemouth 30764, 30765, 30771-30773, 30780-30783
Stewarts Lane 30766-30769, 30793-30795, 30802, 30803
Eastleigh 30770, 30784-30792
Dover 30775-30777, 30797, 30798, 30804, 30805
Hither Green 30796, 30806
Bricklayers Arms 30799-30801.
Before the end of 1958 30765, 30773 and 30794 had been transferred to

Basingstoke as the class began to lose its work on the Eastern Section. By the end of the year the first two Maunsell Arthurs had been withdrawn, 30454 QUEEN GUINEVERE (yet again deserting King Arthur?) in October and 30766 SIR GERAINT in December 1958. As was to be the fate of the rest of the Maunsell Arthurs, (save 30788 and 30804 which met their end at Ashford) they were scrapped at Eastleigh. SIR LAMIEL of course is preserved as part of the National Collection.

In 1959 there were more inroads made into the Maunsell Arthurs; writing was well and truly on the wall now and the following withdrawals (they were threatening to become precipitous) took place in the year:

January 30776
February 30787, 30792
April 30455, 30801
May 30778, 30797
June 30767
July 30779, 30780
August 30452, 30786
October 30784, 30785
November 30805
December 30449, 30789

Transfers during the year concerned those remaining Arthurs moving over to the Western section where they were pitched among a good number of Bulleid Pacifics and BR Standards – withdrawals could only hasten onward. It had been the intention that the class would be reduced to a rump of twenty or fewer by the end of 1960 and though 30457 SIR BEDIVERE got a complete overhaul in the spring of 1960 it could only survive until May 1961. The days

Two comparisons in the early days. Compare 740, yet to be named, in LSWR livery with stovepipe chimney and 742 CAMELOT in Southern days; lined livery, large running number on the tender side complete with E and cabside number plates. Major visual change is the Maunsell chimney. Above encased lock-up safety valves denote Urie boiler; below, Ross pop safety valves indicate Maunsell boiler.

30749 ISEULT at her Basingstoke home; behind is 30787 SIR MENADEUKE, a visitor from Eastleigh. What stands out is the electric lighting that was fitted in November 1947, after running just 66 miles as an oil burner following an A Type overhaul which finished on 11 October. Note that two of them are in the place of the old 'wing' lamp brackets and conventional lamp brackets are still fitted to the smokebox door. Photograph R.C. Riley, www.transporttreasury.co.uk

of the class working to the Kent Coast were very much numbered and it was during this time that I first took a real interest. In a race against withdrawals, I managed to seek out more than thirty as they disappeared from the scene. Despite the gloom the workings carried on, such as 30798 SIR HECTIMERE in March 1959 with the 11.45am Dover Priory to Maidstone East. In April 1959 30453 KING ARTHUR, still of Salisbury, worked the 7.51pm Yeovil Junction to Templecombe made up of two Maunsell coaches, two brake vans and a number of six wheel milk tanks when several stations West of Salisbury used to act as railheads for London milk from local farms. In the same month 30803 SIR HARRY LE FISE LAKE was on one of the last regular N15 turns on the Kent Coast main line, the 11.35am Victoria to Ramsgate made up of six coaches and still with the two Pullmans included. Reports of workings are rather thin on the ground but I recall Basingstoke shed having a number of them allocated in 1959, including 30455 (withdrawn in the April), 30456, 30765 and 30794. Along with the Nine Elms ones we got used to seeing them on the semi-fasts between Waterloo and Basingstoke. One Arthur-hauled train I remember very well was a semi-fast to Salisbury in the evening which must have left Waterloo just before 7pm as it worked past our 'perch' overlooking Oatlands cutting, inevitably at 7.20pm on the down slow,

the line normally dominated by the electric trains on the local services. It would *always* be a King Arthur, until the class became extinct and mainly Salisbury based engines and often one of the first Eastleigh batch 30448-30453 (30454 was withdrawn before my day). The only one of that group I never observed on that working was 30449 SIR TORRE. It was during this time that the SR started giving the names of the twenty withdrawn Urie engines to twenty of the BR 5MT 4-6-0s allocated mainly to Nine Elms, 73080-73089 and 73110-73119.

Soon enough we saw the King Arthurs replaced on the Basingstoke semis by first the Schools and, increasingly, BR Standards; the surviving Arthurs at times were relegated to parcels or goods work. By June 1960 the survivors were all based at sheds in the Western Section as follows:

Nine Elms 30457, 30763, 30774
Feltham 30777, 30793, 30795
Basingstoke 30456, 30765, 30794
Eastleigh 30768, 30770, 30773, 30788, 30790, 30800, 30802-30804, 30806
Bournemouth 30764, 30771, 30772, 30781-30783
Salisbury 30448, 30450, 30451, 30453, 30796, 30798, 30799.

Further withdrawals in 1960 were:

January 30774
February 30769, 30775
May 30456, 30791
August 30448, 30794
September 30450
October 30763.

Late on, surprisingly, 30453, 30765, 30773, 30777, 30782, 30788, 30795 and 30798 all received heavy repairs and repaints. Summer Saturdays still saw them at work on the Bournemouth reliefs, the Basingstoke and Salisbury semi fasts, even the 4.03pm Clapham Junction to Yeovil milk empties. I remember them on summer Saturdays as nearly every free morning in those days saw a number of us by the lineside, bemused by the selection of steam engines still at work on the Western Section. 30453 KING ARTHUR became a firm favourite, for the heroics associated with that name – apart from Launcelot and Guinevere we'd barely heard of any of the others.

Feltham enjoyed an association with the class around this time, from May 1959 when four arrived (30775, 30777, 30793 and 30795) until December 1960 when 30793, the last one, was transferred away to Basingstoke. Feltham was very much a freight shed, notable for the fact that every time I attempted to visit it I was more or less

Two splendid 'original' Maunsell Arthurs, both completed at NBL in May 1925. Snifting valves fitted; Southern lined livery and same style of tender numbering including the 'E' and cabside number plate. That little valve on the smokebox ahead of the works plate was a hot water 'tap' for whenever the crew or a fitter needed it. The works plates seemed to have stayed in place when smoke deflectors were fitted, eventually disappearing when the smokeboxes were renewed. Note the crosshead vacuum pumps on the near lower slidebars. Bulleid had them removed 1939-40 as not worth the maintenance they required.

30457 SIR BEDIVERE at Eastleigh shed on 26th March 1960, waiting entry to the works a few days later for a Light Casual, which was to prove its last visit; it left in the middle of the following month and withdrawal came on 20th May 1961. It was broken up week ending 8/7/61. The boiler has a multi-plug firebox - there were ten like this. Its water cart was replaced by Urie 5,200 gallon tender (note higher sides) 788 ex-H15 30490 in March 1955. Photograph Frank Hornby.

(usually less, considerably so) politely sent on my way. It was not too bad, for the vast majority of the engines worked through Weybridge at some time and to me Feltham shed will always be associated with the S15s, especially those designed by Urie. All the time that Feltham had an Arthur allocated we hoped to see one on the goods trains that regularly worked our way, but, oddly, this never happened. The January 1961 allocation was:

Nine Elms 30457
Bournemouth 30764, 30772, 30781, 30782
Basingstoke 30765, 30777, 30793, 30795
Eastleigh 30768, 30770, 30773, 30788, 30790, 30800, 30802-30804, 30806
Salisbury 30451, 30453, 30771, 30783, 30796, 30798, 30799.

Withdrawals later in 1961:
February 30799
March, 30771, 30783
April 30806
May 30457
July 30453, 30764, 30802
August 30800, 30803
September 30772
October 30777
November 30768, 30790

They then largely disappeared, for most of the survivors spent the winter

in store and in January 1961 30451 SIR LAMORAK was the last to have a general repair. No doubt because of this it was in constant demand and an ever-present regular. If there was a parcels train with an Arthur working it, it had to be 30451; it could be seen on all four running lines; in the end all bets were off when we realised one of the surviving Arthurs was approaching. I even have a very blurred photograph of it working on the down slow line approaching Weybridge station. It was the last of the first Eastleigh batch in service and on 2 September was noted on an up express from Salisbury made up of ten coaches. Needless to say the handful surviving in January, 1961 had all been 'scored' in the well-thumbed Ian Allan ABC. Because of the transfer of more light Pacifics to the Western Section the Arthurs did not see as much work on the busy summer Saturdays. Having said that 30793 SIR ONTZLAKE was on the up Bournemouth Belle on the first Saturday of the summer service and as it was running 45 minutes late passing Esher it was presumably a last minute substitute. June 28th saw 30795 SIR DINADAN on the 7.30am Basingstoke to Waterloo which ran all stations to Woking (not Brookwood) then non-stop to London with ten

heavily laden coaches. 30451 in the summer was often on the 2.45pm Waterloo to Yeovil, a working entrusted to the Arthurs right up to the end of the class. On August 11th it was on the 3pm Waterloo-Exeter train which it took over at Salisbury and 'improved on the schedule by 4 minutes in an attempt to recover loss of time'. On the next day it worked the 10.28am Templecombe to Salisbury stopping train. Salisbury often rostered 30451 for one of the few duties remaining to the class, the 8.46am Salisbury to Waterloo and the 2.45pm return to Yeovil. December 23rd saw 30798 SIR HECTIMERE on the 8.46am Salisbury to Waterloo stopping train composed of two vans and five coaches.

1962 was the final year for the class with the last one withdrawn in November. Allocation for December 1961 was:

Eastleigh 30773, 30788, 30804
Salisbury 30451, 30796, 30798
Bournemouth 30781, 30782
Basingstoke 30765, 30770, 30793, 30795.
Withdrawals came thus:

February 30773, 30788, 30804
March 30796
May 30781
June 30451, 30798

August 30795
September 30765 30782, 30793
November 30770.

The three Eastleigh engines were rostered on the 7.40am Eastleigh to Clapham Junction vans, the noon Clapham Junction stock train and the 7.25pm goods from Nine Elms Yard. All three were withdrawn in the February and while 30773 met its fate at Eastleigh Works in the April, 30788 and 30804 were the only ones scrapped at Ashford Works. 30788 was noted being hauled into Ashford Works on 3 February 1962 by 700 30326, both for scrapping, the 0-6-0 withdrawn from Guildford shed the same month. Of the Salisbury engines 30451 or 30798 were on the 8.46am local, Salisbury to Waterloo and back on the 2.54pm to Basingstoke and then the 4.48pm to Yeovil Junction with 30796 normally employed on station pilot duties. These timetabled duties were taken over by light Pacifics when the last of the Salisbury Arthurs were withdrawn. 30451 was noted on the up working in the April and again on 5 May 1962 with a loading of three vans and five coaches. Basingstoke duties included 30770 on a few Saturday reliefs in the summer and 30765 on the 10.54am Waterloo to Bournemouth West on 13 May in place of the usual Schools.

April 1962 saw 30782 on light passenger trains, parcels and even heavy goods; May 7th had 30798 on an evening goods train at Addlestone, and later in May 30451 was again on the 8.46am from Salisbury and the 2.54pm return from Waterloo. On 14 June 30770 even underwent repairs at Eastleigh; on 22 June 30793 was on a Friday relief to the 6pm Waterloo-Exeter as far as Salisbury. In July and August 1962 30770, 30782 and 30795 were on secondary duties and parcel trains. September 6th had 30770 working a Southampton Docks banana train and with the withdrawal of 30765 in the week ending 22nd September 30770 was the last of the class in service. On 22nd October it worked the 8.24am Basingstoke to Waterloo and later empty stock to Clapham Junction. On October 23rd and 29th it worked the 10.20am slow train Bournemouth to Waterloo and on the 29th returned to Basingstoke on the 1.54pm slow train from Waterloo. 30770 also worked van trains and local goods and on 24th November was at last withdrawn, the final Arthur at work.

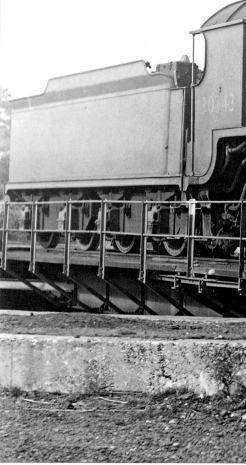

30743 LYONNESSE on the turntable at Bournemouth shed about 1953. Photograph www.transporttreasury.co.uk

Below. E784 (E prefix discarded in the December) SIR NEROVENS at Nine Elms on 28 May 1931. Running number on the tender buffer beam (without a 'No') rather than rear panel; also metal number plate, highlighted with lining. On the right is H15 E524, similarly adorned. Photograph H.C. Casserley, courtesy R.M. Casserley.

Bottom right. Bournemouth shed on 19 July 1937; 777 in the block lettering on rear of tender. It would be another two years before SIR LAMIEL got the Olive Green livery. The engine had in fact just moved from Battersea to Nine Elms, so this was probably its first visit to Bournemouth for a while? Photograph H.C. Casserley, courtesy R.M. Casserley.

Basingstoke shed, Sunday 12th September 1954; a close up of the left-hand side showing how the nameplate sat centrally over the driving wheel. Also a good look at the connecting rod split big end, eccentric crank and eccentric rod. At this time 30745 was based at Basingstoke from where it was withdrawn on 11th February 1956. Photograph R.C. Riley, www.transporttreasury.co.uk

Detail, Differences and Changes

Let the 'engine picking', a well worn term and one grasped to our collective bosom since 'The Book of...' series started with the BR Standards in 1997 by yours truly, commence. It's a serious pursuit, as anyone who has met one of us rivet counters will know. In previous 'Book of' titles covering the Schools and the Lord Nelsons there is a similar chapter using the above title and it is worth repeating the point that engine picking is 'a trade best practised with humour and conducted in the expectancy of Being Wrong, at some point at least'. Happy engine picking.

Some alterations/modifications were applied to the class, or confined to one grouping within the class (on the LNER they'd certainly have been separate classes) while they were also interchangeable to some extent with wholly different classes. They changed tenders with each other and with other classes and shared boilers in a similar way.

Boilers

At the last count thanks to much delving and the surviving boiler record cards it seems that there were 154 N15 type boilers, shared between N15, S15 and certain H15 4-6-0s. Each Arthur started out with a boiler carrying the same number as the engine running number (754 THE GREEN KNIGHT would have boiler no.754 for instance) but this did not last, as boilers were exchanged at works visits. The S15s too, carried boilers with identical running numbers so an Arthur might run at times with a boiler carrying an S15 number.

LSWR practice was to build the same number of boilers as engines which meant no spare boiler was ready and available during a General Overhaul, so an engine spent more time in works than was otherwise necessary. Maunsell had more boilers built, such as eight spares ordered from NBL in December 1924. Other boilers followed before the end of steam hence some of the 'odd' numbering such as nos.1000, 1001, 1047-1057, 1401-1412 and even nos.928-931 (the same as the Schools running numbers). Early boiler records are fragmentary, for a lot of the information was lost or disposed of at the end of steam. Happily, thanks to a near complete set of engine record cards dating from 1936 to the end of the class the boiler exchanges are listed under each individual engine.

Sanding

As on the Schools, sanding was provided to the front of the leading driving wheels but it appears these were the only wheels so served. This was somewhat unusual practice, for it had been widely determined that the 'sanded' wheelset should best be the 'driving' one; that is, the one with the connecting rod. This had been shown to be the best arrangement to avoid rods buckling in difficult circumstances. The sand filler was only visible on closer inspection, with access from the running plate.

Smoke Deflectors

The Urie and later the Maunsell Arthurs appeared without smoke deflectors. Looking at photographs of this early period I feel them to be a bit ordinary looking; they are definitely not the same without the final design of smoke deflectors which so enhanced the appearance. They are what 'marks them out', to my mind at least. What it is, I'm sure, is that locos only ever 'look right' to anybody in the condition in which you first came to know and love them; the Royal Scots are a similar case. On the Maunsell engines, though the boiler pitch was similar the conventional

E753 MELISANDE with a strip of steel across the top of the smokebox, one of those disappointing efforts to disperse the drifting steam caused by larger boilers and much smaller chimneys. Records show MELISANDE carrying this between 21st May 1926 and 16th June 1926. With such a short space of time we are lucky to have shots of it; it's flimsy enough to have flown off above 45 mph! Evidently E774 SIR GAHERIS had a similar strip of metal fitted but the dates don't seem to have been recorded. Photograph Andrew Westlake Collection.

E450 SIR KAY with those delicate wing plates fitted in February 1926 on the back of the chimney that rather reminds me of *The Flash* (a popular American DC comic character of the Sixties m'lud) but I doubt whether the engine could move as fast. More likely, it recalls the Art Deco Hermes Messenger of the Gods look, used on the lamps for the LMS streamlined Coronation Scot for instance. On shed at Nine Elms one can understand why these plates were well, quite useless. They were removed in March 1927 and more realistic studies resulted in the standard smoke deflectors. Crosshead driven vacuum pump. The Nine Elms surroundings are remarkably neat and tidy.

783 SIR GILLEMERE at Eastleigh 'on 7th January 1941' with just two chimneys now, part of the experiment to make the engine less visible from the air to the Luftwaffe during the early part of World War Two. The three chimneys had been fitted in November 1940 and the middle one removed and the side ones lengthened in December. Plates were fitted between the smoke box and deflectors in January 1941, all of the work probably done at Eastleigh shed. In February 1941 the standard Arthur chimney was restored. 783 is in early Malachite Green.

Familiar views of 783 SIR GILLEMERE, one of a few of the class used in experiments or trials to improve smoke removal, and at Oxford on 9th April 1927 (note pannier tank) we have the peculiar arrangement around the chimney in a failed attempt to divert the exhaust up and away. The designers' errors were to (understandably) concentrate on the chimney rather than the front of the locomotive. The arrangement was carried between March and December 1927 so we are lucky, I think, to have Mr Casserley's record of the event. Photographs H.C. Casserley, courtesy R.M. Casserley.

E773 Sir LAVAINE with that mysterious circular hood over the smokebox door, on a Southampton train of LSWR stock running via the Mid-Hants line on 17th May 1930 at Woking station. That is an M7 in the background, when Woking still had LSWR semaphores. Smoke deflectors had been fitted in 1927 but were removed for a short while in 1930 while this hood was carried. Photograph H.C. Casserley, courtesy R.M. Casserley.

chimney was shorter than the Urie stovepipes, so the problem of drifting smoke and steam obscuring the view frontwards was accordingly worse. Though the class continued in service for a time without the deflectors, drifting smoke blocking the view ahead from the footplate was a regular worry.

This was a recent phenomenon, due mainly to the larger boilers and shorter chimneys that were coming into use across the country, and other companies were grappling with it too. The Southern Railway was the first in this country to begin experiments with smoke deflectors; lineside observers of the time (we have always been a conservative lot) considered them an alien feature. It was complaints from footplate crews that had prompted Maunsell to look around for a solution and he is said to have eventually noted that in Germany the answer had been found in large deflector plates either side of the smokebox. Before this, there had been a series of experiments, later paralleled on the LMS and LNER, with E450 SIR KAY fitted with a pair of small wing plates behind the chimney plus the fitting of an additional steam blower at the back of the chimney. It was quite effective but costly in the use of live steam. 1927 saw experiments on six more of the class:

E453 KING ARTHUR had some small side plates fitted which ran in line with the smokebox.

E457 SIR BEDIVERE had a small chimney deflector.

E753 MELISANDE and 774 SIR GAHERIS had curved plates fitted on top and ahead of the smokebox.

E783 SIR GILLEMERE had an open cowling on top of the chimney to deflect airflow and lift exhaust clear.

E772 SIR PERCIVALE had large square plates worthy of a 9F 2-10-0, secured by straps at the top, after Maunsell took a look at practice in Germany. This was the most successful of all.

Eventually Maunsell modified the design and the plates were cut back and set inward on the running plates with a

772 SIR PERCIVALE with those German State Railway pattern smoke deflectors, during its six years of looking like one of those English engines done up for a film set in Europe, which did the loco no justice at all. The lamp irons have not been altered (they were later) so the view forward must have been pretty lousy. It is a Continental Boat Train leaving Dover Marine.

30784 SIR NEROVENS at Eastleigh shed in early BR days, number and BRITISH RAILWAYS in the 'sunshine' lettering'; S15 836 still carrying its SR number in the background. Standard Maunsell smokebox door with horizontal hand rail, the six 'dogs' and so on – the usual details, but in great clarity. As often seen on Eastleigh 4-6-0s the shed code is painted on the buffer beam – E'LEIGH. In October 1954 the spark arrestor chimney was replaced by a standard King Arthur chimney. Photograph W. Hermiston, www.transporttreasury.co.uk

E772 SIR PERCIVALE again in all its glory. Just awful to look at, it ran like this from September 1929 to October 1932 when thankfully standard deflectors were fitted. What if these had become the standard? Just look at those top brackets! They were raised to enable men to walk between smoke box and deflectors. Logical really!

Certainly a different view of an Arthur; 452 SIR MELIAGRANCE in June 1936 at Waterloo, ready to run back out to Nine Elms. Coal rails filled in, panel livery, older style serif numbers on rear; presumably 452 had worked in with SPL 31.

result that all of the class had them fitted as standard. Townroe called them 'smokebox "wings", or deflector plates' and notes that the Arthurs saw the first instance of such features in British practice. These standard smoke deflectors, an improvement and enlargement on the somewhat feeble efforts fitted to E453, were adopted and extended over the front of the running plate with the pleasing curve at the top leading corner, which was so characteristic of all things Southern. As Townroe points out, they served as a neat 'catcher' for game birds, which could be collected at the end of the trip. The outside steam pipes consequently were barely visible. E779 SIR COLGREVANCE was the first of the class to get these standard smoke deflectors, in April 1927 and the rest of the class followed up to 1930 when the job was complete. There were steps (though not at first) between the deflectors and the running plate and cut out handholds in the front of the deflector, nearly level with the running plate, were later made. E773 SIR LAVAINE can be seen with a circular shaped hood in some pictures, fitted to the top of the smokebox, pointing forward; the purpose seems obscure. It was yet another ineffective smoke deflection tinkering, so common in the period. In the 1940s Urie Arthurs 736, 752 and 755 were given vertical smoke deflectors.

Tenders on Urie and Maunsell Engines
Urie
When first built 736-755 were fitted with bogie tenders, an improved version of the type fitted to the H15 4-6-0s (482-491) which carried 5,000 gallons of water and 5 tons of coal. This earliest series of Arthurs was withdrawn in the mid-1950s but many of the tenders survived to work with Maunsell 4-6-0s.

Maunsell
The Maunsell series of King Arthurs had a much more varied time with their tenders. The Eastleigh Arthurs 448-457 had Drummond pattern eight wheel 'water-cart' tenders, 4,300 gallons of water and 5 tons of coal. For the Stockton and Darlington celebrations of 1925 449 SIR TORRE worked north coupled to a Urie 5,000 gallon tender. From new, 763-792 had Urie 5,000 gallon bogie tenders constructed by North British and delivered between May and October 1925 (the so-called 'Scotch Arthurs' or 'Scotchmen'). The final 793-806 started life on the Central Section based at Battersea (Stewarts Lane) shed or Brighton and had the 'Ashford' six wheel 3,500 gallon tenders; the higher drawgear meant the framing below the cab had to be adjusted so if the engines were loaned to Nine Elms the Urie 5,000 gallon tenders could not be used.

763-772 were fitted with 4,000 gallon Eastleigh pattern six wheel tenders between 1928-1930 and their Urie

pattern 5,000 gallon tenders went to S15s 828-837. These Arthurs had the smaller tenders for the shorter journeys on the Eastern Section but 769 SIR BALAN was moved to the Western Section and in January 1933 was at Exmouth Junction, receiving a Maunsell 5,000 gallon bogie tender.

At times 768, 770, 771 and 772 went on loan to the Western Section so in 1930 they regained 5,000 gallon tenders as did 763, 764 and 765 in 1936 and 766 and 767 in 1937. 763-767 were fitted with the Urie pattern, double bogie, flared top 5,000 gallon tenders and 768 and 770-772 with the more modern Maunsell pattern, double bogie, flush sided 5,000 gallon tender which carried auxiliary vacuum cylinders on the tank top. 769 was already fitted with one of these. In 1931-32 768-772 lost these tenders to Lord Nelsons 852, 853 and 858-860 in replacement for Urie double bogie tenders that also carried auxiliary vacuum cylinders.

To sum up after these movement of tenders:
763-767, 773-792 fitted with Urie, double bogie and flared top.
768-772 as above plus auxiliary vacuum cylinders.
793-806 fitted with Ashford pattern six wheel 3,500 gallons
(to meet Central Section restrictions)
448-457 still had the modified Drummond water cart, ex-LSWR 4-6-0s of the same number.

Useful tender detail. 30745 TINTAGEL alongside the coal stage at Basingstoke on 12 September 1954, typical decaying poor 'slack' stuck unused at the rear of the coal space. Two water fillers, one each side. Full BR livery applied in August 1951, smaller (first) totem. I can only assume that the little eyed rods sticking up were for securing the fire irons by their handles and so too, you'd think, were the lamp iron-type projections on the tender side. The tube inside the tender on the far side is thought to carry the cabling for the electric lights fitted to 30745 in 1947. Photograph R.C. Riley, www.transporttreasury.co.uk

In BR days withdrawals commenced with H15, N15X classes and amongst the N15s themselves, which meant the Drummond water carts off 30448-30457 could be replaced as they were now in poor shape. So the following took place:

5/55	30448 got the tender from H15 30478
6/55	30457 got the tender from H15 30490
11/55	30449 got the tender from N15 30753
10/56	30450 got the tender from N15 30737
1/57	30451 got the tender from N15X 32333
4/57	30453 got the tender from N15 30742
6/57	30452 got the tender from N15 30785
6/57	30454 got the tender from N15 30755
12/57	30455 got the tender from N15 30748
8/58	30456 got the tender from N15 30749

With these tenders becoming available some of the Ashford 3,500 gallon tenders were also replaced:

4/58	30795 got the tender from N15 30738
6/58	30802 got the tender from N15 30750
8/58	30806 got the tender from N15X 32331
1/59	30800 got the tender from N15 30755
9/59	30793 got the tender from N15 30776
11/59	30803 got the tender from N15 30792
10/60	30798 got the tender from N15 30450
1/61	30796 got the tender from N15 30766

As noted the tenders of 30798 and 30800 were now riding with their third King Arthur. 30794, 30797, 30799, 30801, 30804 and 30805 kept their Ashford 3,500 six wheel tenders until they were withdrawn. Of these six, five saw their final months out working on the

Western Section, the exception being 30801 SIR MELIOT DE LOGRES which was withdrawn in April 1959 from Bricklayers Arms shed, meeting its fate at Eastleigh in the June. Late on two tender changes are shown taking place at a running shed, both on 7 November 1959; 30785 and 30791 swopped tenders with 30785 getting no.908 and 30791 tender no.854. Both engines are recorded as then being based at Eastleigh shed.

Tender Emblems with BR Green
Second emblem not noted if not used.
30448 1st totem, small
30449 1st totem, large and small
30450 1st totem, large and small; 2nd totem 10/1958
30451 1st totem, large and small; 2nd totem 1/1961
30452 1st totem, small
30453 1st totem, large and small; 2nd totem, Urie tender small 3/57and large 7/58
30454 1st totem, small
30455 1st totem, small
30456 1st totem, small
30457 None.1st totem small, 2nd totem 2/59
30736 1st totem, small
30737 1st totem, small
30738 1st totem. small
30739 1st totem, small
30740 1st totem, small
30741 None. 1st totem, small
30742 1st totem, small
30743 1st totem, small

30744 1st totem, small
30745 1st totem, small
30746 1st totem, small
30747 1st totem, small
30748 1st totem, small
30749 1st totem, small
30750 1st totem, large and small
30751 1st totem, small
30752 1st totem, small
30753 1st totem, small
30754 1st totem, small
30755 1st totem, large and small
30763 1st totem, small; 2nd totem 6/1958
30764 1st totem, small
30765 1st totem, small; 2nd totem 4/1960
30766 1st totem, small
30767 1st totem, small
30768 1st totem, small; 2nd totem 2/1958
30769 1st totem, small
30770 1st totem, small; 2nd totem 8/1957
30771 1st totem, small; 2nd totem 6/1957
30772 1st totem, large and small
30773 1st totem, small; 2nd totem 1/1960;
30774 1st totem, small
30775 1st totem, large and small
30776 1st totem, small; 2nd totem 10/1957
30777 1st totem, small; 2nd totem 1/1960
30778 1st totem, large and small
30779 1st totem, large and small; 2nd totem 5/1957
30780 1st totem, large and small
30781 1st totem, small; 2nd totem 11/1957
30782 1st totem, large and small; 2nd totem 5/1960
30783 1st totem, large and small
30784 1st totem, small
30785 1st totem small, 2nd totem 4/57
30786 1st totem, small; 2nd totem 12/1957

A powerful close up of 30784 SIR NEROVENS with beefeater chimney on foreign soil at Reading General on the Western Region, 14th May 1951. Excellent view of the plain coupling rods, the fluted connecting and eccentric rods and the connecting rod big end. On the front part of the running plate can be seen the access to the valve gear combination lever and the pipe that fed the sand to the front pair of driving wheels. Photograph R.C. Riley, www.transporttreasury.co.uk

30787 1st totem, small
30788 1st totem, small; 2nd totem 3/1960
30789 1st totem, small
30790 1st totem, small; 2nd totem 5/1957
30791 1st totem, small; 2nd totem 11/1959
30792 1st totem, large and small
30793 1st totem, small; 2nd totem 8/1957
30794 1st totem, small
30795 1st totem, small; 2nd totem 5/1958
30796 1st totem, large and small; 2nd totem 11/1957
30797 1st totem, small
30798 1st totem, large and small; 2nd totem 11/1960
30799 1st totem, small
30800 1st totem, large and small; 2nd totem 1/1959
30801 1st totem, small
30802 1st totem, small; 2nd totem 6/1958
30803 1st totem, small
30804 1st totem, large and small; 2nd totem 4/1957
30805 1st totem, small; 2nd totem 6/1957
30806 1st totem, small; 2nd totem 9/1958

Snifting Valves

These were prominent either side of the chimney and were also carried by the Schools and the Nelsons. 1946 saw the decision to start removing them from Southern engines as their unnecessary maintenance was taking up time and money. Urie engines did not have the valves at first, which appeared only as Maunsell superheaters were fitted. Dates of removal can be found in the individual tables.

Superheaters

Urie was one of the first engineers to deal with superheating and used his own design on his H15 4-6-0s, which proved successful. Known as the 'Eastleigh superheater' it was fitted to a lot of the engines Urie had inherited. Maunsell later developed his own type of superheater (not as large as the Eastleigh type) and all the Arthurs built under his regime were fitted from new with his type. Later all the Urie originals, when visiting Works had the Eastleigh type replaced by this Maunsell type superheater. A 'Bolton' superheater was carried on a boiler on E455 SIR LANCELOT, between July 1929 and February 1931. It was then fitted to E454 QUEEN GUINEVERE which carried it from May 1931 to August 1932.

Chimneys

736-755 when built had a stovepipe chimney and capuchin; all later received King Arthur style lipped chimneys of conventional British outline and their look improved no end. In January 1924 742 had a taller chimney with a lipped top, used in trials to improve steaming and later replaced by a standard King Arthur chimney in December, 1925.

In the Second World War Bulleid had 783 fitted with three chimneys, two set forward of the original with the idea to disperse the exhaust to avoid enemy aircraft detecting the engine and attacking it. No real progress was made with it but it did help with 'soot removal from overbridges and tunnels'.

784 SIR NEROVENS in 1947 (at its works visit 30/5/47-4/6/47**D** – see individual table) had a large diameter pre-fabricated chimney and spark arrester ('T2052') fitted. The latter of course, was internal and not visible. Presumably there had been a spate of lineside fires on the Southern blamed on Arthurs but it was a doomed experiment. Arresters could only hinder steaming, in a major or minor way but it was doubtless good to have something 'seen to be done'. It was removed April-May 1948 and a modified version fitted during a works visit in January-February 1949. It was finally removed in 1954, the original reasons for it being installed long forgotten (see 29/9/54-23/10/54**LI**).

There was another Arthur so fitted, 30788 SIR URRE OF THE MOUNT getting a 'Mk 3' version of a large diameter pre-fabricated chimney and spark arrester on works visit 28/12/49-6/1/50**NC**. It was taken off during the period 1/6/51-27/6/51**LI**.

Lemaître Exhausts

Bulleid had greatly improved the Lord

30773 SIR LAVAINE, an Eastleigh engine actually at its home station on the 5.15pm train to Portsmouth, Tuesday 15th August 1961. This close up shows well the lamp irons (original one in the middle), screw coupling correctly hung, upright hand posts, 'dogs' on the smokebox door and the 'half footstep' by the smoke deflector for the running plate. Head code can refer to 'All trains terminating at Portsmouth and Southsea (trains from Salisbury to carry No.17 to Eastleigh).' Photograph Gavin Morrison.

30737 KING UTHER (father of 30453) on shed at Bournemouth, its home from the start of 1949 to withdrawal on 23rd June 1956. The BR classification, 5P, can just be seen over the running number, under the grime. The old A classification that used to be on the running plate is there too, under the running number, just to make sure! It's not often that we get such an intimate view of brake gear, pipe work and injector. Note also the shield over the cab window which was presumably there as a rudimentary sun visor. Those prominent pipes on the side of the Arthur fireboxes, in front of the cab, need to be explained; they carry the steam from that big steam supply valve on top of the firebox to the injectors under the cab behind the footsteps. The little rod leads into the cab to a wheel which operated the valve. Photograph www.transporttreasury.co.uk

Nelson class by fitting the multiple jet Lemaitre Exhaust and started on the Schools class in January 1939 until half of them were so fitted (see *The Book of the Schools 4-4-0s*). The War prevented the rest of the Schools being attended to but it did not stop Bulleid fitting them to some of the Arthurs; below are the works dates during which they were fitted:

736   14/1/41-18/1/41**D**
737   11/2/41-17/2/41**D**
741   16/12/40-1/1/41**C**
752   13/1/41-26/2/41**A**
755   9/12/39-14/2/40**A**

All five were retained until scrapped.

Maunsell Arthur 792 had a Lemaitre Exhaust too, fitted during works visit 6/8/40-25/9/40**A** though it was removed during 29/2/52-29/3/52**GO** and a standard King Arthur chimney returned.

**Urie and Maunsell Cylinders
on Urie Arthurs**
From new they had 22in. cylinders but over a period of time these were replaced by 21in. cylinders (see list below); drivers are said to have felt that performance climbing the West of England banks suffered as a consequence. Bradley, in *Locomotives of the LSWR Part 2* notes that in February 1925, when 741 was found to have a faulty left-hand cylinder, it was equipped with a new pair at 20½in. diameter. The rest of the class were dealt with from 1928 onwards save for 755 which later got 22in. diameter cylinders plus its multiple blastpipe, subsequently building up a reputation for fast running. Maunsell was not satisfied with these improvement and during 1932-1934 added double exhaust ported steam valves to 740, 743, 745, 746, 748 and 752. No doubt all the Urie Arthurs would have been dealt with but Maunsell retired in 1936 and Bulleid had his own ideas.

736   Urie pattern 21in. August 1924
737   Urie pattern 21in. June 1928
738   Urie pattern March 1930; Bulleid pattern April 1939
739   Urie pattern 21in. October 1928
740   Urie pattern 21in. December 1929; Maunsell pattern (double exhaust ports) January 1934
741   Urie pattern 21in. February 1929
742   Maunsell pattern (double exhaust ports) August, 1930
743   Maunsell pattern (double exhaust ports) June 1930
744   Urie pattern 21in. June 1927
745   Maunsell pattern (double exhaust ports) May 1930
746   Urie pattern 21in. January 1929
747   Maunsell pattern (double exhaust ports) March 1933
748   Maunsell pattern (double exhaust ports) March, 1931
749   Maunsell pattern (double exhaust ports) March, 1931
750   Bulleid pattern April 1941
751   Urie pattern 21in. February 1930
752   Maunsell pattern (double exhaust ports) September 1930
753   No record exists
754   Maunsell pattern (double exhaust ports) June 1932
755   Bulleid pattern February 1940

Liveries

LSWR Passenger classes had the Olive Green from the end of 1917; Urie called it Sage Green and it had a three inch black border with a fine white line. Boiler bands were black with white edging and the cylinders were also painted Olive Green with some black band details.

Under Maunsell the first few repaintings of course were of this Urie pattern but from late 1923 white edging was replaced by a yellow one and SOUTHERN added to tender or tank sides.

Oval cabside number plates appeared from the time of the Grouping and the letter E was added to the number on the tender to distinguish the Western section maintained engines (Eastleigh) from the Eastern (A for Ashford) and Central section (B for Brighton). It also helped where duplicate numbers existed.

From February 1925 the Maunsell green livery was applied, a deeper and, some felt, a more attractive shade of green. The edging of the black once again became white.

Dramatic change came with Bulleid, inevitably and in May 1938 749 ISEULT appeared in an unlined lighter and brighter green from Eastleigh, painted numbers replacing the cabside plates. Later still 749 was painted in the bright shade which became known as Malachite Green. It had black and white lining with the lettering 'Southern' applied to the tender side. Bulleid decided on three shades of green but

the Second World War meant that plain black became the norm from spring 1942. The King Arthurs were painted Malachite before and after the War and some continued after BR was formed. A temporary shortage of the malachite paint had seen 765 (7/6/46), 782 (12/4/47), 791 (3/5/47) and 800 (29/3/47) leave works painted black with green driving wheels. Summer 1949 saw the final livery associated with the class, the GW-style dark green ('Brunswick' as it is often misleadingly called – even by the best of us) with orange and black lining. This was the livery I grew up with and which is still my favourite.

Urie Arthur Liveries

After the Grouping 736-745 were painted Maunsell Green, had the prefix E added to their number and received names from the Arthurian legends. Dates of Maunsell livery being applied:

1/24	741, 742
4/24	749-751
5/24	738
7/24	736, 740, 754
9/24	745
10/24	739, 744
12/24	746, 752
1/25	747, 753
4/25	748, 755
6/25	743
10/25	737

1938 saw the livery experiments with 749 and later others of the class were repainted and all had Bulleid lettering and cabside numbers:

Maunsell Green with black and white lining

11/38	748
12/38	736
1/39	751
2/39	743, 754
3/39	752
4/39	737, 738

Olive Green with black and yellow lining

6/39	742
7/39	753
11/39	740, 744
2/40	747, 755
4/40	741
5/40	736

In April 1939 745 was painted as above but with green and yellow lining.

Malachite Green with black and yellow lining:

7/40	737, 739
4/41	750
5/41	743, 751
6/41	745
7/41	746, 748
10/41	754
3/42	744

In March 1939 746 was painted as above but with black and white lining; some non-standard repaints took place while from 742 in 6/42 all repaints were plain black because of the war. At the end of hostilities there was only a limited supply of malachite green paint and it was 4/46 before the first repaint in this livery, 755. Before 1948 736-738, 740-743, 745, 746,

30752 LINETTE (daughter of 780) in rather grimy condition and first British Railways manifestation with the Gill sans lettering and figures; it had been renumbered on 25th September 1948 and though there is no date for this photograph we know the period for removal of the snifting valves at Eastleigh, period ending 24/11/50. Lemaître blastpipe and chimney still in situ. Ex-oil burner, fading Malachite Green, upright deflectors and electric lights. Photograph W. Hermiston, www.transporttreasury.co.uk

Urie 30748 VIVIEN at Eastleigh Works on Sunday 11th September 1955; completed in July 1922 she was a true LSWR product. A good view of the cab showing the regulator handle, injector controls, oil reservoirs; VIVIEN's last recorded visit to Works was its last General in March 1955 but being shedded at 71A at this time it was easy enough to just 'slip it round the corner' for attention. It actually survived until September 1957. Photograph Frank Hornby.

748, 749 and 752 were also dealt with, to be followed after nationalisation by 739, 744, 747, 750, 751, 753 and 754. The last one was 30743 in June 1949.

Finally came the BR dark green:

30736	11/50
30737	6/51
30738	1/53
30739	5/52
30740	5/50
30741	9/49
30742	12/51
30743	6/53
30744	4/51
30745	8/51
30746	9/50
30747	5/50
30748	9/50
30749	11/51
30750	1/50
30751	4/51
30752	11/50
30753	9/50
30754	4/50
30755	10/49

Maunsell Arthur Liveries

These bore the Maunsell Green passenger livery for a number of years but with the arrival of Bulleid as CME changes took place from 1938 (all had Bulleid lettering and cabside numerals):

Maunsell Green with black and white lining:

11/38	784, 785
1/39	451, 764
2/39	776, 782, 787
3/39	802
4/39	449

Olive Green with yellow and green lining:

6/39	450, 770, 793
7/39	453, 457, 800, 805
9/39	788
10/39	777, 803
11/39	778, 781
12/39	774, 786, 795, 799
1/40	454
2/40	772, 780
5/40	773, 806
6/40	456, 768

Malachite Green with black and white lining:

3/39	766, 789

Malachite Green with black and yellow lining:

6/40	801
7/40	765, 769, 785
8/40	779, 791, 798
9/40	452, 792
11/40	449, 783, 787
12/40	451, 776
1/41	767, 784, 789
2/41	450
3/41	453, 790, 796
4/41	797
5/41	766
6/41	457
7/41	775
9/41	794
10/41	448, 763, 782
11/41	455, 802
12/41	788
1/42	454, 764
2/42	785, 804
3/42	805

In April 1942 456 SIR GALAHAD was the first to be painted plain black and this continued as a policy until January, 1946 – see The Record for individual dates. 771 SIR SAGRAMORE kept its Maunsell Olive Green until repainted plain black in July 1942 at Ashford. The repaints into Malachite Green after the War were:

3/46   767, 776, 789
4/46   766, 793
6/46   795
7/46   455, 783
9/46   790
10/46   775, 788, 801
11/46   774, 778
12/46   456, 796, 802
1/47   457, 777, 799
3/47   780
4/47   779, 782, 800
5/47   769, 771, 792, 804, 806
6/47   785
7/47   772
8/47   768
9/47   453, 763, 794
10/47   781, 786, 797
11/47   449, 770, 773, 798
12/47   450, 451

783 was the only one to be repainted at Ashford Works; all the others were dealt with at Eastleigh. Up to the end of 1947 448, 452, 454, 764, 787, 791, 803 and 805 remained in black so did not receive

any general repairs. They were duly dealt with after the formation of British Railways in 1948 and acquired Malachite Green (getting their BR numbers at the same time) as follows:

s787   3/48
30452   5/48
30784   5/48
30803   7/48
30448   8/48
30805   10/48
30791   12/48
30764   2/49
30454   3/49
30791   12/48

The last Malachite Green repaint of a Maunsell Arthur was for 30786 in July 1949. The first BR Green example was 30783 the following month. There was no overlap - there were no more Malachite Green Arthur repaints.

Dates of applying BR dark green:
7/49   30783
8/49   30457
9/49   30449, 30450
10/49   30779, 30782
11/49   30775, 30778, 30798, 30800
12/49   30772
1/50   30780
2/50   30451, 30453, 30796, 30804
3/50   30792
5/50   30455, 30771

6/50   30763, 30776, 30794, 30799
11/50   30784, 30787, 30806
1/51   30802
3/51   30766, 30801
4/51   30454, 30769
5/51   30781, 30791, 30793
6/51   30785, 30788
7/51   30770
9/51   30773
10/51   30767, 30797
12/51   30448, 30777, 30803, 30805
2/52   30765
3/52   30456, 30764
5/52   30452, 30774, 30789
6/52   30768
9/52   30795
10/52   30790
12/52   30786

Lamp Irons

LSWR lamp irons weren't lamp irons, in the conventional sense. On most other railways – probably *all* other railways – the iron was an upright piece of iron about 7in. by 1½in.; this 'male' bit fitted the 'female' bit on the lamp, whether at the rear as on most railways or at the side, as on the GWR. The LSWR perversely reversed this arrangement so that the lamp 'iron' was, in a sense, on the lamp. This was a flat bar on the back of the lamp which slotted into a housing on the upright iron on the buffer beam, smokebox door, or wherever. These LSW features

The back of (I believe) tender 855 which belonged to 30741 JOYOUS GARD (the home of 30455) at Bournemouth shed in BR days. An original Urie pattern 5,000 gallon bogie tender with the number plate long removed; six lamp irons. It's worth taking another look at those lamp irons; three are still the old LSW 'slots' rather than 'irons' proper and 'bars' have been jammed in to turn them into conventional irons. The others have been re-fashioned as 'traditional' lamp irons. It must have been an almighty nuisance in the first few years with the wrong lamps for the right irons and vice versa. No steam heat pipe, so it would be summer time. Photograph www.transporttreasury.co.uk

The front of 764 SIR GAWAIN in September 1936. Six 'lugs/clamps' on the smokebox door plus straight hand rail under top hinge strap; six lamp brackets available; still carries the 'No' with the 'o' underlined with a supporting dot. Wonderful attention to detail! Unused bolt holes in the curved plates denote the pre-deflector wide footstep.

That beautiful form; 779 SIR COLGREVANCE as built, at Nine Elms. The period is between July 1925 and April 1927 when it was the first of the class to be fitted with 'standard' smoke deflectors.

were repeated on the Maunsell Arthurs. There were six lamp irons at the front, three over the buffer beam, one either side of the smokebox door and one centrally placed at the top of the smokebox. On the Uries this was actually welded to the hand rail. The two smokebox rim lamp irons projected out; route indicator discs, when on these irons, projected out even further and obscured vision so they were moved inwards and lower, to the smokebox door – we've seen a similar process on the Nelsons and the Schools.

The LSWR style lamp irons were of course an infernal nuisance on the amalgamated Southern system (the LBSC and SECR being conventional in this regard) and the problem was overcome early on by jamming a bar into the LSW style irons to form a conventional lamp iron. Over the years these LSW relics disappeared, to be replaced by conventional fittings.

Oil Burning

During the coal strike of 1921 the SECR was the first railway company in the south of England to experiment with oil firing on steam locomotives. The LSWR was also exploring the benefits of oil and in April the same year converted 737 KING UTHER using a 'Scarab' system. 739 KING LEODEGRANCE followed in June. Both engines were based at Nine Elms and in this condition worked passenger trains to Bournemouth and Salisbury. Sadly, in July 739 burst into flames at Salisbury shed; the mechanism is unclear but the

fire was said to have been caused by the embers of a nearby locomotive. It was converted back to a coal burner next month and 737 was similarly dealt with in September.

Considerations of fuel supply were made even more pressing in 1926 with the outbreak of the General Strike; this in itself soon collapsed but the miners stayed out for months. This prompted further experimentation, on the part of the Southern this time and oil firing apparatus was fitted to 737 and 739 again, presumably making use of existing fittings on the locos. They worked from Eastleigh under the careful eye of the works, on goods trains between Southampton Docks and Salisbury. In July the pair moved to Nine Elms where they worked goods trains at night and by day passenger trains to Bournemouth and Salisbury.

	Oil burning	To coal burning	Mileage
737	16/6/26	22/12/26	19,046
739	2/6/26	17/12/26	21,998

Oil firing failed to take off because, as was the nature of these things, the immediate crisis always faded; strikes ended, coal supplies resumed. In any case it was not at all clear that oil would ever be particularly cheaper or even be more available than coal. So long as there was the labour, at the right price, to hew it and then to fire steam locos with it, it would remain the fuel of choice for the railways. The changed conditions, economic and technical, for oil to displace coal would not come till the 1950s.

After the Second World War the country was in severe financial crisis, a

great debt hung over it and another fuel crisis was in full swing. The best quality coal was being exported and the railways were running on poor quality coal. So the Government asked all four Companies to convert over 1,000 of their steam locomotives to oil burning, with the total for the Southern set at 110. This was to be confined to the South Western section with the main depot at Eastleigh where a maximum of 40,000 gallons of oil could be stored. The maximum at Fratton was 5,000. Tanks and pumps would also be installed at Salisbury, Exmouth Junction Basingstoke, Bournemouth and Nine Elms which would serve as 'top-up sheds'. Heavy oil fuel was to be used, which also, many forget, had to be warmed before it could be pumped into tender tanks. A number of SR engines were converted but we are only concerned with the Arthurs and the first one dealt with was 740 MERLIN at Eastleigh Works which had an oil tank of 1,600 gallon capacity fixed by a series of bolts to the bottom of the tender. This Arthur worked out of Eastleigh and a number of other Southern sheds and though it was planned to convert another nine of the class only four more were dealt with:

	Converted	Restored to coal burning
740 MERLIN	14/12/46	30/10/48
745 TINTAGEL	4/10/47	18/12/48
748 VIVIEN	27/9/47	20/11/48
749 ISEULT	11/10/47	20/11/48
752 LINETTE	27/9/47	25/9/48

Arthurs 745 and 749 were fitted with

electric headlamps powered by a steam generator and the other oil-burning Arthurs had been dealt with by January 1948; all were based at Eastleigh. 'Come September 1948 the Government-inspired oil scheme had largely collapsed once it was realised that the price in foreign exchange could not be afforded and the Eastleigh Arthurs were laid aside for conversion back to coal firing.

Window Wipers
Eastleigh Test 1207 of 6 December 1927 refers to 'Window Cleaning Arrangements' as fitted to E801 and E766. The latter subsequently lost its wiper - see 30801 later on in the book.

Hand Rails
The Arthurs had hand rails running the length of the boiler to the smokebox, for cleaners and others, the same as all other locomotives. A number of differences are observable at the front over time, with Urie smokebox doors gradually replaced by Maunsell pattern ones a complicating factor. On 736-755 and 448-457 the hand rail curved over the front of the smokebox in the traditional British style, on the rest they did not; instead a third, short straight rail was placed on the smokebox door.

On 736-755 and 448-457 there was a central dart and four retaining 'dogs' on the lower rim of the smokebox door. The later Arthurs had Maunsell pattern doors which eventually became the norm; they had no central dart but six 'dogs', this time disposed around the door.

The boilerside hand rails were finished off 'tacked' to the top of the smoke deflectors when they were fitted and for the earlier engines the 'loop' over the smokebox front was replaced by a separate but short rail curved in line on the top of the smokebox rim.

The various combinations can be seen in the different photographs; it gets worse – 780, 795 and 805 got an earlier Urie smokebox door for instance. Some Maunsell ones without the central dart also had at one time the little 'opening handle' (784 and 793 for instance) just like the Nelsons. In due course this disappeared too. It is impossible to tabulate this sort of detail once we get down to this level of nitty-grittiness so – the usual rule applies, get a photograph if it's essential to model a particular loco at a particular time.

Feedwater Heaters
Some of the Urie Arthurs were fitted with these under the tender, normally between the two bogies but they are not easy to spot on photos of them in LSWR days. Maunsell, it seems, found

little use for them and they were removed early on in his reign.

Crosshead Vacuum Pumps
Maunsell had these fitted to all of his Arthurs, a crosshead-driven vacuum pump which was positioned under the left-hand side lower slidebar. Bulleid found these superfluous, or rather not worth the maintenance, and during his time they were all removed.

Flaman Speed Recorders
In October 1927 E452 SIR MELIAGRANCE and E782 SIR BRIAN were fitted with Flaman Speed Recorders, their presence denoted by a cable from the trailing driving wheel to the cab on the right-hand side. They did not prove reliable and the equipment was removed, from E452 in March 1930 and from E782 in December 1930. For some reason Bulleid felt the equipment ought to be tried again and the following list shows the Arthurs dealt with. It was soon removed again, no doubt because of the outbreak of war.

451: fitted visit ending 11/1/39, removed visit ending 11/12/40
457: fitted visit ending 17/8/38, removed visit ending 25/6/41
767: fitted visit ending 10/8/38, removed visit ending 1/1/41
779: fitted visit ending 17/8/38, removed visit ending 28/8/40
793: fitted visit ending 21/6/39, removed visit ending 9/12/42

E Prefix
At Grouping the Southern inherited over 2,000 steam locomotives made up

of 125 different classes which involved frequently duplicated numbers. To differentiate them the prefix A was applied to Ashford maintained engines, B to Brighton maintained machines and E to those maintained at Eastleigh. All three prefixes were done away with in the early 1930s, with 1000 added to the former A engines, 2000 to the former B engines and the E simply removed from the Eastleigh engines. In 1948 under BR 30000 was added to most Southern Railway engines.

S Lettering
With the formation of BR in 1948 some temporary renumbering took place and for a while four Arthurs ran with the letter S in front of their old SR running number as follows:
453: S added 31/1/48, renumbered 30453 17/2/50
747: S added 24/1/48, renumbered 30747 12/5/50
750: S added 7/2/48, renumbered 30750 6/11/48
753: Gained the S in Eastleigh Works but emerged as 30753
754: S added 17/1/48, and promptly removed - reverted to plain 754, renumbered 30754 2/7/48
787: S added 12/3/48; renumbered 30787 8/4/49

ATC/AWS
Apart from some experiments in the distant past Automatic Train Control was never used on the Southern and it was the BR AWS (Automatic Warning System) that eventually came to be

An oiler's view of **KING UTHER** at Bournemouth shed; feed water clacks, that giant reversing lever and connecting rod big end. Photograph www.transporttreasury.co.uk

adopted, on the Southern Region from 1959. A number of Schools and Nelsons were fitted with it. So far as the more venerable Arthurs were concerned only one, 30802 SIR DURNORE got the gear, on its last visit to Eastleigh, a Light Casual in June 1960. It kept it for just over a year before withdrawal in July 1961.

Electric Lighting
In the late 1940s the five oil burners were equipped with the electric lighting which had become so familiar on the Bulleid Pacifics.
740: 3/1/48
745: 4/10/47
748: 13/12/47
749: 28/11/47
752: 20/11/47

Joyous detail. 30741 JOYOUS GARD has the multiple jet blastpipe and chimney (fitted at Eastleigh 1940-41). Hand rail joined to the top of smoke deflector by brackets, handhold cut-out and step at front, steam sanding to front driving wheel, splasher over rear bogie wheel. Fluted connecting rods, fluted slidebars as normal for 30736-45. Reversing shaft was set an inch further back than on the Maunsell engines and the arm to the lifting link was an inch shorter. Note studded joint halfway down smokebox. Also that fascinating small 'splasher' form on top of the running plate just ahead of the centre of the leading wheel. This was a hinged cover (see also the *Books Of* the Nelsons and Schools) to allow inspection and lubrication of the junction of pivot, radius rod and expansion link beneath.
Photograph www.transporttreasury.co.uk

30448 SIR TRISTRAM, a Salisbury engine for most of its life, in its home city on 13th August 1955 with a three coach local in tow, made up of what looks like LSWR vintage stock performing duty 475. The board carries the train reporting number, 263.

The Record

Although first introduced in 1918 by Robert Urie with the Maunsell version following in 1925 the record cards that are available at the NRM, York are the Southern Railway Wx183 series which only start with some entries from 1935 (but mainly 1936) through to the demise of the class. Considering the rush to get rid of steam in the 1960s very little of this material is missing and the BR entries are later bolstered by information from the BR9637 weekly returns from the Southern Region Works, Eastleigh, Ashford and Brighton, held at the National Archives at Kew [formerly the Public Record Office]. The boiler record cards at the NRM have also been examined.

Abbreviations for repairs under Southern Railway control:-
A = General
B = Intermediate
C = Casual
D = Non-classified

The following codes for repairs under British Railway were based on LMS practice.
GO = General Overhaul
HC = Heavy Casual
HI = Heavy Intermediate
LC = Light Casual
LI = Light Intermediate
Int = Intermediate
NC = Non-classified

Some were upgraded as the work unfolded such as LI-HI but seldom downgraded as in LC-NC and these entries were more prevalent on the BR9637 forms.

'Return' indicates a return visit to works normally soon after a classified repair to rectify (on the LMS for instance it was called 'Rectification') a problem often found during running-in trials. The vast majority of the repairs were carried out at Eastleigh Works as shown in the individual records with some attention at Ashford [AFD] and Brighton [BTN]. Where work was needed elsewhere on shed the abbreviations are entered as follows:-
[NE] = Nine Elms
[EXJ] = Exmouth Junction
[SL] = Stewarts Lane
[BA] = Bricklayers Arms
[DOV] = Dover
[SAL] = Salisbury (entered on the Southern Railway records as Sarum).

Space was saved on the Record Cards and the BR9637 forms to record various repairs/experiments/modifications as a 'Test'. Those listed seemed more common after World War Two and were mainly initiated at Eastleigh. They were denoted by a number with a 'T' prefix, together with abbreviations which we believe meant [R] 'Reconditioned'; [U] 'Undisturbed' and [O] 'Overhauled'. The list is not complete as I am sure some 'Tests' were not listed; moreover all written/typed entries on the records are subject to human fallibility.

T1852: Ashpan down draught
T1891: Thomas 'patent rod piston packing'
T1977: Water gauge protection
T2025: Spring links fitted with copper plated threads
T2052: Spark arrester
T2070: Wear resistance of Cast Iron piston rings (special piston heads and rings)
T2074: Copper stays
T2080: Left and right hand gauge glasses
T2081: Regulator valve special material valve no.8
T2134: Packing jointing material fitted
T2138: Storm sheets fitted
T2149: Ferguson and Timpsons jointing compound
T2189: Standardisation of white metals
T2214: Exhaust injector cones
T2222: Regulator valve, BR alloy
T2256: Tyres turned; apexior paint was probably the brand name, either heat or oil resistant
T2258: Boiler barrel patch plates

Important note: The SR allocated new numbers to all its existing tenders in August 1927. In the following tender lists the number against 1925 pairings is the post-1927 number, on the basis that no tender change occurred between 1925 and 1927.

30448 SIR TRISTRAM with a down train at Andover. Photograph Paul Chancellor Collection.

30448 SIR TRISTRAM

Works order no.C17
To traffic as E448 5/1925
Renumbered 30448 7/8/48

Boilers
No.765 as of 8/1/37
No.827 20/11/37
No.841 3/6/39
No.834 22/10/41
No.1055 22/9/43
No.787 7/9/45
No.1405 7/8/48
No.1406 8/8/53
No.491 1/12/56

Works

2/1929	Smoke deflectors fitted
5/1933	E prefix removed
9/12/36-8/1/37**B**	61,803
15/6/37-30/6/37**C**	81,076 Extension of mileage 10,000
21/10/37-20/11/37**A**	100,107
8/5/39-3/6/39**A**	85,499 Olive Green livery
4/9/41-22/10/41**A**	95,854 Malachite Green livery
17/8/43-22/9/43**A**	88,413 Wartime Black livery
25/7/45-7/9/45**A**	87,472
12/2/46-15/3/46**C[SAL]**	26,247
23/4/46-18/5/46**B**	27,747
3/1/47-8/2/47**B**	61,296
29/9/47-11/10/47**C**	86,297 Extension of mileage 10,000; Snifting valves removed
1/7/48-7/8/48**A**	112,420 Renumbered 30448; T2134 Packing jointing material fitted; Malachite Green livery
6/10/49-21/10/49**LC**	31,440
6/7/50-1/9/50**LC**	73,254
26/11/51-15/12/51**LI**	133,247 BR Green livery
25/2/52-8/3/52**LC**	144,944
30/6/53-8/8/53**GO**	194,742
28/4/55-14/5/55**LI**	70,369
7/11/56-1/12/56**GO**	131,422
27/10/58-8/11/58**LI**	87,207

Tenders
No.870 from new
No.801 from H15 30478, 14/5/55

Sheds
Exmouth Junction 5/1925
Salisbury 7/37

Withdrawn 27/8/60; stored at Eastleigh Works 8/60; cut up at Eastleigh Works w/e 10/9/60
Total 1,483,140 miles

449 SIR TORRE (son of 738) on Honiton bank with a West Country express made up of Maunsell carriages; smoke deflectors were fitted in April 1929. The Arthur is just over three years old, at the start of its career on the Western Section of the SR; Drummond eight wheel water cart tender, four 'dogs' on the smokebox door complete with locking dart, upright hand hold 'posts' and grab irons on frame the latter not yet removed. 449 was one of a minority of King Arthurs to retain its continuous boiler hand rail when fitted with smoke deflectors. Photograph H.C. Casserley, courtesy R.M. Casserley.

30449 SIR TORRE

Works order no.C17
To traffic as E449 6/1925
Renumbered 30449 23/9/49

Works	
4/1929	Smoke deflectors fitted
5/1933	E prefix removed
13/4/35	Stays: 150 holes bushed; Plates: New copper firebox; casing covering, three-quarter sides; Tubes: 169, new "Talbot Stead"; 24 2nd hand Superheater tubes [copper ends]
17/10/36-14/11/36A	74,967
20/3/39-19/4/39A	91,231 Stays: 847 copper renewed; 450 holes bushed Plates: Copper tube, new; Copper wrapping, flanges half-side; Throat welded; Barrel, s.v. seating welded; Tubes: 167 out, 84 welded; 24 new Superheater tubes; Maunsell Green livery
8/10/40-6/11/40A	70,989 Malachite Green livery
18/2/41-26/2/41D	1,897
25/6/42-12/8/42B	65,666 Extension of mileage 10,000
12/7/43-1/9/43A	107,444 Wartime Black livery
28/3/45-12/5/45A	78,068 Stays: 437 copper renewed; 10 roof renewed Plates: Copper wrapping, angle patch; Rivets and seams caulked; Throat, drop plugs; Tubes: 167, new "Howell"; 24 new Superheater tubes; New left hand cylinder
24/1/46-9/3/46B	33,275
20/1/47-8/2/47C	72,587
27/10/47-15/11/47A	97,704 Malachite Green livery from Black
10/8/49-23/9/49A	72,578 Stays: 500 copper renewed; 12 holes bushed Plates: Copper tube, firebox-studs renewed; Protection plate; Rivets, seams and studs repaired; Lead plugs and brick arch studs renewed; Renumbered 30449; BR Green livery; Snifting valves removed
21/3/52-3/5/52GO	73,871 Stays: 634 copper renewed; Longitudinal renewed, all; 50 roof renewed; Plates: Copper tube, new; Copper firehole, 2 angles; Steel tube, new; Fusible plugs renewed; Tubes: Set, new superheater tubes; Foundation ring renewed
12/8/53-22/8/53LC	52,193
27/4/54-15/5/54LI	81,256 Stays: 300 copper repaired; 37 copper renewed; Plates: Copper tube, rivets renewed with studs; Copper firehole, rivets renewed with studs; new fusible plugs; Tubes: 30, new; 2 new Superheater tubes; Combination lever and valve spindle pin E47476
25/7/55-27/8/55LC	139,219
27/2/56-24/3/56GO	158,994 Stays: 682 monel metal renewed; 682 nuts renewed; 310 holes bushed; Plates: Copper tube, 2 angle patches fitted; Tubes: Set, new "Stewart and Lloyds"; Set, new Superheater tubes
15/8/57-17/8/57LC	63,612
13/12/57-4/1/58LI-HI	76,115

Boilers
No.825 13/4/35
No.802 14/11/36
No.451 19/4/39
No.768 6/11/40
No.448 1/9/43
No.451 12/5/45
No.1051 15/11/47
No.782 23/9/49
No.805 3/5/52
No.1402 24/3/56

Tenders
No.871 from new
No.857 from 30753 11/55

Sheds
Exmouth Junction 6/1925
Salisbury 7/1937

Withdrawn 19/12/59; stored at Eastleigh Works 12/59; cut up at Eastleigh Works w/e 26/12/59. Total 1,373,426 miles

A magnificent 30449 SIR TORRE in BR green, at Eastleigh. The bolted inspection panel on the cylinder covers was a late feature.

30449 SIR TORRE (son of 30738) another long term Salisbury servant, at its home shed on 13th May 1958. This is just a few months before its last overhaul at Eastleigh, a heavy intermediate in the autumn. Behind it is one of the three surviving 0415 4-4-2Ts 30584, then based at Exmouth Junction and no doubt dropping in on its way to or from Eastleigh Works. Photograph Brian Morrison.

30449 SIR TORRE at Nine Elms on 10th July 1953 where it is ready to back down to Waterloo and return west to its Salisbury home. The tender has the large version of the first BR totem and the fireman seems to be carrying out final adjustments at the rear of the tender. Behind is MN 35011 GENERAL STEAM NAVIGATION, then a Nine Elms resident. Photograph B.K.B. Green, Initial Photographics.

30450 SIR KAY

Works order no.C17
To traffic as E450 6/1925
Renumbered 30450 20/9/49

Works

2/1926 to 3/1927	Small wing plates behind the chimney
12/1927	Smoke deflectors fitted
11/1929	Boiler changed
6/1932	E prefix removed
24/10/35-23/11/35**C**	49,429
3/6/36-4/7/36**A**	83,267
10/11/37-4/12/37**A**	87,816
8/1/38-12/1/38**D**	[No mileage recorded]
24/5/39-26/6/39**A**	81,920 Plates: Copper tube, flanges welded and studded; Throat, seams welded; Barrel, S.V. seatings welded; Tubes: 167, 2nd hand, welded; 24 new Superheater tubes [copper ends]; Olive Green livery
23/8/40-28/8/40**D**	71,031 Stays: 2 direct crown stays renewed
26/12/40-12/2/41**A**	88,009 Malachite Green livery
24/10/42-18/11/42**A**	83,552 Wartime Black livery
26/4/45-16/6/45**A**	108,024 Stays: 137 copper renewed; PLates: 2 angles; Drop plugs; Tubes: 167, new; Superheater tubes expanded and referruled
4/10/46-26/10/46**C**	57,536 Stays: 350 copper repaired; Plates: Seams caulked and studs repaired; Tubes: 12, 2nd hand
8/11/47-6/12/47**A**	95,100 Stays: 590 copper renewed; Plates: Copper tube, studs and seams caulked; Copper firehole, flanges welded, right-hand side; Casing firehole, welded; Throat welded at left shoulder; Tubes: Set, new "Howell"; 24 2nd hand Superheater tubes; Malachite Green livery from Black; Snifting valves removed; T2025 Spring links with copper plated threads fitted
13/7/48-14/7/48**D**	23,834
31/8/49-20/9/49**A**	77,634 Renumbered 30450; BR Green livery
12/5/52-14/6/52**GO**	92,961
8/3/54-3/4/54**GO**	80,794 Combination lever and spindle valve pin modified E47476
2/9/54-11/9/54**LC**	20,178
18/8/55-20/8/55**LC**	46,102
1/5/56-19/5/56**LC**	59,050
10/10/56-27/10/56**LI-HI**	72,811
8/9/58-11/10/58**GO**	146,272 Stays: 832 monel metal renewed; 832 nuts renewed; 6 longitudinal renewed; Crown, all renewed; 10 crown bars refitted with bolts; Plates: Copper tube, new; Copper firehole, 2 flanges, one-half sides; Steel tube, protection patch Copper wrapping, 2 flanges, one-half sides; Casing covering, 256 holes bushed; 2 fusible plugs renewed; Tubes: 167, new "Tube products";24 new Superheater tubes

Boilers
No.803 as of 23/11/35
No.763 4/7/36
No.786 4/12/37
No.806 26/6/39
No.453 12/2/41
No.1049 18/11/42
No.800 16/6/45
No.454 6/12/47
No.792 20/9/49
No.453 14/6/52
No.791 3/4/54
No.1410 11/10/58

Tenders
No.872 from new
No.851 from 30737 27/10/56

Sheds
Nine Elms 6/1925
Salisbury 1/1933

Withdrawn 3/9/60; stored at Eastleigh Works 9/60; cut up at Eastleigh Works w/e 24/9/60 Total 1,478,783 miles

30450 SIR KAY at Basingstoke shed, 20th June 1956.

450 SIR KAY in pre-war days at Nine Elms on 12th March 1939, three months before a major overhaul and repainting in Olive Green. Smokebox door with six 'dogs', screw coupling hung in right place, fitted for steam heating on front buffer beam, cabside number plate, short name plate, though the running number on the tender looks a bit faded. 'Pep' pipe hanging over cabside and with crew member on Drummond water cart tender it looks like the engine is being prepared to back down to Waterloo to work back home to Salisbury. The 'E' was abolished in mid-1931 and replaced on the buffer beams, in serif style, by 'No' with the little 'o' underlined and a dot below it, as here. Photograph R.J. Buckley, Initial Photographics.

30450 SIR KAY was one we all wanted to see as we had a teacher, Mr Kay and he could never understand the silly schoolboy remarks referring to him as loco. Then at Salisbury, 30450 is taking on water at Nine Elms on 31st May 1960, ready for a journey back home. Staining from the two leaking washout plugs have created a mess right down to the splasher. Just another four months and SIR KAY would head for the great round table in the sky. Photo Peter Groom.

30451 SIR LAMORAK

Works order no.C17
To traffic as E451 6/1925
Renumbered 30451 31/7/48

Works

5/11/25	Stays: 350 copper riveted over
3/3/26	Stays: 350 copper riveted over
25/11/27	Stays: 591 copper renewed; Copper tube, angle patch; Rivets: Foundation ring renewed; Tubes: 96, new, 24 referruled; Smoke deflectors fitted
17/10/28	Stays: 10 copper renewed; 250 copper riveted over; Plates: Copper tube, new plugs; Tubes: 70, new
2/5/29	Stays: 805 copper renewed; Roof renewed, all; Plates: Box and casing caulked; New brick arch studs and plugs; Tubes: 169, new "BM"; 24 Superheater tubes, ferruled, copper ends
5/1932	E prefix removed
25/6/35-13/7/35C	56,503
11/11/35-7/12/35A	80,862
14/4/37-22/5/37A	75,995
8/12/38-11/1/39A	78,724 Stays: 120 holes bushed; Plates: New copper firebox; Casing covering, new;Tubes: 169, new "Talbot and Stead"; 24 2nd hand Superheater tubes; Maunsell Green livery; Flaman speed recorder
3/10/40-11/12/40A	91,352 Stays: 415 copper renewed; Plates: Rivets and seams caulked; Lead plugs,Tubes: 143 out, 84 welded; Superheater tubes expanded; Flaman speed recorder removed. Malachite Green livery
11/4/42-3/6/42A	74,677 Wartime Black livery
4/2/44-16/2/44C	73,559
17/4/45-26/5/45A	110,843 Stays: Monel metal stays on wrapper sides; Copper stays on back plate and tubeplate; 120 holes bushed; Plates: New copper firebox; Drop plugs; Tubes: 169, new "Howell"; 24 new Superheater tubes
17/1/47-22/2/47C	78,115 Stays: 100 copper repaired; Plates: Lead plugs renewed; Seams caulked; Studs renewed and rivets repaired; Extension of mileage 15,000; New right hand cylinder
1/12/47-27/12/47A	109,346 Malachite Green livery from Black; Snifting valves removed
29/7/48-31/7/48D	20,806 Renumbered 30451
24/1/50-24/2/50A	72,863 Stays: 393 copper renewed; Plates: Firebox, seams and studs caulked; Tubes: Set, new "Talbot and Stead"; Set, new Superheater tubes; BR Green livery
20/11/50-11/12/50LC[BTN]	23,000
17/12/51-12/1/52HI	71,122 Stays: 300 copper renewed; Plates: Seams repaired with studs; Fusible plugs renewed; Tubes: Set, new; 3 new Superheater tubes
28/7/52-12/8/52LC	95,009
23/6/53-31/7/53GO	128,408
3/6/54-12/6/54LC	37,658
17/6/55-2/7/55LI	72,146 Live steam injector pipes modified
2/1/57-26/1/57GO	139,739
26/6/57-6/7/57NC	18,185
17/1/58-25/1/58HC	42,172 Stays: 777 copper renewed; 378 copper riveted over; 4 longitudinal renewed; Roof renewed, all; Plates: Copper tube, new; Copper firehole, 12 rivets renewed; Copper wrapping, flanged, one-half sides; Throat patches; Tubes, set 167, new "Stewart and Lloyds"; 24 new Superheater tubes; Rivets; Foundation ring renewed, all.Boiler repaired at Brighton and re-tested at Eastleigh to 200 lbs psi
9/12/58-3/1/59HI	77,289 Stays: 2 copper renewed; 580 copper riveted over; Plates: 112 rivets and seams repaired; 2 fusible plugs renewed; Tubes; 30 out; 3 new Superheater tubes
21/12/60-28/1/61GO	158,908

Boilers

No.451 5/11/25
No.799 2/5/29
No.742 as of 13/7/35
No.773 22/5/37
No.839 11/1/39
No.451 11/12/40
No.828 3/6/42
No.839 26/5/45
No.778 27/12/47
No.457 24/2/50
No.797 31/7/53
No.795 26/1/57
No.451 25/1/58
No.1050 28/1/61

Tenders

No.873 from new
No.3211 from N15X
32333 26/1/57

Sheds

Nine Elms 6/1925
Salisbury 1/33
Basingstoke 8/1/49
Nine Elms 9/10/50
Salisbury 8/12/50

Withdrawn 16/6/62; stored at Eastleigh Works 6/62; cut up at Eastleigh Works w/e 30/6/62
Total 1,579,556 miles

451 SIR LAMORAK, soon after equipping with smoke deflectors (period ending 25/11/27) but before the 'E' prefix was dispensed with (period 5/32). Lamp irons 'adapted' and all period features as originally disposed – lamp irons, crosshead vacuum pump, 'A' on running plate and so on. No hand hole on deflectors or step on front drop.

A subtly changed, BR SIR LAMORAK, at Salisbury shed on 23 April 1962; among all the other little alterations is the extension of the drain cock pipes and their clipping to the front footstep. It was one of the last in service, withdrawn only eighteen months after a General. The tender came from an N15X and has rear footsteps and hand rails. Photograph Gavin Morrison.

30451 SIR LAMORAK at Feltham shed, 11th April 1953; it was a Salisbury engine and is an unusual sight in this period at this largely freight only shed. Alongside is H16 4-6-2T 30518 with that distinctive chimney. Photograph Paul Chancellor Collection.

On a damp 20th June 1956 30451 SIR LAMORAK awaits departure on a local train from Basingstoke, duty no.441.

30452 SIR MELIAGRANCE

Works order no.C17
To traffic as E452 7/1925
Renumbered 30452 29/5/48

Works

12/1927	Smoke deflectors fitted; Flaman speed recorder fitted
3/1930	Flaman speed recorder removed
10/1931	E prefix removed
12/7/35-3/8/35C	56,257
23/9/35-4/10/35C	60,087
25/2/36-28/3/36A	80,491
15/7/37-4/9/37A	79,537
4/5/39-26/5/39A	79,940 Olive Green livery
10/8/40-25/9/40A	75,548 Malachite Green livery
17/1/41-28/1/41D	5,068
27/11/42-9/1/43A	98,053 Wartime Black livery
1/7/44-22/8/44C	73,355
12/9/45-13/10/45A	128,481
8/1/46-26/1/46C	3,214
16/1/47-8/2/47C	42,924
22/4/48-29/5/48A	89,030 Renumbered 30452; Snifting valves removed
9/5/50-9/6/50LI	71,848 Malachite Green livery
18/12/50-5/1/51LC	101,783
23/4/52-31/5/52GO	157,107 BR Green livery
16/4/53-25/4/53LC	42,621
20/6/53-26/6/53LC	51,024
24/11/53-12/12/53LI	71,698
13/4/54-17/4/54LC	85,382
19/9/55-15/10/55GO	154,516
15/10/56-26/10/56LC	54,471
8/5/57-1/6/57HI	75,972
10/9/57-14/9/57LC	89,233
6/12/57-14/12/57LC	98,957
21/1/58-25/1/58LC	103,542
27/2/58-29/3/58LC	106,224

Boilers
No.804 as of 3/8/35
No.452 4/9/37
No.768 26/5/39
No.1001 25/9/40
No.831 9/1/43
No.775 13/10/45
No.766 29/5/48
No.802 31/5/52
No.449 15/10/55

Tenders
No.874 from new
No.902 from 30785 1/6/57

Sheds
Salisbury? 7/1925
Nine Elms 1/33
Salisbury 7/37

Withdrawn 22/8/59;
stored at Eastleigh Works
8-9/59; cut up at Eastleigh
Works w/e 10/10/59
Total 1,494,011 miles

30452 SIR MELIAGRANCE on the turntable at Nine Elms complete with Drummond water cart tender, coal rails filled in. It's midsummer, Saturday 16th July 1955 and it looks like those flats, familiar for so long, are nearing completion. Another long-time Salisbury engine, no doubt 30452 will soon be back to the west. Photograph J.H. Aston.

Early BR days finds 30452 SIR MELIAGRANCE on 21st February 1951 backing out of Waterloo coupled to a Battle of Britain on their way to Nine Elms for servicing, turning and their next duties which should see the Arthur returning to Salisbury, its home shed.

It is the end of the line for 30452 SIR MELIAGRANCE as it waits as Eastleigh on 29th August 1959, withdrawn for a week. Eastleigh didn't hang about for this loco was scrapped by 10 October 1959.

30453 KING ARTHUR

Works order no.B17
To traffic as E453 2/1925
Renumbered 30453 17/2/50

Works

4/1927	Smoke deflectors; worked with small version of standard size smoke deflectors
7/1928	Standard smoke deflectors fitted
7/1931	Stays: 81 copper renewed; Roof renewed, all; Plates: New lead plugs; New casing crown plate; Rivets and stays caulked on casing crown; Tubes: 169, 2nd hand steel, welded; 24 2nd hand Superheater tubes, copper ends; E prefix removed
16/4/32	Boiler off frame for fitters
25/3/33	Stays: 408 copper renewed; Plates: Copper firehole, flanges welded; Lead plugs; Rivets and seams caulked; Tubes: 60, 2nd hand steel, welded; Superheater tubes expanded
31/5/33	Plates: 5 studs in back plate; Steel tube, flanges; Casing back, flanges chipped and caulked
19/4/34	Plates: Copper firehole, flanges welded and studded; Lead plugs
8/6/34	Stays: 8 copper renewed; 300 copper riveted over; Plates: Copper firehole, 1 angle patch
25/9/35-1/11/35**C**	51,498
29/5/36-4/7/36**A**	83,346
2/11/36-3/11/36**D**	17,037
12/11/36-4/12/36**D**	24,527
23/6/37-28/7/37**B**	58,656
28/2/38-6/4/38**A**	91,024
12/6/39-10/7/39**A**	78,443 Olive Green livery
22/6/40-23/7/40**B**	59,926
11/2/41-24/3/41**A**	90,554 Malachite Green livery
14/10/42-11/11/42**A**	79,229 Wartime Black livery
27/6/45-3/8/45**A**	[No mileage recorded]
2/5/46**D**	38,614
20/5/46-1/6/46**C**	42,004
17/7/46-26/7/46**C**	44,127
5/8/47-6/9/47**A**	91,894 Stays: 130 roof renewed; Plates: New copper firebox; Steel tube, new; New three-quarter sides and new crown plate; Tubes: Set, new "Howell"; Set new Superheater tubes; Malachite Green livery from Black
31/12/47-31/1/48	10,570 Stays: 450 copper repaired; Plates: Drop plugs renewed; Renumbered S453; Snifting valves removed
18/1/50-17/2/50**GO**	91,294 Renumbered 30453; BR Green livery
9/4/52-24/5/52**GO**	72,251 Stays: 50 copper renewed; 472 monel metal renewed; 472 nuts renewed; Roof renewed, all; Plates: Copper tube, new; Copper firehole, studded; Tubes: Set, new; Set, new Superheater tubes
12/11/53-5/12/53**LI**	74,359 Stays: 350 monel metal repaired; 350 steel nuts renewed; Plates: Copper tube, rivets renewed with studs; Copper firehole, rivets renewed with studs, Set, new fusible plugs; Barrel ring caulked; Tubes: 30, new; 24 Superheater tubes repaired
17/2/54-26/3/54**LC-HC**	82,058 W/E 20/3/54 awaiting cylinders; New left hand cylinder
18/11/55-30/12/55**GO**	146,642
1/4/57-18/4/57**LI**	62,101
29/5/58-5/7/58**GO**	113,655
7/7/59-8/7/59**NC**	45,030
12/1/60-30/1/60**LI**	68,337

Boilers
No.839 7/1931
No.795 as of 1/11/35
No.774 6/4/38
No.777 10/7/39
No.791 24/3/41
No.787 11/11/42
No.798 3/8/45
No.806 6/9/47
No.453 17/2/50
No.1402 24/5/52
No.803 30/12/55
No.929 5/7/58

Tenders
No.875 from new
No.856 from 30742 18/4/57

Shed
Salisbury 2/1925

Withdrawn 8/7/61; stored at Eastleigh Works 7-9/61; cut up at Eastleigh Works w/e 21/10/61 Total 1,606,428 miles

The doyen, and a favourite of many, 30453 KING ARTHUR with tender no.856; had it not got it in April 1957, it might well have survived into preservation for without the Drummond water cart, it was deemed 'not original'. KING ARTHUR is working a slow train to Basingstoke, first stop Woking I believe, on 11th May 1959. Within two months it was in Eastleigh Works for a non-classified repair. Photograph B.W.L. Brooksbank, Initial Photographics.

KING ARTHUR as s453, at Yeovil Town shed some time in 1948; BRITISH RAILWAYS in sunshine lettering on the tender. The 's' appeared at the end of January 1948, the proper BR number replacing it in February 1950. Photograph Paul Chancellor Collection.

30453 KING ARTHUR at Nine Elms on 23rd March 1956 with original tender; it lost it at Eastleigh during a Light Intermediate in April 1957. Photo Peter Groom.

KING ARTHUR at Basingstoke on 20th June 1953 heading five coach set no.833 which consisted of BSK, SK, CK, SK and BSK, the BSK being a Semi-saloon brake second.

Two more of KING ARTHUR at Basingstoke on 20th June 1953, with the same coaching set no.833 and the loco still carrying duty no.432. With the angles of the photos the train must have either had a long lay over or the photographer had a lineside permit.

30454 QUEEN GUINEVERE

Works order no.B17
To traffic as E454 3/1925
Renumbered 30454 11/3/49

Works

6/1925	New Boiler no.454
6/7/28	Stays: 180 copper renewed; 150 copper riveted over; Plates: New studs in flanges; New brick arch studs; Lead plugs; Tubes: 84, new, 85 expanded; Smoke deflectors fitted
5/1931-8/1932	Bolton Superheater
8/1932	E prefix removed
5/8/33	Stays: 124 copper renewed; Plates: Flanges welded; Copper wrapping, top seams welded; Lead plugs; Tubes: 169, 2nd hand, electrically welded; 24 2nd hand Superheater tubes, copper ends
22/10/35-22/11/35**A**	89,826
17/2/37-19/3/37**A**	78,968
3/6/38-6/7/38**A**	66,956 Stays: 443 copper renewed; 2 roof renewed; Plates: Studs in flanges; Lead plugs; Throat, seams welded; Barrel seating welded Tubes: 169, new "Howell"; 24 new Superheater tubes, copper ends
22/12/39-31/1/40**A**	70,559 Olive Green livery
25/7/40-14/8/40**B**	19,903 Stays: 471 copper renewed; Plates: Copper tube, 2 angles; Flanges welded; Lead plugs; Throat, seams welded; Barrel, safety valve seatings welded; Tubes: 169, 2nd hand, welded; 24 2nd hand Superheater tubes, welded
15/12/41-28/1/42**A**	76,174 Malachite Green livery
26/1/44-25/2/44**A**	92,114 Wartime Black livery
3/8/45-15/9/45**A**	63,254 New right hand cylinder
22/3/46-7/6/46**B**	15,025
15/9/47-3/10/47**C**	63,833
8/2/49-11/3/49**A**	112,618 Malachite Green livery from Black; Renumbered 30454; Snifting valves removed
16/3/51-12/4/51**LI**	79,985 BR Green livery
22/8/52-20/9/52**GO**	144,587
27/8/53-12/9/53**HC**	45,123
29/1/54-19/2/54**NC**	64,151 (at Salisbury shed)
27/8/54-18/9/54**LI-GO**	88,076 Stays: 885 copper renewed; 30 direct and 3 sling renewed; Plates: Copper tube, new; 2 new fusible plugs; Steel tube, levelled; 2 protection patches fitted; 2 angles and 2 flanges half sides fitted on wrapping plate; Tubes: All renewed; All Superheater tubes renewed; 430 holes bushed in casing covering plate; T2256 Apexior paint [U]
5/9/56-8/9/56**NC**	47,884 Plates: Vacuum seating re-caulked and rivets repaired
2/10/56-5/10/56**NC**	51,127 Plates: Vacuum injector seating welded and caulked; T2256 [U]
29/5/57-15/6/57**LI**	77,779 Stays: 590 copper riveted over; Plates: Seams repaired; 112 studs renewed; 2 fusible plugs renewed; Vacuum seating, welded and caulked; Tubes: Set, new "Stewart and Lloyds"; 3 new Superheater tubes; T2256: Tyres turned

Boilers
New no.454 6/1925
No.800 5/8/33
No.834 22/11/35
No.455 19/3/37
No.454 6/7/38
No.795 31/1/40
No.781 14/8/40
No.770 28/1/42
No.766 25/2/44
No.783 7/6/46
No.830 11/3/49
No.789 20/9/52
No.806 15/6/57

Tenders
No.876 from new
No.878 at Nine Elms shed 31/7/46 from 30456
No.868 from 30755 on 15/6/57

Sheds
Salisbury 3/1925
Exmouth Junction 12/12/49
Salisbury 12/5/51

Withdrawn 18/10/58; stored at Eastleigh shed 10/58; cut up at Eastleigh Works w/e 22/11/58. Total 1,421,676 miles

30454 QUEEN GUINEVERE, a Salisbury engine for most of its life, at Nine Elms on Saturday 2nd October 1954 on the coaling line, ready for the return west. Still attached to the Drummond water cart no.878, I believe. Pondering Arthurian legend, was it just a coincidence that 30454 and 30455 were withdrawn before 30453? Photograph P. Edwards, Norman Preedy Archive.

30454 QUEEN GUINEVERE, the most renowned of the Arthurian ladies, at Salisbury. That's the GWR box (Salisbury 'C' after nationalisation) on the right and the signals beyond the train are GWR. The duty number is not 47 but 47-something, with the last digit missing; the 470 series were all Salisbury duties and No.470 covered, on Saturdays in 1956 for example, an Exeter-Salisbury semi-fast. The rolling stock is all Southern. Behind the 3 car Bulleid set is a Maunsell set in red and cream. 30448-30457 never seemed to stray from the LSWR main lines to the West, indeed all the works attention seems to have taken place at Eastleigh and all ten were scrapped there. Photograph Paul Chancellor Collection.

30455 SIR LAUNCELOT

Works order no.B17
To traffic as E455 3/1925
Renumbered 30455 8/5/48

Works

3/1928	Smoke deflectors fitted
16/7/29	Stays: 799 copper renewed; 120 holes bushed; Plates: Copper wrapping, 2 flanges, half-side; New brick arch, studs and plugs; Tubes: 100, new; 24 new Superheater tubes
7/1929-2/1931	Bolton Superheater
3/1932	E prefix removed
27/12/35-25/1/36A	95,796
7/7/36-13/7/36D	11,032
27/4/37-15/5/37C	75,985
24/8/37-24/9/37A	93,486
1/3/38-11/5/38B	30,674
	To Eastleigh Works, [Tisbury accident] 8/2/38 working the 1.05pm to Salisbury left-hand side connecting rod broke - piston forced out of the back end of the cylinder - demolished slide bars and motion - damaged platform at Tisbury.
18/4/39-20/5/39A	94,125 Olive Green livery
17/1/40-31/1/40C	24,635
4/10/41-12/11/41A	94,085 Malachite Green livery
31/7/42-2/10/42C	31,898 Wartime Black livery
9/5/44-15/7/44A	102,112
25/5/45-16/6/45C	46,631
28/6/46-20/7/46A	88,854 Malachite green livery from Black
9/4/48-8/5/48A	81,508 Renumbered 30455; Snifting valves removed
28/9/48-16/10/48C	16,279
30/3/50-5/5/50A	85,316 BR Green livery
26/11/51-5/12/51LC	55,945
4/11/52-29/11/52HI	92,207
14/10/53-22/10/53LC	[No mileage recorded]
15/1/54-6/2/54LI	138,683 Combination lever and valve spindle pin [modified]
10/11/55-9/12/55GO	196,108
14/12/56-22/12/56LC	33,748
25/11/57-7/12/57HI	57,970

Boilers
No.451 16/7/29
No.1001 25/1/36
No.841 24/9/37
No.802 20/5/39
No.776 12/11/41
No.879 15/7/44
No.766 20/7/46
New boiler no.1404 8/5/48
No.840 5/5/50
No.785 9/12/55

Tenders
No.877 from new
No.862 from 30748 on 7/12/57

Sheds
Salisbury 3/1925
Exmouth Junction 5/8/50
Salisbury 8/12/50
Exmouth Junction 20/3/51
Salisbury 12/5/51
Nine Elms 7/6/52
Basingstoke 8/10/57

Withdrawn 18/4/59; stored at Eastleigh Works 4/59; cut up at Eastleigh Works w/e 9/5/59
Total 1,475,829 miles

30455 SIR LAUNCELOT on the Nine Elms disposal roads, 31 January 1959; red tail lamp on for journey from Waterloo and then back again. Something needs looking at on that screw coupling. Photograph Philip J. Kelley.

30455 SIR LAUNCELOT on 23rd May 1953 with a down train at Southampton Central; just look at that signal gantry. A daily sight. The Lord Nelson on the right will take over a Fareham to Bournemouth stopper that provides a connection to the down 'Belle'. The head code on both engines refers to Waterloo or Nine Elms and Brockenhurst and Bournemouth West via Sway. Photograph R.C. Riley, www.transporttreasury.co.uk.

30456 SIR GALAHAD

Works order no.B17
To traffic as E456 4/1925
Renumbered 30456 16/10/48

Works

18/7/27	Stays: 387 copper renewed; 150 copper riveted over; Tubes: 42, new, 127 expanded; 24 Superheater tubes expanded
3/1928	Smoke deflectors fitted
23/4/29	Stays: 325 copper renewed; Plates: Rivets and seams caulked; New brick arch studs and plugs; Tubes: 169, new "Chesterfield"; 24 Superheater tubes ferruled, copper ends
7/1931	E prefix removed
13/10/34	Stays: 150 holes bushed; Plates: New copper firebox; Tubes: 169, new "Howell"; 24 2nd hand Superheater tubes
2/9/36-1/10/36**A**	90,045
5/5/37-4/6/37**B**	39,282
9/7/37-23/7/37**C**	39,282
12/1/38-15/1/38**D**	58,102
28/2/38-10/3/38**D**	26,277
8/9/38-5/10/38**A**	87,844 Stays: 402 copper renewed; Plates: Studs in flanges; Lead plugs; Brick arch studs; Throat, seams welded; Barrel S.V. seating welded; Tubes: 169, new "Talbot Stead"; 24 new Superheater tubes
13/5/40-5/6/40**A**	78,780 Olive Green livery
14/2/42-28/4/42**A**	96,806 Wartime Black livery
9/8/44-28/9/44**A**	105,632
23/1/46-23/2/46**B**	61,358 Extension of mileage 5,000; New right hand cylinder; Malachite Green livery from Black
2/12/46-21/12/46**A**	88,046
16/9/48-16/10/48**A**	72,769 Renumbered 30456; Snifting valves removed
19/10/50-27/10/50**LC**	54,148
13/2/52-15/3/52**GO**	101,977 BR Green livery
6/7/53-10/7/53**LC**	63,846
28/5/54-19/6/54**LI**	91,983
15/11/55-17/12/55**GO**	137,829 T2222: Regulator valve, BR alloy, new test
11/12/56-15/12/56**LC**	29,971 T2222 [U]
29/5/57-28/6/57**LC**	44,171 (at Brighton shed)
5/12/57-14/12/57**LC**	57,780
25/6/58-2/8/58**LI**	66,203

Boilers
No.456 4/1925
No.833 13/10/34
No.452 1/10/36
No.742 4/6/37
No.456 5/10/38
No.789 5/6/40
No.802 28/4/42
No.788 21/12/46
No.764 16/10/48
No.823 15/3/52
No.834 17/12/55

Tenders
No.878 from new
No.876 at Bournemouth shed 31/7/46 from 30454
No.863 2/8/58 from 30749

Sheds
Salisbury 4/1925
Exmouth Junction 12/12/49
Basingstoke 7/1/50
Salisbury 8/12/50
Nine Elms 27/6/51
Basingstoke 1/4/57

Withdrawn 14/5/60; stored at Eastleigh Works 5/60; cut up at Eastleigh Works w/e 21/5/60
Total 1,386,742 miles

No.456 SIR GALAHAD (son of no.455 and no.747) at Waterloo in February 1939. A Salisbury engine at the time, 456 has worked up from the west in an era in which they were the premier passenger locomotives for the Waterloo-Exeter line. It is now waiting to run light to Nine Elms for servicing and turning. The following June, despite the War, it got Olive Green livery; the austerity black did not come until April 1942. You suppose that, if the paint was there and paid for, why not use it?

Nine Elms' 30456 SIR GALAHAD, one of my favourites, at Reading shed on 11 July 1952. Still running with its Drummond water cart tender; coal rails filled in, no steam heating pipe in front buffer beam and front coupling hung in correct position. Not often would a named engine be seen here at this out of the way shed, though Schools turned up in later years. Photograph B.K.B. Green, Initial Photographics.

30456 SIR GALAHAD, 'the most noblest of Knights', in Malachite Green with Drummond water cart, backing in to Waterloo on 21 February 1951. The next duty will be no.437 and one of the fireman's jobs will be to place that disc on the front of the loco before departure. It has an original Drummond eight wheeled tender no.876 but 30456 had only got this, at Bournemouth shed, on 31 July 1946 from 30454 QUEEN GUINEVERE. The coal rails were filled in during the 1930s to give more support to the coal within and the tender today is well topped up for the work home to the west for it was in its second period based at Salisbury shed. It is unusual is to see a BR loco running number on the rear of the tender, normal for a Malachite Green loco, as here.

A mournful 30456 SIR GALAHAD at Eastleigh on 14th May 1960, the very day it was officially withdrawn; according to official records it was cut up within seven days, before the end of May 1960. It has one of the boilers with multi-plug fireboxes.

Now what is 30456 SIR GALAHAD doing at Feltham shed on 14th June 1959? In May 1959 four Arthurs were transferred to this freight only shed but 30456 was not one of them. Still the shed foreman would no doubt have found a job for SIR GALAHAD which has that panel on the cylinder cover, something that appeared in BR days. Photograph Peter Groom.

30457 SIR BEDIVERE
Works order no.B17
To traffic as E457 4/1925
Renumbered 30457 26/8/49

Works	
19/9/25	Stays: 200 copper riveted over; Tubes: 168 expanded; New plugs
2/9/26	Stays: 300 copper riveted over; Tubes: All expanded
13/1/27	Stays: 36 copper renewed; 250 copper riveted over; Tubes: All expanded; 16 new Superheater tubes
9/4/27	Stays: 43 copper renewed; 200 copper riveted over
14/2/28	Stays: 382 copper renewed; 100 copper riveted over; Tubes: 60, new: 24 Superheater tubes, ferruled. Smoke deflectors fitted
31/8/29	394 copper renewed; Plates: New studs in flanges; Copper wrapping, flat patch, right side; New brick arch studs and plugs; Tubes: 109, new "Chesterfield"; 24 new Superheater tubes
28/2/30	Stays: 250 copper riveted over; Plates: New plugs
6/31	Stays: 964 copper renewed; 300 holes bushed; Plates: Copper tube, new; Copper wrapping, flange one-half sides; Tubes: 169 2nd hand steel; 24 2nd hand steel Superheater tubes [copper ends]
8/1932	E prefix removed
1/1/36-1/2/36**A**	84,279
12/8/36-14/8/36**D**	16,202
8/3/37-11/3/37**D**	54,978
4/6/37-3/7/37**B**	65,629 Extension of mileage 10,000
20/12/37-19/1/38**A**	96,665
11/5/38**D**	[No mileage recorded]
5/7/38-17/8/38**D**	29,548 Flaman speed recorder fitted
22/6/39-18/7/39**A**	83,664 Olive Green livery
14/5/41-25/6/41**A**	88,334 Stays: 457 copper renewed; Plates: 1 rivet and seams caulked; Lead plugs; Tubes: 169 2nd hand welded; Flaman speed recorder removed; Malachite Green livery
22/9/41-26/9/41**D**	250 Stays: 11 roof renewed
16/4/43-26/5/43**A**	89,170 Wartime Black livery
2/5/45-23/6/45**A**	84,629
2/1/47-25/1/47**A**	77,389 Malachite Green livery from Black
5/11/47-8/11/47**D**	37,000
5/7/49-26/8/49**A**	99,286 Stays: 247 holes bushed; Plates: New copper firebox; Three-quarters, casing sides; Head crown patch; Throat, new; Tubes: Set, new " TalbotStead"; Set, new Superheater tubes. Renumbered 30457; BR Green livery; Snifting valves removed
6/7/50-13/7/50**LC**	11,150
8/8/52-6/9/52**GO**	74,197
19/5/55-18/6/55**GO**	105,267
2/5/57-25/5/57**LI**	66,567 T2256: New test [Engine bogie only]
13/2/59-7/3/59**GO**	115,104 T2256; Stays: 449 monel metal renewed; 506 nuts renewed; Plates: 3 rivets replaced by studs; 2 fusible plugs; Tubes: 167, new "Phoenix"; 24 new Superheater tubes
31/3/60-16/4/60**LC**	33,206 T2256

Tenders
No.879 from new
No.788 18/6/55 from 30490

Sheds
Salisbury 4/1925
Exmouth Junction 5/8/50
Salisbury 8/12/50
Exmouth Junction 20/3/51
Salisbury 12/5/51
Nine Elms 27/6/51
Basingstoke 8/10/57
Nine Elms 6/6/58

Withdrawn 20/5/61; stored at Eastleigh Works 5-6/61; cut up at Eastleigh Works w/e 8/7/61
Total 1,429,723 miles

Boilers
No.457 6/1925
No.806 6/1931
No.767 1/2/36
No.787 19/1/38
No.452 18/7/39
No.824 25/6/41
No.767 26/5/43
No.453 23/6/45
No.783 26/8/49
No.780 6/9/52
No.841 7/3/59

Another engine changeover by the look of it. The fifth one of the first Eastleigh batch, 30457 SIR BEDIVERE (as we all know, he threw 30736 into the lake at 30453's behest) approaching Yeovil Junction some time in BR days on what looks like a parcels train. 30450 awaits it next move. Photograph J. Davenport, Initial Photographics.

This is the 10.05 Waterloo-Bournemouth on 20th June 1959. Even at this late stage the engines were still performing top link duties and this ten coach train should be no problem for 30457 SIR BEDIVERE. Untold times I saw them roar beneath us at Haines Bridge and loads like this were never a struggle. 30457 had become a Nine Elms loco a year before, surviving until the late spring of 1961. When 30457 lost its Drummond tender it got a 5,200 gallon tender from one of the first batch of H15s. These were taller and narrower than the standard Urie 5,000 gallon tender. Once more, 431 is the train reporting number. These rectangular boards had the number attached at the starting station while the number on the disc, the loco roster number, was attached at the shed. Photograph Peter Groom.

30457 SIR BEDIVERE on 22nd August 1959 at Basingstoke shed, which had been its home for a few months from October 1957. By now its final base was Nine Elms and it would have come to Basingstoke from Waterloo on one of the semi-fasts that the engines were now working. Series of firebox plugs clearly shown.

30457 SIR BEDIVERE at home shed Nine Elms; the usual post-apocalypse landscape. Behind is a modern BR Class 5 built to replace the like of the Arthurs, though not by long as it turned out; SIR BEDIVERE went in May 1961. High sided 5,200 gallon tender, ex-H15 30490.

SIR BEDIVERE awaiting departure from Waterloo with the headcode suggesting a train to Southampton Terminus, though not a boat train. The loco spent its second period at Nine Elms from mid-1958 to withdrawal.

Splendid side on provided by the Nine Elms turntable. 30457 spent two periods in the 1950s at the big London shed; unusually large crowd around the table. Photograph Paul Chancellor Collection.

30736 EXCALIBUR

Works order no.N15
To traffic as 736 8/18
Renumbered 30736 19/2/49

Boilers
No.478 13/7/35
No.824 18/2/37
No.798 14/12/38
No.750 15/5/40
No.747 22/7/42
No.522 5/7/47
No.828 24/11/50

Works

8/1924	SR livery; E prefix; Urie pattern 21" cylinders
2/1925	Named
9/1928	Smoke deflectors fitted; King Arthur chimney
9/1930	Maunsell Superheater
9/1932	E prefix removed
27/5/35-13/7/35A	102,582
13/1/37-18/2/37A	85,284 Fitted with Ross pop valves
20/10/37D	[No mileage recorded]
11/11/38-14/12/38A	90,667 Maunsell Green livery
15/4/40-15/5/40A	65,803 Olive Green livery
14/1/41-18/1/41D	21,839 Multiple blastpipe; large diameter chimney
30/5/42-22/7/42A	78,176 Wartime Black livery
28/6/44-19/8/44C	60,274 Extension of mileage 5,000
2/10/45-9/11/45A	101,084
9/6/47-5/7/47A	71,980 Malachite Green livery from Black
30/9/47-4/10/47D	2,977
11/1/49-19/2/49CLI	50,222 Renumbered 30736; Fitted with vertical smoke deflectors
25/10/50-24/11/50A	140,867 BR Green livery; snifting valves removed
12/4/54-1/5/54LI	71,974 Steam heating relief valve repositioned

Tender
No.850 from new

Sheds
Nine Elms 8/1918
Bournemouth by mid 1930
Nine Elms 1935
Eastleigh by spring 1945
Bournemouth 6/46
Eastleigh 4/9/48
Bournemouth 8/1/49

Withdrawn 3/11/56; cut up at Brighton Works w/e 26/1/57. Total 1,455,334 miles

Ex-LSWR N15 736 EXCALIBUR at the old Nine Elms coal stage in 1933. Already fifteen years old it had started life here but was now at Bournemouth, though it would soon return to London. The tender needs a repaint, its markings faded almost to extinction.

30736 EXCALIBUR in Brighton shed yard on 17th November 1956 for the sad reason that withdrawal had taken place on 3rd November. The loco was to be cut up at the nearby works in January 1957. The smoke deflectors are not set at an angle as usual but are vertical, while the hand rail is not attached to the top. Photo Peter Groom.

30737 KING UTHER

Works order no.N15
To traffic as 737 10/1918
Renumbered 30737 22/7/49

Works

23/4/21	Converted to Oil burning [Scarab system]
26/9/21	Converted back to Coal burning
10/1925	Southern livery; Named; E prefix; King Arthur chimney
16/6/26	Converted to Oil burning again
22/12/26	Converted back to Coal burning, having run 19,046 miles as an Oil burner
6/1928	Smoke deflectors fitted; Urie pattern 21" cylinders
6/1929	Maunsell Superheater
2/1932	E prefix removed
29/7/35-1/8/35C	65,298
30/10/35-29/11/35A	83,276
23/3/37-24/4/37A	75,874
10/3/39-5/4/39A	94,887 Maunsell Green livery
18/6/40-24/7/40A	53,135 Malachite Green livery
11/2/41-17/2/41D	13,355 Multiple blastpipe; Large diameter chimney
2/3/42-11/4/42C	65,176 Extension of mileage 5,000
8/10/42-10/11/42A	82,808 Wartime Black livery
20/6/44-30/6/44C	50,025
5/3/45-7/4/45A	64,268
7/5/46-7/6/46B	49,340
22/7/46D	49,340
12/9/46-5/10/46C	58,692 Malachite Green livery from Black
2/2/47-24/2/47C	68,277 Eastleigh shed
9/12/47-10/1/48A	90,005 Stays: 175 holes bushed; plates: new firebox; Steel tube, new; Casing back, new; Casing covering, three-quarter sides and crown plate; Snifting valves removed
15/6/49-22/7/49LI	52,411 Stays: 398 copper repaired; plates: Firebox, studs, seams and rivets repaired; Lead plugs renewed; Tubes: Repaired; 15 Superheater tubes repaired and ferruled; Renumbered 30737
28/5/51-30/6/51GO	123,215 BR Green livery
14/9/54-2/10/54LI	72,013 Steam heating relief valve repositioned
6/4/56-24/4/56LC [BTN]	105,803 V and P exam only

Boilers
No.500 as of 1/8/35
No.745 24/4/37
No.508 5/4/39
No.737 24/7/40
No.752 10/11/42
No.738 7/4/45
No.515 7/6/46
No.755 10/1/48
No.508 30/6/51

Tender
No.851 from new

Sheds
Salisbury 10/1918
Nine Elms 4/1921
Exmouth Junction Summer 1925
Eastleigh early 1929
Nine Elms 1935
Eastleigh 5/1937
Nine Elms 7/1937
Eastleigh 9/1943
Bournemouth 31/5/48
Eastleigh 4/9/48
Bournemouth 8/1/49

Withdrawn 22/6/56; cut up at Brighton Works w/e 15/9/56
Total 1,412,683 miles

30737 KING UTHER at his home shed Bournemouth, with the shed code 71B clear enough on the smokebox door. Fitted with the Lemaître exhaust it received in 1941 under Bulleid's regime. Here on Sunday 17th July 1955 it is awaiting its next duty in the usual field of clinker and ash. The venerable push-pull M7 30107, though older than 30737, outlasted the Arthur by at least eight years; KING UTHER was withdrawn in June 1956, the 0-4-4T in May 1964. Photograph B.K.B. Green Collection, Initial Photographics.

30737 a wet Bournemouth on 27th July 1954. Apart from 792, locos which were fitted with the Lemaître exhaust kept them until withdrawal. KING UTHER was a Bournemouth engine at the time; this Urie loco had two more years at work. Photograph Paul Chancellor Collection.

Basingstoke on 28th August 1954 and 30737 KING UTHER (father of 30453) has brought in a passenger train of mixed coaches, *Great Western Hotel* in the background. The train is the 11.50am ex Bournemouth Central to Birmingham Snow Hill which was due at Basingstoke at 1.49 pm. The loco will come off the train here (seen below running light to the shed) and return to Bournemouth at 3.13 pm with the 11.55 am ex Wolverhampton.

30738 KING PELLINORE

Works order no.N15
To traffic as 738 12/1918
Renumbered 30738 13/5/49

Boilers
No.741 29/10/36
No.753 18/5/38
No.749 12/4/39
No.777 28/5/41
No.749 4/3/44
No.1000 22/3/47
No.477 13/5/49
No.745 10/1/53
No.521 26/6/55

Works

5/1924	Southern livery
8/1925	E prefix; named
7/1928	Smoke deflectors fitted; King Arthur chimney
3/1930	Maunsell Superheater; Urie pattern 21" cylinders
10/1932	E prefix removed
29/9/36-29/10/36**A**	88,636
25/5/37-18/6/37**C**	18,738
31/3/38-18/5/38**B**	52,430 Extension of mileage 5,000
17/3/39-12/4/39**A**	90,381 Maunsell Green livery; Bulleid pattern cylinders
7/4/41-28/5/41**A**	82,984 Malachite Green livery, unlined
9/8/41-19/8/41**C**	3,813
30/12/42-9/1/43**C**	62,932
3/2/44-4/3/44**A**	93,677 Wartime Black livery
3/4/46-4/5/46**C**	77,068 Extension of mileage 5,000
14/2/47-22/3/47**A**	111,919 Light version of Malachite Green livery from Black
6/4/49-13/5/49**A**	78,708 Renumbered 30738; Snifting valves removed; T2256
12/7/51-14/8/51**LC**	53,266 (At Bournemouth shed)
3/12/52-10/1/53**GO**	85,060 BR Green livery
27/5-25/6/55**LI-GO**	63,594 T2256 Tyres turned

Tender
No.852 from new

Sheds
Nine Elms 12/1918
Eastleigh Summer 1923, on loan, returned to Nine Elms
Exmouth Junction 3/1944
Nine Elms 11/1946
Exmouth Junction 3/1950
Nine Elms 22/4/50
Salisbury 17/6/50
Bournemouth 12/5/51
Basingstoke 12/6/57

Withdrawn 8/3/58; stored at Eastleigh Works 3/58; cut up at Eastleigh Works w/e 15/3/58 Total 1,460,218 miles

A Malachite Green Arthur, 30738 KING PELLINORE at Eastleigh on 17th September 1949; Urie 5,000 gallon bogie tender. The engine had been renumbered and repainted in Malachite with unlettered tender in the spring; it did not get BR Green until 1952. Deflector nicely lined green as normal for a Malachite Arthur. This engine's first post-war green application was a light shade, virtually Apple Green which resulted from a shortage of regular Malachite in March 1947. Photograph J.H. Aston.

Nine Elms yard on 21st September 1957 with 30738 KING PELLINORE (father of a number of the Knights of the Round Table) awaiting a return duty to Basingstoke where it had been based since June 1957; most likely a semi-fast which the class seemed to work so many of in their latter days. This loco survived until March the following year, the last of the series.

30739 KING LEODEGRANCE

Works order no.N15
To traffic as 739 2/1919
Renumbered 30739 19/2/49

Boilers
No.774 4/12/35
No.473 9/2/38
No.504 10/7/40
No.750 18/8/42
No.755 22/9/45
No.477 24/5/47
No.750 19/2/49
No.505 30/5/52

Works

18/6/21	Converted to Oil burning [Scarab system]
6/8/21	Converted back to coal burning having burst into flames at Salisbury shed on 28/7/21
10/1924	Southern livery; E prefix
11/1925	Named
12/6/26	Converted to Oil firing again [Scarab system]
17/12/26	Converted back to Coal burning having run 21,998 miles as an Oil burner
1/1928	Smoke deflectors fitted; King Arthur chimney
10/1928	Urie pattern 21" cylinders
5/1930	Maunsell Superheater
8/1931	E prefix removed
7/11/35-4/12/35A	72,929
29/12/36-3/2/37B	48,077 Extension of mileage 5,000
11/1/38-9/2/38A	94,603 Ross pop valve boiler replaced
12/6/40-10/7/40A	96,584 Malachite Green livery
13/7/42-18/8/42A	75,979 Wartime Black livery
18/8/45-22/9/45A	103,521 Stays: 483 copper renewed; Roof renewed, direct 30; Plates: 2 lead plugs Tubes: 167, 93 new "Howell", 74 2nd hand: 24 new Superheater tubes
22/3/46-29/3/46C	24,803 Stays: 450 copper renewed; 3 crown bolts renewed Plates: Seams and rivets repaired
18/11/46-30/11/46C	44,865 Stays: 450 copper repaired; Plates: Seams and studs repaired
3/5/47-24/5/47B	52,508
15/1/49-19/2/49A	108,298 Malachite Green livery from Black; Renumbered 30739; Snifting valves removed
28/4/52-30/5/52GO	110,182 BR Green livery
3/3/55-25/3/55LI	67,820

Tender
No.853 from new

Sheds
Nine Elms 2/1919
Exmouth Junction Summer 1925
Salisbury by 6/1928
Nine Elms by mid-1930
LNER, Heaton shed 1/1943
Eastleigh 9/1943
Bournemouth 31/5/48
Salisbury 8/1/49
Nine Elms 3/5/49
Bournemouth 8/12/50

Withdrawn 4/5/57; stored at Eastleigh Works 5/57; cut up at Eastleigh Works w/e 18/5/57
Total 1,399,989 miles

Early BR times at Nine Elms shed, 25th September 1949 with 30739 KING LEODEGRANCE (very important to the Arthurian legend, father of 30454) still in Malachite Green but without tender marking. It received an 'A' overhaul in the late winter of this year though renumbering had taken place in the February. Steam heating fitted on front buffer beam, cylinder drain cock pipes fixed to front footsteps. Photograph J.H. Aston.

30740 MERLIN with a through working to Bradford on 28th August 1954. The train is the ex 9.31am Bournemouth Central to Bradford train arriving at Basingstoke at 12.39pm. 30739 will work through to Oxford and return with the 3.10pm, arriving back at Basingstoke at 4.17pm and finally Bournemouth at 7.34pm.

30740 MERLIN

Works order no.N15
To traffic as 740 4/1919
Renumbered 30740 30/10/48

Boilers
No.740 21/11/25
No.784 as of 11/12/36
No.523 23/10/37
No.514 1/11/39
No.502 28/10/42
No.521 9/9/44
No.837 24/8/46
No.773 19/5/50

Works
7/1924	Southern livery
21/11/1925	Plates: Copper tube, two; Copper firehole, 2 angle patches; E prefix; Named
25/1/1927	Stays: 250 copper riveted over; King Arthur chimney
5/1928	Smoke deflectors fitted
12/1929	Maunsell Superheater; Urie pattern 21" cylinders
11/1931	E prefix removed
1/1934	Maunsell pattern cylinders [double exhaust ports]
21/10/36-11/12/36**B**	66,816 Extension of mileage 5,000
27/9/37-23/10/37**A**	98,791
10/10/39-1/11/39**A**	70,452 Olive Green Livery
30/9/42-28/10/42**A**	89,929 Wartime Black livery
1/7/44-9/9/44**B**	58,863 Extension of mileage 10,000
9/6/45-28/7/45**C**	85,254 Extension of mileage 15,000
11/3/46-23/3/46**C**	101,759
16/7/46-24/8/46**A**	109,889 Boiler with Ross pop valves; Malachite Green livery from Black
6/11/46-14/12/46**C**	8,726 Converted to Oil burning
19/12/46-21/12/46**D**	8,726
3/2/47**D**	9,239
23/12/47-3/1/48**D**	27,261 Stone's turbogenerator; Electric lighting
11/10/48-30/10/48**C**	40,462 Converted back to Coal burning; Renumbered 30740; Kept electric lighting; tubular ladders fitted to tender
18/4/50-19/5/50**A**	99,728 BR Green livery; Snifting valves removed; T1891 Thomas "patent piston rod packing"
7/4/53-25/4/53**LI**	77,517
12/3/54-20/3/54**NC**	99,228
	BR 9637 form reported at Brighton "To be withdrawn 10/12/55 see LA/RS/201 1 DEC 1955"

Tender
No.854 from new

Sheds
Nine Elms 4/1919
Exmouth Junction by 5/1920
Nine Elms by Grouping
Exmouth Junction Summer 1925
Nine Elms 1935
Eastleigh 1/7/40
LNER, Heaton shed 1/1943
Eastleigh 9/1943
Bournemouth 8/1/49
Eastleigh 5/2/51
Bournemouth 14/3/51

Withdrawn 10/12/55; cut up at Brighton Works w/e 30/6/56
Total 1,357,971 miles

30740 MERLIN again at Basingstoke on 28th August 1954, a few minutes later.

30741 JOYOUS GARD

Works order no.P15
To traffic as 741 4/1919
Renumbered 30741 20/11/48

Boilers
No.473 18/4/36
No.738 12/1/38
No.504 4/1/39
No.510 17/4/40
No.744 30/3/45
No.752 6/3/48
No.768 9/9/49
No.524 25/4/53

Works

1/1924	Southern livery
2/1925	Faulty left-hand cylinder, replacements 20½ in
6/1925	E prefix; King Arthur chimney; named
1/1928	Smoke deflectors fitted
2/1929	Maunsell superheater; Urie pattern 21" cylinders
9/1932	E prefix removed
13/3/36-18/4/36A	90,624
4/12/37-12/1/38A	89,169
26/10/38-4/1/39B	40,320
14/3/40-17/4/40A	94,964 Olive Green livery
16/12/40-1/1/41C	19,586 Multiple blastpipe; large diameter chimney
27/10/42-25/11/42A	69,481 Wartime Black livery
21/2/45-30/3/45B	72,708 Extension of mileage 10,000
30/5/45-28/7/45B	72,753 Extension of mileage 10,000
8/8/45-11/8/45D	72,753
23/7/46-31/8/46A	110,586 Malachite Green livery from Black
28/5/47-21/6/47C	37,438
12/2/48-6/3/48B	54,769 Snifting valves removed
15/11/48-20/11/48C	74,973 Renumbered 30741
19/7/49-9/9/49A	98,490 BR Green livery
6/7/50-11/7/50NC	15,830
13/9/51-15/9/51LC	31,303
18/3/53-25/4/53GO	75,551 New left-handside cylinder

Tender
No.855 from new

Sheds
Nine Elms 4/1919
Exmouth Junction 5/1920
Nine Elms by Grouping
Eastleigh 27/2/40
Feltham 21/7/42
Eastleigh by spring 1945
Basingstoke 3/5/49
Salisbury 3/1950
Bournemouth 17/6/50

Withdrawn 18/2/56; cut
up at Brighton Works w/e
18/2/56
Total 1,346,891 miles

30741 JOYOUS GARD at Eastleigh shed, cleaned and ready to go on 23rd April 1949; renumbered in November 1948 in SR style, still Malachite Green. Photograph J.H. Aston.

It is 28th August 1954 again and we seem to have a sequence of Arthurs at Basingstoke that day with 30741 JOYOUS GARD on duty no.396. Her home shed then was Bournemouth. It was one of the Urie Arthurs that was fitted with the multiple jet blast pipe and large diameter chimney which I think did nothing for their appearance. Leaking front washout plug has left a nasty streak down the side of the outer casing.

30742 CAMELOT

Works order no.P15
To traffic as 742 6/1919
Renumbered 30742 23/10/48

Boilers
No.754 as of 2/11/35
No.500 16/6/37
No.753 14/6/39
No.521 22/6/42
No.499 14/9/44
No.829 24/8/46
No.506 23/10/48
No.510 1/12/51

Tender
No.856 from new

Sheds
Nine Elms 6/1919
Summer 1923 on loan to Bournemouth, returned to Nine Elms
Exmouth Junction 5/1920
Nine Elms by Grouping
Eastleigh 27/2/40
LNER Heaton shed 1/1943
Eastleigh 9/1943
Nine Elms 7/1947
Exmouth Junction 3/1950
Nine Elms 22/4/50
Bournemouth 9/10/50

Withdrawn 9/2/57; stored at Eastleigh Works 2/57; cut up at Eastleigh Works w/e 23/3/57.
Total 1,386,007 miles

Works
1/1924	Southern livery [lipped chimney etc.]
12/1925	Boiler change; Named; E prefix; King Arthur chimney
6/1928	Smoke deflectors fitted
8/1930	Maunsell superheater; Maunsell pattern cylinders [double exhaust ports etc.]
2/1932	E prefix removed
3/10/35-2/11/35**A**	100,759
28/4/37-16/6/37**A**	79,795
24/6/38-17/8/38**B**	40,884
17/5/39-14/6/39**A**	71,519 Olive green livery
22/4/42-22/6/42**A**	98,236 Wartime Black livery
17/7/44-14/9/44**B**	63,290 Extension of mileage 10,000
16/6/45-3/8/45**B**	88,849 Extension of mileage 25,000
22/9/45-2/10/45**C**	89,425 Extension of mileage 5,000
17/7/46-24/8/46**A**	119,133 Stays: 150 holes bushed; Plates: New copper firebox; Throat, new; Barrel, three-quarter sides crown plate; Tubes: 169, new "Tubes ltd"; Set, new Superheater tubes; Malachite Green livery; Boiler with Ross pop safety valves
11/2/47-13/2/47**D**	14,230
21/9/48-23/10/48**A**	74,797 Renumbered 30742; Snifting valves removed
1/11/51-1/12/51**GO**	75,238 BR Green livery
12/11/54-27/11/54**LI**	79,522

An unusual place to see one of the class, especially this early on, 742 CAMELOT at Feltham shed around 1947, which did not get any Arthurs until May 1959 though it was home to a good number of S15s. Presumably lined up for duty 77 the engine has the usual Maunsell smokebox, horizontal hand rail and longer door hinges plus the three cylinder drain cock pipes attached to the front footsteps. Photograph R.J. Buckley, Initial Photographics.

An early portrait of 742, before it carried the name CAMELOT, in LSWR livery at Nine Elms on 21st April 1923. An Arthur in original state, very clean with the peculiar LSW lamp 'irons', the slightly potty Urie chimney and the Spartan lettering. This year saw 742 still a Nine Elms engine, spending the summer on loan to Bournemouth. While at Heaton, on 18th December 1942 it was famously taken off a goods train at Berwick to replace an ailing LNER Pacific on the 10am Edinburgh-Kings Cross express as far as Newcastle. Photograph H.C. Casserley, courtesy R.M. Casserley.

742 CAMELOT at Clapham Junction (what a caption 'Clapham Junction at Camelot' would have been) on 30th August 1924 fitted with a shelter during a series of test runs between Waterloo and Salisbury. 742 was reckoned at the time to be the weakest of the Urie engines and was used on these trials 'to enhance their performance without resorting to costly and extensive reconstruction'. Experimental chimney to LSWR loading gauge; no number plate. Photograph H.C. Casserley, courtesy R.M. Casserley.

30743 LYONNESSE

Works order no.P15
To traffic as 743 8/1919
Renumbered 30743 10/6/49

Boilers
No.740 14/1/33
No.504 as of 9/1/36
No.803 25/7/36
No.511 6/3/37
No.505 8/2/39
No.499 7/5/41
No.475 12/8/44
No.754 7/12/46
No.797 10/6/49
No.833 27/6/53

Works

6/1925	Southern livery; Named; E prefix; King Arthur chimney
11/1927	Smoke deflectors fitted
6/1930	Maunsell Superheater; Maunsell pattern cylinders [double exhaust ports etc.]
14/1/1933	Plates: New copper firebox; Steel tube, new; Casing covering, half sides; Tubes: 169, new "Chesterfield"; 24 2nd hand Superheater tubes [copper ends] E prefix removed
12/1/1934	Stays: 325 copper renewed; Plates: Lead plugs; Rivets and seams caulked; E prefix removed
17/12/35-9/1/36**B**	37,327
30/6/36-25/7/36**B**	55,330 Extension of mileage 5,000
5/2/37-6/3/37**A**	79,882 Ross pop safety valves removed
13/1/39-8/2/39**A**	88,839 Maunsell Green livery
22/3/41-7/5/41**A**	84,358 Malachite Green livery
23/1/43-15/2/43**C**	57,708
20/6/44-12/8/44**A**	100,806 Wartime Black livery
5/9/45-20/9/45**C**	41,614
13/11/46-7/12/46**A**	82,779 Malachite Green livery from Black
2/5/49-10/6/49**A**	95,185 Renumbered 30743; Snifting valves removed
3/6/53-27/6/53**GO**	99,485 Stays: Monel metal renewed, all; Longitudinal renewed, all; Roof renewed, all; 230 holes bushed; Plates: New copper firebox; Tubes: Set, new; Set, new Superheater tubes; BR Green livery

Tender
No.857 from new

Sheds
Nine Elms 8/1919
Salisbury 5/1920
Bournemouth by 6/1928
Exmouth Junction 1931
Eastleigh 12/1942
Bournemouth 6/1946

Withdrawn 6/10/55; stored at Eastleigh Works 10/55; cut up at Eastleigh Works w/e 12/11/55
Total 1,301,442 miles

30743 LYONNESSE at Bournemouth Central, 27th June 1954, a stone's throw from its home shed and presumably awaiting a job west to Weymouth. It has just over a year left in service before withdrawal in October 1955. Photograph R.C. Riley, www.transporttreasury.co.uk

30744 MAID OF ASTOLAT

Works order no.P15
To traffic as 744 9/1919
Renumbered 30744 5/6/48

Boilers
No.750 2/11/35
No.502 13/11/37
No.523 29/11/39
No.501 4/3/42
No.506 7/7/45
No.515 5/6/48
No.501 6/4/51
No.835 16/10/54

Works
10/1924	Southern livery
4/1925	Named; E prefix
6/1927	King Arthur chimney; Urie pattern 21" cylinders
11/1927	Smoke deflectors fitted
1/1930	Maunsell Superheater
1/1932	E prefix removed
7/10/35-2/11/35**A**	84,279
12/10/37-13/11/37**A**	97,279
27/10/39-29/11/39**A**	93,117 Olive Green livery
1/1/42-4/3/42**A**	75,004 Malachite Green livery
31/5/45-7/7/45**A**	116,301 Wartime Black livery
24/2/47-22/3/47**C**	77,400
9/9/47-20/9/47**C**	85,204
7/5/48-5/6/48**A**	108,222 Malachite Green livery from Black; Renumbered 30744; Snifting valves removed
2/3/51-6/4/51**GO**	105,972 BR Green livery
19/11/52-11/12/52**HI**	53,449
15/9/54-16/10/54**GO**	117,120

Tender
No.858 from new

Sheds
Salisbury 9/1919
Exmouth Junction by 6/1928
LNER, Heaton shed 1/1943
Salisbury 7/1943
Exmouth Junction 1/4/48
Nine Elms 12/8/49
Salisbury 4/2/50
Eastleigh 8/12/50
Basingstoke 5/2/51
Feltham 27/6/51
Nine Elms 6/12/51
Basingstoke 27/3/53
Nine Elms 26/5/53
Basingstoke 30/9/55

Withdrawn 7/1/56; cut up at Brighton Works w/e 4/2/56
Total 1,463,292 miles

30744 MAID OF ASTOLAT; 'on the first puff out of Tisbury, 3.05pm slow Salisbury to Exeter, 26th June 1948'. Renumbered a few weeks before, 30744 is still without smokebox numberplate and instead has that novel painting on the buffer beam As 744, on return from Heaton in the summer of 1943 it had been sent to Salisbury while the other nine 'returnees' went to Eastleigh shed. It had been repainted from black in June 1948 and renumbered at the same time. Photograph J.H. Aston.

Nine Elms on 27th August 1949; the Merchant Navy in front, nearly 20 months after Nationalisation, remains in Southern livery while 30744 MAID OF ASTOLAT still has Malachite Green with BR lettering/numbering. This maiden died for the love of Sir Launcelot while her name, Elaine, was carried by 30747. Photograph H.C. Casserley, courtesy R.M. Casserley.

30745 TINTAGEL

Works order no.P15
To traffic as 745 11/1919
Renumbered 30745 18/12/48

Boilers
No.502 21/12/35
No.506 30/7/37
No.824 26/4/39
No.830 11/6/41
No.477 23/6/44
No.521 8/11/46
No.791 3/6/49
No.738 10/8/51

Works

9/1924	Southern livery
4/1925	Named; E prefix
7/1928	Smoke deflectors fitted; King Arthur chimney
5/1930	Maunsell pattern cylinders [double exhaust ports]
1/1932	Maunsell Superheater; E prefix removed
23/11/35-21/12/35A	101,282
18/7/36-30/7/36D	27,576
29/6/37-30/7/37A	85,091
23/2/39D	[No mileage recorded]
29/3/39-26/4/39A	82,772 Stays: 200 holes bushed; Plates: New copper firebox; Steel tube, new; Casing covering; three-quarter sides; Tubes: 169, 134 new "Howell", 35 2nd hand; 24 second hand Superheater tubes; New foundation ring; Olive Green livery; Boiler with Ross pop safety valves 200 lbs psi
16/4/41-11/6/41A	88,848 Malachite Green livery
13/5/44-23/6/44A	117,624 Wartime Black livery
17/10/46-8/11/46A	93,356 Malachite Green livery from Black
19/9/47-4/10/47C	34,939 Converted to Oil burning; Electric lighting; Snifting valves removed
4/48	T1977 Water gauge protection at M.P.D.
29/11/48-18/12/48C	58,166 Converted back to coal burning and kept the electric lighting. Renumbered 30745
9/5/49-3/6/49HC	67,399
27/3/50-5/5/50LC	93,523
3/7/51-10/8/51A	136,706 BR Green livery
28/4/53-16/5/53HI	57,811
25/5/53-30/5/53LC	57,865
2/7/54-20/8/54LC-GO	97,106

Tender
No.859 from new

Sheds
Salisbury 11/1919
Nine Elms by 6/1928
Bournemouth 1935
Salisbury 7/1937
Bournemouth 16/10/37
Salisbury 11/7/38
Bournemouth 2/12/38
Salisbury 20/3/39
Eastleigh 12/1947
Nine Elms 3/5/49
Basingstoke 9/10/50
Eastleigh 8/12/50
Basingstoke 5/2/51

Withdrawn 11/2/1956; cut up at Brighton Works w/e 17/3/56
Total 1,464,032 miles

The clean lines of a Urie Arthur, enhanced by the King Arthur chimney and the bogie tender; of course, large capacities were essential on the SR main line to the west, lacking as it did any water troughs. This is Eastleigh, on 15th August 1951 and just a few days earlier 30745 TINTAGEL (above and below) had emerged from the nearby works after a General Overhaul, in newly applied BR Green. What stands out is the electric lighting which had been fitted to the post-war oil fired locos (all Urie Arthurs; see *The Record*). On the front of the loco the three around the smokebox were in the original lamp socket positions allowing the existing lamp sockets to carry discs. The three along the buffer beam had disc irons mounted on them. The six lamps on the back of the tender all had disc irons mounted on top; the electric lighting was retained after the locos reverted to coal burning.

Gorgeous low lighting on malachite 'SR/BR' 30745 TINTAGEL at Nine Elms on 22nd June 1950 amid those familiar concrete lumps, looking like the remnants of some ancient civilisation – as indeed they were, after a fashion! Behind is 30454 QUEEN GUINEVERE then enjoying its short period at Exmouth Junction; 30746 was a Bournemouth engine. Photograph Paul Chancellor Collection.

30746 PENDRAGON

Works order no.L16
To traffic as 746 6/1922
Renumbered 30746 21/9/50

Works

12/1924	Southern livery
10/1925	Named; E prefix
1/1929	Smoke deflectors fitted; King Arthur chimney; Urie pattern 21" cylinders; Maunsell Superheater
10/1932	E prefix removed
22/4/36-12/6/36**B**	52,183 Extension of mileage 5,000
19/4/37-28/5/37**A**	89,063
20/2/39-15/3/39**A**	92,209 Malachite Green livery, black and white lining
23/5/41-9/7/41**A**	93,511 Malachite Green livery, black and yellow lining
15/12/43-12/1/44**A**	100,574 Wartime Black livery
3/7/46-27/7/46**A**	100,656 Stays: 120 holes bushed; Plates: New copper firebox; Steel tube, new; Throat, new; Tubes: 169, new "Talbot and Stead"; 24 2nd hand Superheater tubes; Malachite Green livery from Black
10/12/46-21/1/47**B[NE]**	21,110 Boiler tested in steam; Fusible plugs renewed
29/12/47-17/1/48**C**	42,779 Stays: 110 copper renewed; 450 steel repaired and 1 renutted; Plates: Obstructions cleared from waterways; Right side fusible plugs renewed; Firebox seams chipped and caulked; Corner rivets caulked; 110 bushes [steel casing] caulked on Casing back plate; Tubes: Superheater tubes expanded, rebeaded and referruled
9/2/48-14/2/48**D**	42,821
21/12/48-31/12/48**C[NE]**	74,832
16/8/50-21/9/50**A**	132,283 Renumbered 30746; BR Green livery; Snifting valves removed
24/1/51-3/2/51**LC**	6,946
20/8/51-27/8/51**NC**	20,964
12/9/51-22/9/51**NC**	21,032
2/12/52-20/12/52**LI**	68,953
15/10/53-23/10/53**LC**	99,739
3/9/54-11/9/54**LC**	132,528
25/5/55-28/5/55**LC**	154,652
25/8/55-27/8/55**LC**	160,083

Boilers

No.506 as of 12/6/36
No.477 28/5/37
No.744 15/3/39
No.749 9/7/41
No.746 12/1/44
No.833 27/7/46
No.837 21/9/50

Tender

No.860 from new

Sheds

Nine Elms 6/1922
Exmouth Junction by 6/1928
Bournemouth 1935
Salisbury 7/1937
Bournemouth 16/10/37
Salisbury 1/9/38
Bournemouth 2/12/38
Salisbury 20/3/39
Exmouth Junction 1/4/48
Eastleigh 4/9/48
Bournemouth 3/5/49
Eastleigh 8/12/50

Withdrawn 22/10/55; stored at Eastleigh Works 10/55; cut up at Eastleigh Works w/e 19/11/55 Total 1,388,102 miles

30745 TINTAGEL working a train from its home shed Basingstoke and looking in fine fettle on 28th August 1954 only eight days after its final General Overhaul at Eastleigh works; no wonder it looks so good.

Eastleigh shed on 30th June 1953 and on one of those fifteen roads we have 30746 PENDRAGON 'all suited up' and ready to go. BR cycling totem – the first emblem – on the side of the bogie tender and how tidy the foreground looks. Bolted plate where snifting valve used to be; these disappeared as smokeboxes were renewed. Photograph B.K.B. Green, Initial Photographics.

30747 ELAINE

Works order no.L16
To traffic as 747 7/1922
Renumbered 30747 12/5/50

Boilers
No.799 30/3/35
No.750 27/11/37
No.522 28/2/40
No.507 8/7/42
No.501 30/8/45
No.512 24/1/48
No.747 12/5/50
No.753 20/11/52

Works

1/1925	Southern livery
9/1925	Named; E prefix; King Arthur chimney
8/1928	Smoke deflectors fitted
11/1930	Maunsell superheater
6/1932	E prefix removed
3/1933	Maunsell pattern cylinders [double exhaust ports etc.]
30/3/35	Stays: 100 holes bushed; Plates: New copper firebox; casing covering, three-quarters sides; Tubes: 169, 2nd hand welded; 24 2nd hand Superheater tubes
11/11/35-14/11/35**D**	24,089
2/11/36-16/12/36**B**	70,396 Extension of mileage 10,000
23/10/37-27/11/37**A**	Ex.Works 30/11/37 Lord Nelson chimney fitted in error; later fitted to no.786; To Works 6/12/37 Standard King Arthur chimney fitted [No mileage figures given]
9/11/38-11/1/39**B**	53,945
1/2/40-28/2/40**A**	100,268 Olive Green livery
28/10/40-5/11/40**D**	24,936
7/5/42-8/7/42**A**	77,366 Wartime Black livery
10/7/45-30/8/45**A**	108,364
17/7/46-23/8/46**C**	40,184
6/9/46-12/9/46**D**	40,184
2/1/48-24/1/48**A**	93,590 Renumbered S747; Snifting valves removed
13/4/50-12/5/50**A**	80,817 Test 2256: Tyres turned; Renumbered 30747;BR Green livery
25/1/52-2/2/52**NC**	67,184
17/10/52-20/11/52**GO**	91,908
12/1/55-29/1/55**LI-HI**	58,726 T2256 Apexior paint [U]

Tender
No.861 from new

Sheds
Nine Elms 7/1922
Summer, 1923 on loan to Bournemouth, returned to Nine Elms
Exmouth Junction by Summer 1925
Salisbury 1935
Bournemouth 1/10/37
Salisbury 16/10/37
Feltham 21/7/42
LNER, Heaton shed 1/1943
Eastleigh 7/1943
Salisbury 4/1946
Exmouth Junction 7/1947
Salisbury 4/9/48
Nine Elms 8/12/50
Basingstoke 14/3/51
Eastleigh 12/5/51

Withdrawn 20/10/56; cut up at Brighton Works w/e 11/5/57 Total 1,296,927 miles

If there was a spiritual home to the Arthurs then it surely would be Eastleigh. 30747 ELAINE is there on 17th May 1953 having joined the complement two years earlier. Photograph R.C. Riley, www.transporttreasury.co.uk

30748 VIVIEN

Works order no.L16
To traffic as 748 8/1922
Renumbered 30748 20/11/48

Boilers
No.799 21/3/31
No.504 19/12/36
No.448 23/11/38
No.524 23/7/41
No.752 19/5/45
No.507 27/9/47
No.456 22/9/50
No.830 26/3/55

Works	
4/1925	Southern livery; named; E prefix
11/1929	Smoke deflectors fitted; King Arthur chimney; Maunsell Superheater
21/3/31	Stays: 702 copper renewed; 50 roof renewed; 250 holes bushed Plates: Copper tube, new; Copper wrapping, flanges, one-half sides; Crown plate altered and flat patch; Tubes: 169, new "BM"; 24 2nd hand Superheater tubes, ferruled; Maunsell pattern cylinders [double exhaust ports etc.]
5/1932	E prefix removed
23/11/36-19/12/36**A**	86,465
29/10/38-23/11/38**A**	88,489 Maunsell Green livery
10/6/41-23/7/41**A**	85,773 Malachite Green livery
21/4/45-19/5/45**A**	133,993 Wartime Black livery
9/7/45-12/7/45**C**	1,983
27/7/45-2/8/45**D**	3,132
9/9/46-21/9/46**C**	61,688
2/9/47-27/9/47**A**	93,029 Malachite Green livery from Black; Snifting valves removed; Converted to Oil burning
8/12/47-13/12/47**D**	983 Electric lighting fitted; Stone's turbo generator
26/10/48-20/11/48**C**	23,947 Reverted to coal burning; Renumbered 30748
21/8/50-22/9/50**A**	79,881 Stays: 575 copper renewed; 4 roof stays renewed; Plates: Copper tube, flange rivets renewed by studs; Copper firehole, flange rivets renewed by studs; Fusible plugs renewed; Set of new barrel stays; Tubes: Set, new tubes; Set of new Superheater tubes; BR Green livery
24/2/53-7/3/53**LI**	77,234 Stays: 2 copper renewed; 300 copper repaired; Plates: Rivets renewed with studs; Fusible plugs renewed; Tubes: 167, new; 2 new Superheater tubes
25/2/54-13/3/54**LC**	112,517
25/2/55-26/3/55**GO**	144,497

Tender
No.862 from new

Sheds
Nine Elms 8/1922
Salisbury 1935
Nine Elms 13/3/37
Salisbury 1937
LNER, Heaton shed 1/1943
Eastleigh 7/1943
Salisbury 4/1946
Exmouth Junction 7/1947
Eastleigh 12/1947
Nine Elms 12/8/49
Salisbury 20/5/50
Eastleigh 8/12/50
Basingstoke 12/6/57

Withdrawn 7/9/57; stored at Eastleigh Works 9/57; cut up at Eastleigh Works w/e 5/10/57
Total 1,298,717 miles

One of the few carrying the name of a Lady, 30748 VIVIEN, at Nine Elms on 16 July 1955. This is almost the furthest point from the shed, the lines coming together for the turntable to the right. She was also the Lady of the Lake and it seems odd that none of the engines carried such a pretty name; perhaps it was felt the LNW had already bagged it. It still has the electric lighting; the Fireman, incidentally, is taking a spanner to the top clamp to ensure the smokebox is air tight and, thinking about it, this clamp arrangement had one drawback in that a special tool was always needed. When one went AWOL from the engine it was a long walk to the stores and back. Photograph J.H. Aston.

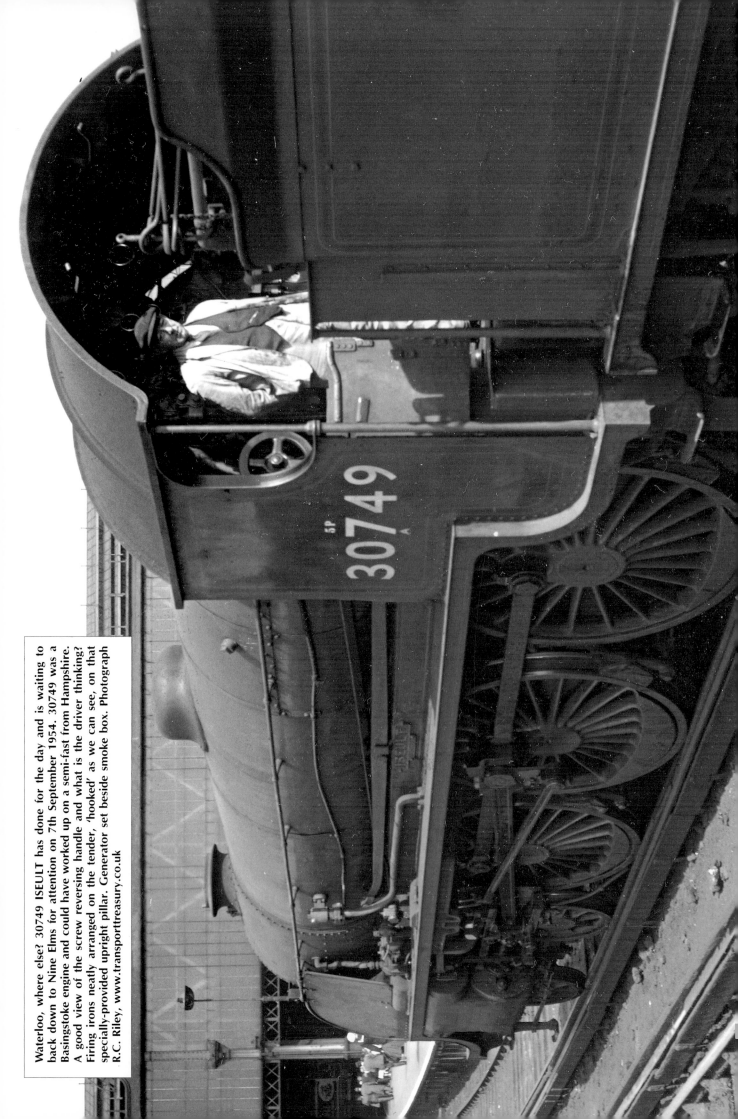

Waterloo, where else? 30749 ISEULT has done for the day and is waiting to back down to Nine Elms for attention on 7th September 1954. 30749 was a Basingstoke engine and could have worked up on a semi-fast from Hampshire. A good view of the screw reversing handle and what is the driver thinking? Firing irons neatly arranged on the tender, 'hooked' as we can see, on that specially-provided upright pillar. Generator set beside smoke box. Photograph R.C. Riley, www.transporttreasury.co.uk

30749 ISEULT

Works order no.L16
To traffic as 749 9/1922
Renumbered 30749 20/11/48

Works

4/1924	Southern livery
9/1925	Named; E prefix; King Arthur chimney
8/1927	Smoke deflectors fitted
12/1928	Maunsell superheater
3/1931	Maunsell pattern cylinders [double exhaust port etc.]
5/1932	E prefix removed
4/7/35-24/8/35**B**	35,883
5/6/36-11/7/36**A**	80,632
9/9/36-17/9/36**D**	2,142
10/11/36-19/11/36**D**	5,775
12/3/38-13/4/38**A**	68,777
8/7/38	Maunsell Dark Green livery
1/8/40-4/9/40**A**	86,055 Maunsell Dark Green livery
17/10/40-30/10/40**D**	[No mileage figure]
8/7/42-2/9/42**A**	52,950 Wartime Black livery
11/10/43-20/10/43**C**	31,570
1/11/44-2/12/44**A**	66,549
6/5/46-7/6/46**B**	54,093
11/3/47-14/3/47**D**	77,226 Malachite Green livery from Black
19/9/47-11/10/47**A**	89,888 Stays: 563 copper renewed; 414 holes bushed Plates: 2 angle patches on back plate; Converted to Oil burning; Snifting valves removed
21/11/47-28/11/47**D**	66 Electric lighting
27/10/48-20/11/48**C**	17,686 Stays: 300 copper repaired; Plates: Seams and studs caulked; Lead plugs renewed; Tubes: Expanded and rebeaded; Superheater tubes referruled; Reverted to coal burning; Renumbered 30749; Kept electric lighting
2/3/50-31/3/50**LI**	54,069 Stays: 250 repaired; Plates: Internal tube, firehole and wrapping plates - studs and seams repaired; Tubes: Set, new; Set, new Superheater tubes; BR Green livery
7/9/50-29/9/50**LC**	72,556 on Eastleigh shed
23/10/51-24/11/51**GO**	110,662
9/10/53-7/11/53**HI**	61,205
5/8/55-3/9/55**GO**	114,711

Boilers
No.515 as of 24/8/35
No.474 13/4/38
No.498 4/9/40
No.522 2/9/42
No.741 2/12/44
No.740 11/10/47
No.513 24/11/51
No.473 3/9/55

Tender
No.863 from new

Sheds
Exmouth Junction 9/1922
Salisbury by 6/1928
Exmouth Junction by mid 1930
Salisbury 1931
Eastleigh 1935
LNER, Heaton shed 1/1943
Eastleigh 7/1943
Bournemouth 7/1946
Eastleigh 9/1946
Basingstoke 26/5/53
Eastleigh 30/9/55
Basingstoke 5/6/56

Withdrawn 22/6/57; stored at Eastleigh Works 6/57; cut up at Eastleigh Works w/e 13/7/57
Total 1,261,799 miles

Another of the Ladies, ISEULT at Basingstoke shed on 30th June 1953, after transferring there in May. 30749 was the wife of King Mark of Cornwall and, typically for the Arthur stories, was smitten by one of the Knights of the Round Table. Photograph B.K.B. Green, Initial Photographics.

30750 MORGAN LE FAY

Works order no.L16
To traffic as 750 10/1922
Renumbered 30750 6/11/48

Boilers
No.521 as of 21/9/35
No.499 20/6/36
No.741 28/9/38
No.511 30/4/41
No.510 12/5/45
No.511 7/2/48
No.448 6/1/50
No.775 8/11/52
No.523 17/9/55

Works

4/1924	Southern livery
10/1925	Named; E prefix
1/1928	Smoke deflectors fitted; King Arthur chimney
2/1930	Maunsell superheater
11/1931	E prefix removed
25/8/35-21/9/35**B**	74,376 Extension of mileage 15,000
8/5/36-20/6/36**A**	102,545
12/8/38-28/9/38**A**	93,777
7/11/38-8/11/38**D**	[No mileage recorded]
12/3/41-30/4/41**A**	86,362 Bulleid pattern cylinders; Malachite Green livery
13/6/42-14/7/42**C**	26,499
5/10/43-8/12/43**C**	63,011 Wartime Black livery
9/4/45-12/5/45**A**	104,400 T2256 Tyres turned
15/1/47-8/2/47**B**	9,239
16/4/47-26/4/47**D**	65,362
13/1/48-7/2/48**A**	86,192 Renumbered S750; Malachite Green livery from Black; Snifting valves removed
3/11/48-6/11/48**D**	28,231 Renumbered 30750
2/12/49-6/1/50**A**	75,097 BR Green livery
7/10/52-8/11/52**GO**	75,931
18/8/55-17/9/55**GO**	111,964 T2256 Tyres turned; T2258 deleted

Tender
No.864 from new

Sheds
Salisbury 10/1922
Nine Elms by 6/1928
Salisbury by 1934
Eastleigh 1935
LNER, Heaton shed 1/1943
Eastleigh 7/1943
Bournemouth 3/5/49
Eastleigh 8/12/50
Nine Elms 12/5/51
Eastleigh 30/9/55
Nine Elms 29/1/56
Basingstoke 31/10/56
Nine Elms 17/12/56
Basingstoke 12/6/57

Withdrawn 10/7/57; stored at Eastleigh Works 7/57; cut up at Eastleigh Works w/e 10/8/57
Total 1,298,672 miles

We are back at Basingstoke on 28th August 1954, a favoured spot for Urie Arthurs this day. 30750 MORGAN LE FAY (evil half sister of King Arthur, who plotted his downfall) is approaching the station from the west; on the right is the shed where the loco would spend two short periods after this date; she was withdrawn a month after its second transfer to Basingstoke shed.

Nine Elms on 23rd March 1956 and 30750 MORGAN LE FAY at her then home. During its short BR life this loco had at least eight transfers between Western Section sheds. Alongside is U class 31634, a Nine Elms resident for a number of years. Jolly 'Edwardian' cover to the safety valves, as per the Urie boilers. Photograph Peter Groom.

30751 ETARRE

Works order no.N16
To traffic as 751 11/1922
Renumbered 30751 26/6/48

Boilers
No.755 22/6/29
No.824 23/3/35
No.724 11/1/36
No.508 23/1/37
No.738 11/1/39
No.741 20/5/41
No.473 16/4/44
No.748 2/3/46
No.736 26/6/48
No.473 12/4/51
No.824 11/2/55

Works
4/1924	Southern livery
3/1927	Named; E prefix
12/1928	Smoke deflectors fitted; King Arthur chimney
22/6/29	Stays: 65 copper renewed; Roof renewed, all; Plates: Copper tube, new; Copper wrapping, flat patch; New brick arch studs and 2 plugs; Tubes: 169, new; 24 Superheater tubes, ferruled, copper ends; Alteration of crown; Maunsell Superheater
29/10/29	Minor fitting
2/1930	Urie pattern 21" cylinders
10/1931	E prefix removed
23/3/35	Stays: 892 copper renewed; 500 holes bushed; Plates: Copper tube, angle patches; Copper wrapping, flanges, one-half sides; Tubes: 29 2nd hand welded and ferruled; Superheater tubes expanded
12/12/35-11/1/36**B**	39,531
23/12/36-23/1/37**A**	89,260
10/12/38-11/1/39**A**	93,997 Maunsell Green livery
2/4/41-20/5/41**A**	75,489 Malachite Green livery
15/3/44-16/4/44**A**	92,842 Wartime Black livery
7/1/46-2/3/46**B**	44,307
7/10/46-12/10/46**D**	66,747
11/3/47-12/4/47**B**	79,080
1/6/48-26/6/48**A**	113,435 Renumbered 30751; Snifting valves removed: Malachite Green from black
8/3/51-12/4/51**GO**	76,012 BR Green livery
5/2/53-21/2/53**LI**	74,800
20/5/54-29/5/54**LC**	127,244
13/1/55-11/2/55**GO**	151,398 Stays: 421 copper renewed; Plates: Copper tube, new; Copper firehole, 2 angle patches; 2 fusible plugs; Casing back, holes bushed; Throat, 110 holes bushed; Tubes: Set, new "Stewart and Lloyds"; Set new Superheater tubes

Tender
No.865 from new

Sheds
Nine Elms 11/1922
Salisbury by 6/1928
Eastleigh by 1934
LNER, Heaton shed 1/1943
Eastleigh 7/1943
Bournemouth 12/12/49
Eastleigh 8/12/50
Nine Elms 12/5/51
Basingstoke 5/6/56

Withdrawn 15/6/57; stored at Eastleigh Works 6/57; cut up at Eastleigh Works w/e 13/7/57
Total 1,362,472 miles

Another Lady, ETARRE. 751 is in its later Southern railway guise. Curved hand rail over smokebox. But look at those fashions and the social contrast they indicate, between the Driver and the platform group. Maunsell boiler 824.

30751 ETARRE, one of the Arthurian ladies who were unlucky in love, like most of them it seems. This is Nine Elms on 23rd March 1956 with a former Brighton loco, E4 0-6-2T 32492 receiving attention. Like most Arthurs it has split big ends which lasted most of the class for life. The paintwork looks a bit weary; well, it had undergone its last works visit in 1955, and was withdrawn in June 1957. Maunsell boiler 824 (again) returned in February 1955. Photograph Peter Groom.

30752 LINETTE

Works order no.N16
To traffic as 752 12/1922
Renumbered 30752 25/9/48

Boilers
No.768 2/1/37
No.511 22/3/39
No.743 26/2/41
No.502 10/2/45
No.473 1/3/47
No.1048 24/11/50

Works

12/1924	Southern livery
3/1927	Named; E prefix
12/1927	Smoke deflectors fitted
12/1928	King Arthur chimney
3/1930	Maunsell Superheater
9/1930	Maunsell pattern cylinders [double exhaust ports]
9/1932	E prefix removed
1/12/36-2/1/37**A**	84,505 New boiler with Ross pop valves
30/3/38-4/5/38**B**	55,965
27/2/39-22/3/39**A**	94,313 Maunsell Green livery
13/1/41-26/2/41**A**	84,249 Maunsell Green livery [non standard]; Large diameter chimney, multiple jet blastpipe
3/4/41-5/4/41**D**	[No mileage figure]
25/6/41-9/8/41**C**	1,515
10/1/45-10/2/45**A**	98,860 Wartime Black livery
18/7/45-28/7/45**C**	19,806
7/2/47-1/3/47**A**	84,305 Malachite Green livery from Black
11/9/47-27/9/47**C**	24,464 Converted to Oil firing. Vertical deflectors
12/12/47-20/12/47**D**	28,399 Stone's turbogenerator and electric lighting
7/9/48-25/9/48**C**	44,870 Converted to coal burning; Renumbered 30752
24/6/49-22/7/49**LI**	70,405
9/10/50-24/11/50**A**	118,832 BR Green livery; Snifting valves removed
18/4/52-9/5/52**HC**	47,469
28/1/53-31/1/53**LC**	75,663
19/10/53-7/11/53**HI**	108,615
7/12/53-12/12/53**Return**	112,312
27/8/54-18/9/54**LC**	148,824

Tender
No.866 from new

Sheds
Nine Elms 12/1922
Eastleigh 1935
Bournemouth 7/1946
Eastleigh 9/1946
Bournemouth 3/5/49
Eastleigh 12/12/49
Nine Elms 12/5/51

Withdrawn 10/12/55;
cut up at Brighton
Works w/e 21/1/56
Total 1,287,576 miles

Truly something from another age, E752 **LINETTE** on what would be (according to the headcode) a Waterloo or Nine Elms to Bournemouth West via Brockenhurst and Sway, arriving at Bournemouth West. Inspection pit in the foreground from the days when drivers went underneath to oil *during* the journey.

30752 LINETTE, looking very smart in green, is at home at Eastleigh shed on 3rd December 1950 having been released from a General a week or so before. Linette was the daughter of Sir Persant, the name carried by 30780. Vertical deflectors, Maunsell boiler 1048. Photograph Les Elsey.

30753 MELISANDE

Works order no.N16
To traffic as 753 1/1923
Renumbered 30753 3/4/48

Boilers
No.523 7/9/35
No.803 10/4/37
No.503 12/7/39
No.491 3/11/42
No.736 2/2/46
No.509 3/4/48
No.507 29/9/50
No.747 14/2/53
No.501 11/12/54

Tender
No.867 from new

Sheds
Exmouth Junction 1/1923
Nine Elms 1923
Eastleigh early 1929
Exmouth Junction 3/1944
Nine Elms 11/1946
Salisbury 20/5/50
Eastleigh 8/12/50
Nine Elms 12/5/51
Basingstoke 8/10/51
Nine Elms 6/12/51
Basingstoke 7/6/52
Nine Elms 30/9/55
Basingstoke 10/10/55

Withdrawn 16/3/57; stored at Eastleigh Works 3-4/57; cut up at Eastleigh Works w/e 4/5/57
Total 1,241,374 miles

Works	
1/1925	Southern livery
8/1925	Named; E prefix
5/1926	King Arthur chimney
1/1928	Smoke deflectors fitted
7/1928	Maunsell Superheater
9/1931	E prefix removed
29/8/35-7/9/35**D**	[No mileage figure]
3/1/36-18/1/36**C**	32,837
15/5/36-27/6/36**B**	46,915
20/2/37-10/4/37**A**	86,886 Boiler with Ross pop safety valves
31/1/38-23/2/38**C**	30,701
9/4/38-12/4/38**D**	[No mileage figure]
19/6/39-12/7/39**A**	71,736 Olive Green livery
20/10/42-3/11/42**A**	101,519 Wartime Black livery
9/1/45-22/1/45**C[EXJ]**	75,897 Extension of mileage 5,000
18/6/45-1/7/45**C[EXJ]**	103,385 Extension of mileage 10,000
4/1/46-2/2/46**A**	123,598
5/3/48-3/4/48**A**	85,985 Renumbered 30753; Malachite Green livery from Black; Snifting valves removed
9/6/49-17/6/49**C[LC]**	50,390
5/9/50-29/9/50**GO**	97,405 BR Green Livery; T2189 Standardisation of white metals
23/11/51-1/12/51**LC**	31,621
22/1/53-14/2/53**GO**	66,829
11/11/54-11/12/54**GO**	60,675
23/3-13/4/56**LC[BTN]**	42,644 V and P only

30753 MELISANDE at Nine Elms in BR guise but minus shed plate though this is hardly surprising as it had eight transfers in BR days including three to Basingstoke, its final shed, in October 1955. How could you keep up? Photograph B.K.B. Green, Initial Photographics.

MELISANDE's safety valves gently discharge at Basingstoke on 30th August 1955; this shed would soon be its home, until withdrawal in March 1957. Photograph B.K.B. Green, Initial Photographics.

30753 MELISANDE (some confusion exists as to what part this maiden played in the Arthurian legend) at Basingstoke on 20th June 1956. She appears to be doing some shunting, maybe as station pilot. For her last eighteen months MELISANDE was at Basingstoke shed.

30754 THE GREEN KNIGHT

Works order no.N16
To traffic as 754 2/1923
Renumbered 30754 2/7/48

Boilers
No.783 9/1/30
No.507 13/7/35
No.475 13/12/35
No.749 14/11/36
No.748 22/2/39
No.751 15/11/45
No.747 17/1/48
No.749 14/4/50

Works

7/1924	Southern livery
9/1925	Named; E prefix; King Arthur chimney
7/1928	Smoke deflectors fitted
9/1/1930	Stays: 600 copper renewed Plates: Copper wrapping, 2 flanges, one-half sides; Rivets and seams caulked; New brick arch studs and plugs; Tubes: 43 new "BM" Maunsell Superheater fitted
14/3/31[BTN]	Stays: 1 copper renewed; 660 copper riveted over; Plates: Rivets caulked; new plugs; Tubes: 127 2nd hand; 24 Superheater tubes ferruled
6/1932	E prefix removed; Maunsell pattern cylinders [double exhaust ports]
7/6/35-13/7/35A	74,250
27/11/35-13/12/35B	18,656
13/10/36-14/11/36A	71,898
25/1/38-12/3/38C	49,155
31/1/39-22/2/39A	83,757 Maunsell Green livery
23/7/41-8/10/41A	84,790 Malachite Green livery
15/11/43-19/1/44C	64,526 Extension of mileage 10,000
9/10/45-15/11/45A	115,883 Wartime Black livery
29/10/46-2/11/46C	38,506
16/12/47-17/1/48A	67,959 Renumbered S754 briefly only; Snifting valves removed
28/6/48-2/7/48D	18,781 Renumbered 30754
10/3/50-14/4/50A	89,631 BR Green livery
7/6/50-23/6/50LC	[No mileage recorded]
19/9/51-28/9/51NC	32,531

Tenders
No.868 from new
No.869 5/2/53 at Eastleigh shed from 30755 (for scrapping only)

Sheds
Exmouth Junction 2/1923
Nine Elms 1923
Salisbury by 6/1928
Eastleigh 1935
LNER, Heaton shed 1/1943
Eastleigh 7/1943
Bournemouth 17/6/50
Eastleigh 8/12/50
Nine Elms 12/5/51
Basingstoke 8/10/51
Nine Elms 6/12/51
Basingstoke 7/6/52

Withdrawn 10/2/53; cut up at Eastleigh Works w/e 1/3/53
Total 1,151,285 miles

Proud Driver and 30754 THE GREEN KNIGHT at Bournemouth shed on 9th May 1925; LSW livery, 'wing' lamp irons and so on. Photograph H.C. Casserley, courtesy R.M. Casserley.

The 'Super Urie Arthur', 755 THE RED KNIGHT with Bulleid pattern cylinders and Lemaître multiple blast pipe chimney and vertical deflectors. Within a few weeks of it leaving works (visit ending 19/4/40) the Nine Elms shed master heard of the engine's improved performance and got it transferred. All Urie Arthurs had Maunsell smokebox doors by about the middle 1930s.

30755 THE RED KNIGHT

Works order no.N16
To traffic as 755 28/3/1923
Renumbered 30755 21/10/49

Works

6/1923	New Boiler no.755
29/12/24-9/4/25**GO**	66,584 Southern livery; Named; E prefix
31/10/25	Stays: 250 copper riveted over
5/10/26	Stays: 250 copper riveted over
2/4/27-9/7/1927**GO**	75,044 King Arthur chimney; Stays: 301 copper renewed; 150 copper riveted over; Tubes: 169, new; Foundation ring, 20 rivets repaired
1/1928	Smoke deflectors fitted
3/1929	Maunsell Superheater
4/10/30-15/11/30**A**	61,297
12/1/32-13/2/32**A**	55,551 E prefix removed
11/8/33-12/9/33**A**	73,582
5/7/35-17/8/35**A**	91,956
7/12/36-16/1/37**A**	73,160
3/9/37-2/10/37**B**	32,559
15/6/38**D**	[No mileage recorded]
1/11/38-14/12/38**B**	67,236 Extension of mileage 5,000
9/12/39-14/2/40**A**	95,156 Bulleid pattern 22" cylinders; Olive Green livery; Large diameter chimney
17/4/40-19/4/40**C**	1,105
30/7/41-3/9/41**C**	47,343
26/6/42-5/8/42**A**	86,014 Wartime Black livery
1/8/44-23/9/44**A**	105,340
2/1945	Vertical smoke deflectors fitted
20/3/46-13/4/46**B**	62,582 Malachite Green livery from Black
31/10/46-16/11/46**C**	96,241 Extension of mileage 5,000
25/6/47-2/8/47**A**	125,322
15/9/49-21/10/49**GO**	92,198 Renumbered 30755; BR Green livery; Snifting valves removed
27/11/51-29/12/51**GO**	62,913 Stays: 410 copper renewed; Roof renewed all Plates: Copper tube, seams repaired; Copper firehole, 2 angle patches; Fusible plugs renewed; Tubes: Set, new; Set, new Superheater tubes
29/9/53-17/10/53**HI**	77,621 Stays: 370 copper repaired; Plates: Copper tube, studded; Copper firehole, studded [22]; 2 plugs renewed; Tubes: Set, new; Set, new Superheater tubes
21/1/54-17/2/54**LC**	85,369 T2256 Apexior paint
11/8/54-14/8/54**LC**	104,748 T2256 [U]
1/9/55-24/9/55**GO**	141,734 T2256 [R]

Tenders
No.869 from new
No.868 at Eastleigh shed,
6/2/53 from 30754

Sheds
Exmouth Junction 3/1923
Nine Elms 1923
Eastleigh 1931
Nine Elms 1/7/40
Eastleigh 5/2/51
Nine Elms 12/5/51
Basingstoke 8/10/51
Eastleigh 30/9/55
Nine Elms 29/1/56
Basingstoke 5/6/56

Withdrawn 11/5/57;
stored at Eastleigh Works
5/57; cut up at Eastleigh
Works w/e 2/6/57
Total 1,330,274 miles

Boilers
No.755, brand new, 6/23
No.1000 17/8/35
No.510 16/1/37
No.1000 14/2/40
No.509 5/8/42
No.476 23/9/44
No.507 13/4/46
No.475 2/8/47
No.752 21/10/49
No.755 29/12/51
No.522 24/9/55

The last of the Urie Arthurs, completed in March 1923; 30755 THE RED KNIGHT, once it was fitted with 22 inch Bulleid pattern cylinders and Lemaître exhaust, gained a reputation as a strong engine and was often used on the most arduous of duties when based at Nine Elms in the 1940s. A couple of months before withdrawal it is on empty stock working out of Waterloo, in March 1957; bound for Clapham Junction, it is passing Vauxhall. Photograph Peter Groom.

30763 SIR BORS DE GANIS

NBL works no.23209
To traffic as E763 5/1925
Renumbered 30763 16/6/50

Boilers
No.928 19/8/27
No.780 23/11/35
No.776 15/6/38
No.832 8/10/41
No.1051 13/1/45
No.798 27/9/47
No.742 16/6/50
No.929 11/4/53
No.766 7/6/58

Works

19/8/27	73,884
23/6/28	33,682 Stays: 64 copper renewed; 200 copper riveted over; Roof renewed, all; Plates: Three-quarter seams and rivets caulked: New brick arch studs and plugs; Tubes: New, all "BM"; 24 Superheater tubes ferruled, copper ends; smoke deflectors fitted
16/8/29	Stays: 279 copper renewed; Plates: Rivets and seams caulked; New brick arch studs and plugs; Tubes: 24 Superheater tubes ferruled
25/7/30	Stays: 2 copper renewed; 100 copper riveted over; Plates: New plugs; Tubes: 24 Superheater tubes ferruled
2/1931	79,143
4/1932	E prefix removed
3-7/1933	Carried rail washing equipment for this period
4/1933	89,929
23/10/35-23/11/35**A**	91,448
6/12/35-7/12/35**D**	[No mileage recorded]
2/10/36**D**	35,128
15/2/37-25/3/37**B**	51,231
4/9/37-17/9/37**C**	64,539
10/5/38-15/6/38**A**	91,172
9/8/41-8/10/41**A**	78,859 Malachite Green livery
11/1/43-9/3/43**C**	54,993 Wartime Black livery
23/7/43-6/10/43**B**	65,127
5/2/44-24/3/44**C[SL]**	69,028
3/11/44-13/1/45**A**	91,909
6/9/45-12/9/45**C**	23,310
30/9/46-19/10/46**B**	54,618
21/6/47	T2080 Left and Right-hand gauge glasses at Stewarts Lane
4/9/47-27/9/47**A**	74,532 Malachite Green livery from Black; Snifting valves removed; T2025 Spring links fitted with copper plated threads
9/5/50-16/6/50**GO**	70,658 Renumbered 30763; BR Green livery
11/3/53-11/4/53**GO**	74,996
28/9/54-18/11/54	[No mileage recorded] at Ashford shed
30/1/56-25/2/56**LI-HI**	67,772
28/9/56-13/10/56**LC**	93,488 Test oilbox on right-hand top slidebar [rear position] [U]
15/5/58-7/6/58**GO**	133,028 Right-hand side injector and feed gear modified
9/12/59-23/1/60**NC**	[No mileage recorded]

Tenders
No.3231 from new
No.880 23/6/28
No.3212 from S15 no.833 2/10/36
No.3213 from N15x 32330 25/2/56

Sheds
Stewarts Lane 5/1925
Ramsgate 13/11/37
Stewarts Lane 27/2/40
Ramsgate 4/9/48
Stewarts Lane 12/5/51
Basingstoke 12/8/55
Eastleigh 5/6/56
Bournemouth 12/6/57
Nine Elms 8/10/57

Withdrawn 1/10/60; stored at Eastleigh Works 9/60; cut up at Eastleigh Works w/e 28/10/60 Total 1,050,454 miles

763 SIR BORS DE GANIS (nephew of 455) at Teynham on the North Kent line in 1935; early features such as snifting valves and crosshead vacuum pump present, straight sided six wheel 4,000 gallon tender. This was the first of the Scotch Arthurs, completed in May 1925. The first of the Maunsell Arthurs was E453 February 1925.

30763 SIR BORS DE GANIS (brother to 30797) at Basingstoke on duty SPL30 from Waterloo on 20th June 1956; it looks like a boat train heading for Southampton. SIR BORS had just transferred to Eastleigh shed.

30764 SIR GAWAIN

NBL Works no.23210
To traffic as E764 5/1925
Renumbered 30764 25/2/49

Boilers
No.783 26/4/28
No.454 3/11/29
No.828 as of 19/10/35
No.491 22/8/36
No.794 25/1/39
No.1053 3/1/46
No.1412 25/2/49
No.798 10/6/55

Works	
26/4/28	Stays: 475 copper renewed; 80 roof renewed; Plates: Copper tube, new; New studs in flanges: Box and casing caulked; New brick arch studs and plugs; Tubes: Set, new "BM"; 24 Superheater tubes ferruled, copper ends fitted; Smoke deflectors fitted; Ashford pattern tender
3/11/29	Stays: 640 copper renewed; Plates: Copper wrapping, 2 flanges; New brick arch studs and plugs; Tubes: 93, new; 24 Superheater tubes, ferruled, copper ends
8/1932	E prefix removed
3-7/1933	Carried rail washing equipment for this period
19/9/35-19/10/35**B**	53,811
16/7/36-22/8/36**A**	80,618
28/10/36-13/11/36**D**	3,511
5/8/37-28/8/37**B**	38,035
21/12/38-25/1/39**A**	84,587 Maunsell Green livery
28/1/42**A**	[No mileage recorded] Malachite Green livery
4/3/44-8/4/44**C[SL]**	68,002 Wartime Black livery
13/11/45-3/1/46**A**	102,641
8/1/49-25/2/49**A**	87,624 Malachite Green livery from Black; Renumbered 30764; Snifting valves removed
15/11/49-25/11/49**HC**	24,568 Stays: 150 monel metal riveted over; 150 nuts renewed; Plates: Seams and studs repaired
11/2/52-1/3/52**LI**	93,403 Stays: 500 monel metal repaired; 565 new nuts; Plates: Seams repaired; New fusible plugs; Tubes: Set, new; 3 new Superheater tubes; BR Green livery
16/5/55-10/6/55**GO**	159,277
25/2/57-2/3/57**LC**	48,977
12/2/58-28/2/58**LI**	70,277

Tenders
No.3230 from new
No.881 26/4/28
No.3231 from S15 no.834 on 13/11/36

Sheds
Stewarts Lane 5/1925
Ramsgate 13/11/37
Dover 27/2/40
Stewarts Lane 1/7/40
Ramsgate 4/9/48
Stewarts Lane 3/5/49
Eastleigh 7/7/55
Bournemouth 12/8/55
Salisbury 5/10/60
Bournemouth 24/11/60

Withdrawn 22/7/61; stored at Eastleigh Works 7/61; cut up at Eastleigh Works w/e 26/8/61
Total 979,213 miles

An unusual sight at Feltham shed, a named engine and an Arthur at that, on Saturday 8th August 1959. Our footplate crew seem intent on something in the smokebox, leaking tubes perhaps? The engine is 30764 SIR GAWAIN (nephew of 30453) at the time based at Bournemouth. For a short while in 1959-1960 in fact Feltham had its own Arthurs, 30775, 30777, 30793 and 30795 and Haines Bridge oiks looked forward to seeing them on the twice nightly Nine Elms-Southampton goods which always passed us on the down slow at 7.35pm and 8.10pm. Normally it was in the hands of S15 4-6-0s, and mainly Urie ones at that. Photograph J.H. Aston.

You don't often see an Arthur keeping company with a Terrier but here's one, 30764 SIR GAWAIN at Eastleigh shed on 15th April 1960.

Despite the unfortunate lamp post still a good solid portrait of 30764 SIR GAWAIN at Eastleigh shed, 14 May 1960.

30765 SIR GARETH

NBL Works no.23211
To traffic as E765 5/1925
Renumbered 30765 4/3/49

Boilers
No.786 30/8/35
No.804 16/10/37
No.456 24/7/40
No.791 17/2/43
No.1047 4/3/49 ['Repaired at Derby']*
No.796 2/10/54
No.804 9/4/60
*An odd entry, otherwise without explanation

Works

11/1927	Smoke deflectors fitted
3-7/1933	Carried rail washing equipment
4/1933	E prefix removed
25/7/35-30/8/35**A**	82,417
11/12/36-27/12/36**B**	49,292
28/6/37**D[AFD]**	[No mileage recorded]
21/9/37-16/10/37**A**	81,707
6/1/39-22/2/39**B**	55,833 Extension of mileage 5,000
28/6/40-24/7/40**A**	96,564 Stays: 530 copper renewed; Plates: Copper tube, 2 angles; Copper firehole, 2 angles; Lead plugs; Tubes: 169, new "Tubes Ltd"; 24 new Superheater tubes; Malachite Green livery
15/1/43-17/2/43**A**	78,722 Wartime Black livery
7/2/45-24/3/45**C**	73,074 Extension of mileage 10,000
8/5/46-7/6/46**A**	109,764 Black livery with green driving wheels
23/6/47**[SL]**	T2080 Left and right-hand gauge glasses
4/7/47**[SL]**	Left-hand gauge glass removed
2/2/49-4/3/49**A**	77,476 Plates: New firebox; Tubes: Set, new "Howell"; Set, new Superheater tubes; Malachite Green livery from Black; Snifting valves removed; Renumbered 30765
29/1/52-23/2/52**LI**	106,324 Stays: 406 monel metal repaired and 406 new nuts; 18 roof renewed; Plates: Copper tube, studded; Copper firehole, studded; Fusible plugs renewed; Tubes: Set, new; 3 new Superheater tubes; BR Green livery
7/8/53-22/8/53**LC**	126,066 Stays: 475 steel repaired; 475 new nuts; Plates: Copper tube, flanges repaired; Copper firehole, flanges repaired; Fusible plugs renewed; Tubes: 6 renewed; All Superheater tubes renewed
6/9/54-2/10/54**GO**	158,735 Combination lever and valve spindle modified
22/1/58-14/2/58**LI**	74,027
15/3/60-9/4/60**GO**	123,730

Tenders
No.3227 from new
No.882 1/29
No.3232 from S15 no.835 on 27/12/36
No.3234 at Eastleigh Works on 10/11/59 from 30767

Sheds
Stewarts Lane 5/1925
Hither Green 27/2/40
Stewarts Lane 1/7/40
Ramsgate 4/9/48
Nine Elms 3/5/49
Salisbury 9/10/50
Nine Elms 8/12/50
Stewarts Lane 5/2/51
Bournemouth 12/8/55
Basingstoke 13/10/58

Withdrawn 29/9/62; stored at Eastleigh Works 9-10/62; cut up at Eastleigh Works w/e 10/11/62
Total 1,116,054 miles

765 SIR GARETH, then a Stewarts Lane engine, with a down continental Pullman boat train – it would be the Golden Arrow – at Downsbridge Road, Shortlands about 1931. The shed had a good complement of the class at the time, supporting the Lord Nelsons on the main expresses to the Kent Coast before the Second World War. In certain areas of south-east London the fourth conductor rail was bonded to the running rails either side, to provide a better return of current. For Stage 1 of the Kent Coast electrification in 1959 the four tracks through Shortlands were extended over the allotments in the foreground to pointwork just below the bridge.

30765 SIR GARETH in Eastleigh Works, 14th April 1960. It is of interest for the way, for instance, the running plate unbolts ahead of the cylinders to afford access to the valves. *The Record* shows it to have undergone a General but gives its completion as 9th April; beware the Accountants!

30765 SIR GARETH (brother of 30764) on one of the workings the class were famed for, the 'inter regionals' between Bournemouth and Oxford. 30765 is at the latter place on 3rd May 1957. 30765 was at the time a Bournemouth engine and the headcode refers to trains between Bournemouth Central and Weymouth, and also Basingstoke to Oxford. Photograph R.M. Casserley.

30765 SIR GARETH at Basingstoke, its home shed from October 1958 until withdrawal; an interesting side-on in that the delicate taper from the dome to the smokebox is actually fairly apparent for once. Photograph J. Davenport, Initial Photographics. *Inset.* Eastleigh, 20th September 1962, nine days before SIR GARETH's withdrawal; as for the missing bolt, in the Second World War one was removed for the scrap drive from all N15 nameplates! A problem was that if the other bolt at that end worked free the plate would flap about and occasionally fracture part way. Thus around 1945 790 had one plate reading simply VILLIARS and 454 had the remaining part plate reading QUEEN G. Photograph John Scrace.

30766 SIR GERAINT

NBL Works no.23212
To traffic as E766 5/1925
Renumbered 30766 8/1/49

Boilers
No.839 19/10/29
No.454 16/6/34
No.829 27/7/35
No.831 21/7/37
No.785 8/3/39
No.826 28/5/41
No.783 17/3/44
No.773 6/4/46
No.792 6/9/47
No.1411 8/1/49
No.841 8/8/53

Works	
2/1928	Smoke deflectors fitted
19/10/29	169 new tubes
25/9/30	Stays: 300 copper riveted over; Plates: Rivets and seams caulked; New plugs; Tubes: All expanded
7/1931	E prefix removed
3-7/33	Carried rail washing equipment for this period
16/6/34	Stays: 197 copper renewed; Plates: Copper tube, flanges welded; Copper wrapping, top seams of one-half sides welded; Lead plugs; Rivets and seams caulked; Tubes: 169, new "Chesterfield": 24 Superheater tubes, 2nd hand, copper ends
24/6/35-27/7/35**A**	86,723 Plates: New copper firebox; Casing covering, three-quarter sides [Reinforcing plate]; Tubes: 169, 2nd hand welded; 24 2nd hand ; Superheater tubes [copper ends]
21/7/36-25/8/36**C**	43,551 Stays: 350 copper riveted over; Plates: Rivets and seams caulked; Lead plugs; Tubes: 6, new
21/6/37-21/7/37**A**	80,327
14/2/39-8/3/39**A**	72,884 Malachite Green livery
22/4/41-28/5/41**A**	70,101 Stays: 425 copper renewed; Plates: Copper tube, new; Copper wrapping, flanges, one-half sides; Lead plugs; Tubes: 167 2nd hand, welded: 24 new Superheater tubes
4/9/42-7/10/42**B**	48,193 Extension of mileage 10,000
18/2/44-17/3/44**A**	107,198 Stays: 468 copper renewed; Plates: Rivets and seams caulked; Lead plugs; Tubes: 167 2nd hand; 24 2nd hand Superheater tubes; Wartime Black livery
20/2/45-22/3/45**C[NE]**	42,927
26/9/45-4/10/45**C[NE]**	68,013
27/2/46-6/4/46**A**	82,698 Malachite Green livery from Black
2/7/46-20/7/46**C**	12,912
13/8/47-6/9/47**B**	62,427
10/10/47-1/11/47**B**	65,091 Snifting valves removed
10/12/48-8/1/49**A**	111,366 Renumbered 30766
28/2/51-31/3/51**HI**	76,465 BR Green livery
13/11/51-15/11/51**LC**	95,295
26/6/52-2/8/52**HC**	105,125 New right-hand cylinder
24/6/53-8/8/53**GO**	143,271 Tubes: 167, new; 24 new Superheater tubes; Foundation ring, all rivets renewed
4/1954	Live steam injector [Railway Observer 1954 pg.144]
7/1/57-26/1/57**LI**	93,106 30, new tubes "Stewart and Lloyds"; 3 new Superheater tubes; "Internal examination extended from 8/58 to 12/58" then "Internal examination extended from 12/58 to 4/59"

Tenders
No.3226 from new
No.883 1/29
No.3233 from S15 no.836 on 21/7/37
No.905 at Nine Elms shed on 22/3/45 from 788

Sheds
Stewarts Lane 5/1925
Nine Elms 22/11/42
Stewarts Lane 3/5/49

Withdrawn 27/12/58; stored at Eastleigh Works 12/58; cut up at Eastleigh Works w/e 31/1/59 Total 1,141,019 miles

Below. SIR GERAINT (actually E766) in original condition looking quite stunning as usual with fine lining even to the panels of the footsteps. Quite breathtaking; under a glass the wording of the North British builders plate on the smokebox side can even be read. Snifting valves, crosshead vacuum pump, 'oven door handle' to the smokebox door and so on.

Long-standing Stewarts Lane Arthur 30766 SIR GERAINT (cousin of 30454) hauls an up Continental boat train at Ashford, Kent on Saturday 20th April 1957, just over a year before withdrawal and disposal. Withdrawal came in December 1958 with scrapping at Eastleigh Works. Photograph B.W.L. Brooksbank, Initial Photographics.

30767 SIR VALENCE

NBL Works no.23213
[Originally to be named SIR MORDRED]
To traffic as E767 5/1925
Renumbered 30767 6/11/48

Boilers
No.824 25/10/33
No.772 21/3/36
No.929 10/8/38
No.780 1/1/41
No.788 7/7/43
No.824 26/1/46
No.788 6/11/48
No.785 12/10/51
No.1050 3/6/55

Works

4/1928	Smoke deflectors fitted
9/1931	E prefix removed
3-7/1933	Carried rail washing equipment for this period
25/10/33	Stays: 104 copper renewed; 80 roof renewed; Plates: Copper tube, new; Copper firehole, flanges welded; Lead plugs; Steel reinforcing plate; Tubes: 169 2nd hand welded; 24 2nd hand Superheater tubes [copper ends]
13/3/34	Stays: 3 copper renewed; 350 copper riveted over; Plates: Studs and seams chipped and caulked; Mud plugs seating caulked
19/2/36-21/3/36A	93,979
23/4/37-22/5/37C	47,074
6/12/37C[SL]	[No mileage recorded]
23/6/38-10/8/38A	92,835 Flaman speed recorder fitted
22/11/40-1/1/41A	79,837 Malachite Green livery; Flaman speed recorder removed
24/5/43-7/7/43A	90,867 Wartime Black livery
4/8/44-21/8/44C[NE]	46,761
31/12/45-26/1/46A	83,859 Stays: 700 copper renewed; 30 direct renewed; 120 SS bolts; 550 holes bushed; Plates: Copper tube, new; Copper wrapping, flanges, one-half sides; Tubes: 169, new "Howell"; 24 new Superheater tubes; Malachite Green livery from Black; T1891 Thomas patent piston rod packing Ref TT6/42/1/1891
26/2/46-23/3/46C	385 Plates: Left hand expansion bracket re-fixed and studded; 50 steel bushed; 48 rivets caulked
3/10/47-25/10/47C	59,677 Stays: 6 copper renewed and 725 repaired Plates: Studs renewed; Seams, rivets and studs repaired; Lead plugs renewed; Tubes: 60 expanded; Superheater tubes expanded, re-beaded and new ferrules; Snifting valves removed
9/10/48-6/11/48A	87,591 Renumbered 30767
20/4/51NC [AFD]	66,595 Weighing only
14/9/51-12/10/51GO	79,855 BR Green livery
4/5/55-3/6/55GO	60,251

Tenders
No.3229 from new
No.884 2/30
No.3234 from S15 no.837 at Stewarts Lane shed on 6/12/37

Sheds
Stewarts Lane 5/1925
Dover 27/2/40
Stewarts Lane 1/7/40
Nine Elms 22/11/42
Dover 23/4/45
Stewarts Lane 4/1946
Dover 6/1946
Stewarts Lane 27/6/51
Bournemouth 12/8/55
Stewarts Lane 30/9/55
Eastleigh 14/6/59

Withdrawn 27/6/59; stored at Eastleigh Works 6-8/59; cut up at Eastleigh Works w/e 12/9/59 Total 1,029,937 miles

Eastleigh, which saw all the Arthurs at one time or another, on 29th August 1959 with 30767 SIR VALENCE in store having been withdrawn on 27 June 1959, two months before. Everything still looks complete though the tender seems empty. The end came in September 1959. Behind is 30778 SIR PELLEAS which was withdrawn before 30763 and scrapped the week after SIR VALENCE.

SIR VALENCE in his pomp as E767, first on the 10.35am Continental Pullmans at Victoria Grosvenor Bank (above the middle of the train is one of the American-style 3-position upper quadrant semaphores installed in 1919 and replaced by colour lights in 1939, as well as the LBSC catenary) and (below) at full flight through Bromley South with the 11.00am Victoria-Dover boat in 1927. The SECR matchboard continental coaches were used almost exclusively on such 'boats' at the time. Note yet again the 'wing' lamp brackets in use and the prominent snifting valves, along with the astonishing level of cleaning or, rather, burnishing. No 'hood' over cab windows in these Spartan days. The Bromley passengers, presumably waiting for an imminent excursion, would have seen their reflections flashing by in the boiler!

30768 SIR BALIN

NBL Works no.23214
To traffic E768 5/1925
Renumbered 30768 30/10/48

Boilers
No.782 10/3/34
No.765 12/1/38
No.771 12/6/40
No.1050 8/9/43
No.772 30/10/48
No.452 21/6/52
No.767 15/2/58

Works

6/1928	Smoke deflectors fitted
3/1932	E prefix removed
10/3/34	Stays: 50 holes bushed; Plates: New copper firebox; Casing covering, three-quarters sides; Tubes: 169, new "Tubes ltd"; 24 2nd hand Superheater tubes, copper ends
9/12/35-11/1/36A	81,241 Stays: 439 copper renewed; Plates: Copper firehole, flanges welded; Rivets and seams caulked; Studs in flanges; Lead plugs; Tubes: 60, 2nd hand, welded; 24 Superheater tubes, expanded and referruled
2/12/37-12/1/38A	82,350
30/8/39 [BTN]	[No mileage recorded]; Extension of mileage 5,000
15/5/40-12/6/40A	82,500 Olive Green livery
16/7/43-8/9/43A	87,515 Wartime Black livery
25/5/45-14/7/45A[AFD]	74,724
16/4/46-4/5/46C	18,874
11/8/47-5/9/47B	56,203 Malachite Green livery from Black
2/10/48-30/10/48A	86,740 T2070 Special piston heads and rings; Renumbered 30768; Snifting valves removed
23/5/52-21/6/52GO	90,210 BR Green livery
19/8/53-5/9/53HC	42,788 New left-hand side cylinder
12/10/54-6/11/54LI	85,627 T2222 Regulator valve BR alloy [R]
8/10/55-21/10/55LC[BTN]	124,895
23/1/58-15/2/58GO	165,897
20/10/59-21/10/59NC-LC	37,414
5/1/60-21/1/60LC	39,615
28/6/60-30/7/60LI	47,821

Tenders
No.3232 new 5/25 Urie
No.705 6/28 6 wheel 4,000 gal
No.1008 1/30 LN
No.885 3/32 Urie

Sheds
Stewarts Lane 5/1925
Hither Green 27/2/40
Stewarts Lane 1/7/40
Nine Elms 22/11/42
Dover 23/4/45
Stewarts Lane 4/1946
Dover 6/1946
Stewarts Lane 27/6/51
Eastleigh 14/6/59

Withdrawn 4/11/61; stored at Eastleigh Works 10-12/61; cut up at Eastleigh Works w/e 13/1/62
Total 1,078,112 miles

Stewarts Lane's 30768 SIR BALIN on 25th August 1954 heading the 'Kentish Belle' made up of Pullman coaches. This train was timed to leave London at 11.35 running to Ramsgate and returning at 5.05pm on Mondays to Fridays with different timings at the weekend. The loco has been spruced up for the work with special attention paid to the buffers and smokebox door hinge.

Compared with its time on the 'Kentish Belle' SIR BALIN looks very run down here at Eastleigh on 25th June 1960. But it is not withdrawn and was to enter the works three days later for its last Light Intermediate. It had been an Eastleigh loco for at least a year and was a regular in my Surrey haunts.

768 SIR BALIN with the Lord Nelson pattern tender that it ran with from January 1930 until February 1932. Seen here on a down express at Axminster.

An Bournemouth express for SIR BALIN, storming out away from Waterloo on 20th June 1959. Photograph Peter Groom.

30769 SIR BALAN

NBL Works no.23215
To traffic as E769 6/1925
Renumbered 30769 7/4/51

Boilers
No.769 as of 21/7/35
No.796 9/11/35
No.1001 30/10/37
No.823 24/7/40
No.795 10/11/44
No.796 17/5/47
No.784 6/4/51
No.831 10/4/54

Works
3/1928	Smoke deflectors
7/1931	E prefix removed
21/7/35**[EXJ]**	Extension of mileage 5,000
14/10/35-9/11/35**A**	106,550
5/10/37-30/10/37**A**	83,407
11/5/39-17/6/39**B**	59,146
25/6/40-24/7/40**A**	88,090 Malachite Green livery
11/8/42-15/9/42**C[NE]**	60,381
12/10/44-10/11/44**A**	139,357 Wartime Black livery
26/11/46-14/12/46**D-C**	68,413
20/2/47**D[SL]**	69,732
14/4/47-17/5/47**A**	73,758 Malachite Green livery from Black
20/4/50-1/5/50**LC[BA]**	85,669
26/2/51-6/4/51**GO**	107,026 Renumbered 30769; BR Green livery; Snifting valves removed
17/3/54-10/4/54**GO**	67,580 Steam heat relief valve repositioned; Combination lever and valve spindle pin E47476
20/9/56-27/10/56**LI[BTN]**	56,873 New piston heads and rings

Tenders
No.3228 6/25 new Urie
No.1002 12/29 LN
No.886 7/31 Urie

Sheds
Stewarts Lane 6/1925
Exmouth Junction mid-1929
Dover 11/1936
Stewarts Lane 20/2/37
Hither Green 27/2/40
Nine Elms 22/11/42
Stewarts Lane 2/1944
Dover 26/4/45
Stewarts Lane 27/6/51
Dover 27/3/53
Stewarts Lane 20/7/53
Eastleigh 14/6/59

Withdrawn 27/2/60; stored at Eastleigh Works 2/60; cut up at Eastleigh Works w/e 13/2/60
Total 1,036,794 miles

Delightful view of 769 SIR BALAN (brother of 768) at Orpington Junction, Petts Wood, emerging into the light on 20th July 1929. A Stewarts Lane engine, it was soon to move to Exmouth Junction for a few years and while there got a Maunsell pattern double bogie tender and then, in 1931, a Urie one once attached to Lord Nelson 852. Photograph H.C. Casserley, courtesy R.M. Casserley.

Sole Street Bank with third rail and encroaching vegetation; 30769 SIR BALAN (observe usual changes at front end, including shorter hand rail) hard at work with at least ten coaches in the load. Photograph P. Ransome-Wallis.

30769 SIR BALAN at Ashford on 28th March 1959, having spent nearly fifteen years working in this corner of the country, except for the odd visit to Eastleigh Works. According to *The Record* it never visited Ashford Works though of course it could often be found at the shed. Within three months it was on the way to Eastleigh shed where it spent about eight months before withdrawal.

Sittingbourne on 31st August 1954 30769 SIR BALAN was in its fifth spell at Stewarts Lane shed. It is still coupled to the Urie double bogie tender it had got from Lord Nelson 852 SIR WALTER RALEIGH back in July 1931.

30770 SIR PRIANIUS

NBL works no.23216
To traffic as E770 6/1925
Renumbered 30770 7/1951

Boiler (most of record missing)
No.800 17/8/44

Works	
6/1927	75,288
3/1928	Smoke deflectors fitted
3/1931	72,667
7/1932	E prefix removed
2/1933	87,032
10/1934	79,835
10/1936	86,425
6/1939	86,457 Olive Green livery
1/1943	89,882 Wartime Black livery
17/8/44	Stays: 436 copper renewed; Plates: Flanges welded and studded; Lead plugs; Brick arch studs; Tubes: 167, 2nd hand; 24 new Superheater tubes, copper ends
6/1945	107,086
11/1947	75,340 Malachite Green livery from Black; Snifting valves removed
7/1951	102,629 BR Green livery; renumbered 30770
16/3/54-17/4/54**GO**	63,999 Combination lever and valve spindle modified E47476; Steam heat relief valve repositioned
14/2/56-10/3/56**LI**	55,473 T2256 Tyres turned
31/7/57-24/8/57**GO**	95,176 T2256 Tyres turned; Live steam injector right hand side and feed gear
19/5/59-30/5/59**LC**	52,478 T2256 [U]
25/2/60-12/3/60**LC**	70,261 T2256 Apexior paint
22/12/60-21/1/61**LI**	81,532 T2256
10/5/61-9/6/61**HC**	108,372
14/1/62**NC**	

Tenders
No.3225 new 6/25 Urie
No.708 12/28 6 wheel 4,000 gal
No.1009 5/30 LN
No.887 7/32 Urie

Sheds
Stewarts Lane 6/1925
Dover 5/1934
Stewarts Lane Autumn 1934
Dover 12/1935
Nine Elms 11/1936
Stewarts Lane 20/2/37
Ramsgate 10/11/38
Stewarts Lane 2/12/38
Dover 21/6/39
Stewarts Lane 1/7/40
Nine Elms 22/11/42
Dover 8/2/46
Stewarts Lane 7/6/52
Basingstoke 12/8/55
Eastleigh 5/6/56
Basingstoke 22/10/62

Withdrawn 24/11/62; stored at Eastleigh Works 11/62-1/63; cut up at Eastleigh Works w/e 23/2/63
Total 1,144,608 miles

Eastleigh, 20th September 1962; note small welded repair in the splasher. This name should have read SIR PRIAMUS but someone at North British misread the 'M' on his list as 'NI' with the above result; surprisingly it was never corrected. Photograph John Scrace.

770 SIR PRIANIUS at Dover shed, its home for about six years, on 24th May 1951. It is still in Southern Malachite Green and although its Engine History Card is missing we know it visited Eastleigh Works in July 1951 where it was renumbered and received BR Green. The little upright hand 'posts' are visible for once (they seem to have replaced the grab irons on the main frame) and the six lamp irons are in their final and 'correct' locations. Photograph B.K.B. Green, Initial Photographics.

Well it may once have been LORD K KENT (Dover and Ramsgate were amongst its sheds) but by now, on 22nd November 1962 30770 stands at Eastleigh on the very day of withdrawal. It survived until February 1963 before meeting the cutter's torch. Photograph Gavin Morrison.

30771 SIR SAGRAMORE

NBL works no.23217
To traffic as E771 6/1925
Renumbered 30771 19/5/50

Boilers
No.783 21/3/33
No.1055 29/8/36
No.793 12/10/38
No.806 23/9/44
No.777 3/5/47
No.737 19/5/50
No.777 5/9/53
No.829 22/6/57

Works	
10/1928	Smoke deflectors fitted; Ashford pattern tender
4/1932	E prefix removed
21/3/33	Stays: 3 tube plate renewed; 450 holes bushed; Plates: New copper firebox
23/2/34[BTN]	Stays: 489 copper riveted over; Plates: Flanges caulked; Lead plugs; Tubes: 8, new; 24 Superheater tubes ferruled, Foundation ring, corner rivets renewed
23/2/35	Stays: 508 copper renewed; Plates: Lead plugs; Studs in flanges; Rivets and seams caulked; Tubes: 68 2nd hand welded; 24 2nd hand Superheater tubes, copper ends
20/7/36-29/8/36A	77,332
13/9/38-12/10/38A	72,492
16/6/41-23/7/41C[BA]	[No mileage recorded]
7/42	Wartime Black livery
29/7/44-23/9/44A	89,072 Stays: 423 copper renewed; 4 roof renewed; Plates: Copper tube, 2 angles; Copper firehole, 2 angles; Lead plugs; Tubes: 167, new "Howell"
8/3/46-23/3/46C	53,850 At Dover
8/4/47-3/5/47A	79,194 Malchite Green livery
26/4/50-19/5/50A	83,775 Renumbered 30771; BR Green livery; Snifting valves removed
21/11/51-14/12/51LI	58,951
6/8/53-5/9/53GO	95,483
6/1954	New type of live steam injector [Railway Observer 1954 page 144]
29/9/55-4/11/55LI[BTN]	71,061 Left hand cylinder fitted with new steam chest, liners
6/12/55-10/12/55LC	71,341 T2256 Tyres turned [U]
27/5/57-22/6/57GO	104,475 Stays: 650 copper riveted over; Tubes: 167, new "Stewart and Lloyds"; Set, new Superheater tubes; T2256 Tyres turned [U]

Tenders
No.3233 new 6/25 Urie
No.707 10/28 6 wheel 4,000 gal
No.1003 5/30 LN
No.888 4/31 Urie

Sheds
Stewarts Lane 6/1925
Dover 5/1934
Stewarts Lane Autumn 1934
Dover 12/1935
Stewarts Lane 20/2/37
Nine Elms 22/11/42
Dover 8/2/46
Stewarts Lane 7/6/52
Basingstoke 30/9/55
Bournemouth 5/6/56
Salisbury 24/11/60

Withdrawn 1/4/61; stored at Eastleigh Works 3-4/61; cut up at Eastleigh Works w/e 6/5/61
Total 1,054,549 miles

30771 SIR SAGRAMORE in its final days, at Eastleigh on 14th May 1960 looking very weary; smokebox open to the elements but coal still in the tender; all it needs is COND daubed somewhere. Withdrawal did not actually take place for another year. Auxiliary vacuum reservoirs visible on rear of tender.

30771 SIR SAGRAMORE catches the sun at Bournemouth in August 1956; newly transferred here, its main duties would have been up to Waterloo or inter-regional work to Oxford on the Western Region. This profile demonstrates what a handsome class they were. 768-772 had these auxiliary vacuum cylinders on their tenders for many years. Photograph B.K.B. Green, Initial Photographics.

30772 SIR PERCIVALE

NBL works no.23218
To traffic as E772 6/1925
Renumbered 30772 24/4/48

Boilers
No.793 as of 28/9/35
No.767 23/2/38
No.764 28/2/40
No.1047 23/9/42
No.792 16/6/45
No.776 12/7/47
No.787 2/12/49
No.774 31/3/51
No.1403 18/2/55
No.763 14/2/59

Works

9/1926	German State Railway pattern smoke deflectors
10/1932	E prefix removed; Standard smoke deflectors fitted
30/8/35-28/9/35A	86,173
17/2/37-13/3/37C	54,908
19/1/38-23/2/38A	90,846
25/1/40-28/2/40A	108,732 Olive Green livery
20/8/42-23/9/42A	92,926 Stays: 668 steel renewed; 200 steel riveted over; 200 nuts renewed; Plates: Copper tube, 3 tube holes plugged, 2 angles, flanges one-half sides; Lead plugs; Tubes: 166, new "Jarrow"; 24 new Superheater tubes
6/2/43-2/3/43C	6,053 Wartime Black livery
28/4/45-16/6/45A	95,178
13/6/47-12/7/47A	87,884 Malachite Green livery from Black; Snifting valves removed
2/4/48-24/4/48B	31,978 Renumbered 30772
31/10/49-2/12/49A	99,693 BR Green livery
20/2/51-31/3/51GO	45,649
2/7/53-7/8/53LI	53,056
21/1/55-18/2/55GO	93,792 Stays: 80 copper renewed; 472 monel metal renewed; 472 nuts renewed; 30 roof renewed; Plates: Copper tube, new; Copper firehole, 2 angles fitted: Set, new fusible plugs; Tubes: 167, new "Howell"; Set, new Superheater tubes
28/3/56-29/3/56NC-LC	31,034
14/3/57-5/4/57HI	57,275 Stays: 19 copper renewed; 70 copper riveted over; 382 nuts renewed; 382 monel metal stays repaired; Plates: Seam and 84 studs repaired; 3 fusible plugs renewed; Tubes: 167, new "Stewart and Lloyds"; 24 new Superheater tubes; Foundation ring, 40 rivets repaired
12/8/57-17/8/57LC	67,270 Stays: 2 copper renewed; 130 copper riveted over; Plates: Copper firehole, lap welded; Tubes: Firehole, 14 rivets renewed
22/1/59-14/2/59GO	92,686
30/6/60-5/7/60NC	17,374

Tenders
No.3234 new 6/25 Urie
No.709 10/29 6 wheel 4,000 gal
No.1010 7/30 LN
No.889 6/31 Urie

Sheds
Stewarts Lane 6/1925
Exmouth Junction 2/1936
Stewarts Lane 14/7/36
Nine Elms 7/1937
Stewarts Lane 27/2/40
Nine Elms 22/11/42
Eastleigh 12/1942
Bournemouth 7/1943
Dover 8/2/46
Eastleigh 3/5/49
Stewarts Lane 8/12/50
Dover 5/2/51
Stewarts Lane 7/6/52
Ramsgate 27/3/53
Stewarts Lane 20/7/53
Hither Green 20/8/54
Bournemouth 12/6/57

Withdrawn 30/9/61; stored at Eastleigh Works 9-11/61; cut up at Eastleigh Works w/e 9/12/61
Total 1,187,768 miles

Spick and span but in fact more than a year out of a General, Bournemouth's 30772 SIR PERCIVALE (brother of 30451) is at Eastleigh shed on 14th May 1960. With at least sixteen transfers recorded was this one of the dud 'Scotchmen'? In views of earlier years it certainly looked to have suffered more than most from priming. In very many of these views it is possible to see a distinctive Maunsell feature; this is the small curved splasher-like form immediately above the leading wheel with an open rectangular slot at the front, as here, on the running plate. This was actually a hinged cover to allow inspection and lubrication of the junction of pivot, radius rod and expansion link beneath. The hole in the front of it is actually the handhold. It is readily visible on both the Nelsons and the Schools, as noted here and there elsewhere in the book.

30773 SIR LAVAINE

NBL works no.23219
To traffic as E773 7/1925
Renumbered 30773 19/6/48

Boilers
No.768 6/7/35
No.930 28/11/36
No.737 7/6/38
No.767 15/5/40
No.775 21/4/43
No.454 21/9/45
No.835 8/11/47
No.930 3/6/49
No.786 22/9/51
No.793 30/12/55
No.838 9/1/60

Works

12/1927	Smoke deflectors fitted
c.1930	Fitted with circular hood over smokebox door; eventually changed to smoke deflectors
3/1932	E prefix removed
31/5/35-6/7/35**A**	91,830
29/10/36-28/11/36**A**	79,110
6/5/38-7/6/38**A**	80,216
17/4/40-15/5/40**A**	101,171 Olive Green livery
14/11/41-5/1/42**C[EXJ]**	[No mileage recorded]
22/3/43-21/4/43**A**	98,470 Wartime Black livery
13/10/44-25/11/44**C**	64,408 Extension of mileage 10,000
11/8/45-21/9/45**A**	92,536 Stays: 270 holes bushed; Plates: New copper firebox; Casing covering, three-quarters sides; Tubes: 166, 103 new, "Howell" 63 2nd hand; 24 2nd hand Superheater tubes
29/10/46-16/11/46**C**	56,440 Stays: 300 copper riveted over; Plates: Studs and seams caulked; Lead plugs; Tubes: 12, new "Howell", 169 rebeaded; 24 Superheater tubes, expanded and rebeaded
1/7/47**[NE]**	T2080 Left-hand and right-hand gauge glasses fitted
16/10/47-8/11/47**A**	88,688 T2025 Spring links with copper plated threads fitted; Malachite Green livery from Black; Snifting valves removed
8/6/48-19/6/48**C**	29,224 Renumbered 30773
6/4/49-3/6/49**A**	63,779
27/8/51-22/9/51**GO**	84,945 BR Green livery
2/10/51-11/10/51**NC**	[No mileage recorded]
24/10/51-5/11/51**NC**	229
16/11/54-27/11/54**LC**	52,357
18/11/55-30/12/55**GO**	146,642
14/2/57-21/2/57**LC**	43,674
25/9/57**LC [1 day]**	56,544
19/6/58-30/7/58**LI-HI**	71,202
20/10/59-21/10/59**NC**	99,272
4/12/59-9/1/60**GO**	101,523
4/8/60-11/8/60**LC**	44,084

Tender
No.890 from new

Sheds
Nine Elms 7/1925
Stewarts Lane 27/2/40
Bournemouth 7/1941
Salisbury 3/1944
Nine Elms 6/1946
Stewarts Lane 26/9/49
Salisbury 9/10/50
Stewarts Lane 8/12/50
Dover 5/2/51
Stewarts Lane 7/6/52
Nine Elms 16/9/55
Bournemouth 12/6/57
Basingstoke 13/10/58
Eastleigh 1/5/59

Withdrawn 10/2/62; stored at Eastleigh Works 2-3/62; cut up at Eastleigh Works w/e 21/4/62
Total 1,296,365 miles

An Eastleigh Arthur at home, 30773 SIR LAVAINE which had moved shed over a dozen times during its career, the last to Eastleigh coming in May 1959. But look at the debris in the foreground, like the Luftwaffe's just been over – as it once did of course. This is Sunday 18th February 1962 and although fully coaled this engine will not steam again; it had been withdrawn on the 10th of the month and was cut up at Eastleigh week ending 21st April 1962. So it carried the LSW lamp 'iron' in the middle of the buffer beam to the grave. Photograph B.K.B. Green, Initial Photographics.

Eastleigh on 29th August 1959 with 30773 SIR LAVAINE who seems to have existed in the Arthurian legends by name alone; nothing else is known about him.

30773 SIR LAVAINE at Eastleigh on 14th May 1960 only four months after its final General. This was one of the last Arthurs withdrawn, being scrapped at Eastleigh in April 1962.

An heroic pile of coal on SIR LAVAINE's bogie tender, which like the loco must now be over thirty-five years old. On 17th August 1961 it awaits its next duty at Eastleigh; it would never get further attention in the nearby works, being withdrawn in February 1962 and disposed of in the works yard. These two photographs show well the multiple washout plug boiler (838) with five plugs on the left side and four on the right. Photograph Gavin Morrison.

30774 SIR GAHERIS
NBL works no.23220
To traffic as E774 6/1925
Renumbered 30774 14/4/49

Works

6/1927	Smoke deflectors fitted
7/1931	E prefix removed
2/10/35-26/10/35**B**	51,349 Stays: 300 copper riveted over; Plates: Lead plugs; Rivets and seams caulked; Tubes: 42, 2nd hand, welded; Superheater tubes expanded and referruled
24/6/36-25/7/36**A**	88,735
27/4/38-25/5/38**A**	89,721
11/11/39-13/12/39**A**	82,337 Olive Green livery
17/7/41**D**	[No mileage recorded]
11/11/41-3/12/41**C**	62,843
29/6/42-12/8/42**A**	78,523 Stays: 902 copper renewed; 272 copper riveted over; 31 roof renewed; 31 roof nuts renewed; 459 holes bushed; Plates: Copper tube, new; 2 x one-half side, flanged and cleaned; Lead plugs; Barrel, cleaned; Tubes: 167, new "Chesterfield"; 24 new Superheater tubes [copper ends]Wartime Black livery
1/12/43-16/12/43**C[EXJ]**	54,853
25/8/44-23/9/44**A**	86,442 Stays: 330 copper renewed; Plates: Studs in flanges; Rivets and seams caulked; Tubes: 169 2nd hand
22/2/46-23/3/46**C**	48,199 Stays: 350 copper repaired; Plates: Seams caulked; Drop plugs renewed; 4 rivets replaced by studs; 24 rivets caulked; Throat plate welded - left side; Tubes: 24 Superheater tubes expanded, re-beaded and re-furruled; Malachite Green livery from Black
2/11/46-30/11/46**A**	73,517
29/10/47-15/11/47**C**	40,009
10/3/49-14/4/49**A**	91,843 Renumbered 30774; Snifting valves removed
3/4/52-3/5/52**LI**	82,267 BR Green livery
26/7/54-31/7/54**LC**	109,703 T2222 Regulator valve BR alloy
24/8/55-17/9/55**GO**	124,706 Stays: 773 monel metal renewed; 803 nuts renewed; 6 longitudinal renewed; Roof renewed, all; 10 crown bars stays renewed Plates: Copper tube, new; 2 copper flanges, one-half sides; 2 fusible plugs renewed; Crown channel replaced and riveted; Tubes: Set, renewed by 2nd hand set; Set, new Superheater tubes; Rivets: 24 renewed by studs in Copper back plate
17/10/56-10/11/56**LC[BTN]**	40,601
19/8/57-7/9/57**HI**	62,042 Stays: 450 monel metal repaired; 8 copper riveted over; 450 nuts renewed; Plates: Seams and 104 studs repaired; 2 fusible plugs renewed; Tubes: 167, new "Tubes ltd"; 3 new Superheater tubes
16/1/59-24/1/59**LC**	104,729

Boilers
No.826 as of 26/10/35
No.453 25/7/36
No.795 25/5/38
No.491 13/12/39
No.825 12/8/42
No.768 30/11/46
No.834 14/4/49
No.1404 17/9/55

Tender
No.891 from new

Sheds
Nine Elms 6/1925
Stewarts Lane 27/2/40
Bournemouth 22/1/42
Salisbury 3/1944
Nine Elms 6/1946
Stewarts Lane 26/9/49
Dover 5/2/51
Stewarts Lane 7/6/52
Nine Elms 7/7/55

Withdrawn 9/1/60; stored at Eastleigh Works 1/60; cut up at Eastleigh Works w/e 16/2/60
Total 1,121,270 miles

Stewarts Lane shed, with the Depository building once hit by a German rocket, in the background. 30774 SIR GAHERIS (brother of 30764) in its final BR guise with cycling totem (it never got the second emblem) and the BR Green it received in 1952. The 73A shed plate dates the photograph between June 1952 and its final move, to Nine Elms, in July 1955. Multi-plug boiler No.834. Photograph J. Davenport, Initial Photographics.

30775 SIR AGRAVAINE

NBL works no.23221
To traffic as E775 6/1925
Renumbered 30775 18/11/49

Boilers
No.779 5/12/35
No.806 19/6/37
No.832 26/5/39
No.455 6/7/41
No.780 24/11/43
No.803 26/10/46
No.1050 18/11/49
No.765 19/3/55

Works
12/1927	Smoke deflectors fitted
5/1932	E prefix removed
4/11/35-5/12/35A	103,284
13/5/37-19/6/37A	81,356 Stays: 200 holes bushed; Plates: New copper firebox; Casing covering, three-quarter sides; Throat, new
2/5/39-26/5/39A	87,213 Olive Green livery
8/8/40-14/8/40D	[No mileage recorded]
4/6/41-16/7/41A	77,694 Malachite Green livery
10/2/42-18/2/42C	19,332
13/11/42-5/1/43B	52,697 Extension of mileage 5,000
20/10/43-24/11/43A	91,673 Wartime Black livery
28/3/45-26/5/45B	56,606 Extension of mileage 20,000
8/10/46-26/10/46A	112,543 Malachite Green livery from Black
12/10/49-18/11/49A	71,321 Renumbered 30775; BR Green livery; Snifting valves removed
26/4/51-4/5/51NC[AFD]	21,859
13/3/53-2/4/53HI	69,611
16/2/55-19/3/55GO	131,037
28/9/56-13/10/56LC	43,339
29/8/57-14/9/57LI-HI	65,827
24/10/58-29/11/58LC-HC	93,766

Tender
No.892 from new

Sheds
Nine Elms 6/1925
Stewarts Lane 8/2/46
Dover 5/2/51
Feltham 14/6/59

Withdrawn 27/2/60;
stored at Eastleigh Works
2/60; cut up at Eastleigh
Works w/e 27/2/60
Total 1,136,498 miles

On Saturday 20th April 1957 Dover's 30775 SIR AGRAVAINE has empty stock at Ashford, Kent. Ashford has certainly changed since the 1950s and the signal gantry and water cranes have long since gone. Even the new 'international' station is moribund. Photograph B.W.L. Brooksbank, Initial Photographics.

30775 SIR AGRAVAINE on the Central Section, passing London Bridge on duty no.422, ferry vans from Ewer street to Dover (no doubt for passage over the English Channel) on Monday 3rd June 1957. The engine was based at Dover at the time and though it moved to Feltham in June 1959 survived only a few months there before its final demise. When on this duty the engine left Bricklayers Arms at 12.45pm (having arrived at 6.25am from Dover) and was due at Dover Marine at 3.47pm. Photograph L. Elsey.

Dover shed on 24th May 1951 with 30775 SIR AGRAVAINE, very obviously coaled up and ready. It had been on Dover's complement for three months and didn't go to the Western Section until June 1959, only to be withdrawn in February 1960. First emblem, large size. Photograph B.K.B. Green, Initial Photographics.

30776 SIR GALAGARS

NBL works no.23222
To traffic as E776 6/1925
Renumbered 30776 8/7/49

Works	
12/1927	Smoke deflectors fitted
11/1932	E prefix removed
14/8/35-7/9/35**A**	72,747
5/3/36-28/3/36**C**	28,521
11/2/37-13/3/37**A**	78,790
20/1/38-9/3/38**B**	45,281
11/1/39-8/2/39**A**	91,552 Maunsell Green livery
13/5/40-5/6/40**B**	59,743
18/11/40-24/12/40**A**	78,033 Malachite Green livery
7/5/41-7/6/41**B**	3,140
20/7/42-12/9/42**C**	59,274 Extension of mileage 5,000 Wartime Black livery
12/10/43-24/11/43**A**	103,403 Stays: 50 roof renewed; 350 holes bushed; Plates: Copper tube, new; Copper wrapping, flanges, one-half sides; Lead plugs; Tubes: 167, new "Howell"; 24 2nd hand Superheater tubes
10/6/44-6/7/44**C**	18,641
30/1/46-2/3/46**A**	74,040 Malachite Green livery from Black; first post-war Malachite Arthur
3/1/47-5/2/47**C[SL]**	21,788
25/11/47-20/12/47**B**	41,327 Snifting valves removed
21/6/49-8/7/49**HC[B]**	66,024 Renumbered 30776
26/4/50-2/6/50**A**	93,016 Stays: 463 copper renewed; Plates: Internal tube, 2 angle patches; Firehole plates, rivets renewed on flanges; Foundation ring, seams caulked; BR Green livery
10/2/53-28/2/53**HI**	64,878 Stays: 6 copper renewed and 302 repaired Plates: Renewed with studs; Fusible plugs renewed; Tubes: 167 new; 3 new Superheater tubes
15/3/54-9/4/54**LC-HC**	102,031
25/3/55-9/4/55**LC**	127,125
8/9/55-24/9/55**LI-HI**	139,831
13/9/57-15/10/57**GO**	189,048 Stays: Copper renewed, all; Longitudinal renewed, all; Roof renewed, all; Plates: New copper firebox; Casing back; 150 holes bushed; Casing covering, 2 x three-quarters sides fitted; New one-half throat; Tubes: 167, new "Phoenix"; 24 new Superheater tubes; Live steam injector and feed gear

Boilers
No.775 as of 7/9/35
No.785 13/3/37
No.775 8/2/39
No.766 24/12/40
No.799 24/11/43
No.765 2/3/46
No.763 8/7/49
No.806 2/6/50
No.931 9/4/54
No.800 15/10/57

Tender
No.893 from new

Sheds
Nine Elms 6/1925
Stewarts Lane 27/2/40
Nine Elms 1/7/40
Stewarts Lane 26/4/45
Dover 5/2/51

Withdrawn 24/1/59; stored at Eastleigh Works 1/59; cut up at Eastleigh Works w/e 28/2/59
Total 1,094,727 miles

776 SIR GALAGARS in Southern Railway days, on a down express approaching Surbiton; the code indicates a Waterloo - West of England service irrespective of destination west of Exeter.

30776 SIR GALAGARS extravagantly coaled up (in a fashion quite typical of the Arthurs, it appears) and ready to go home to Dover, on the turntable at Bricklayers Arms shed in London on 25th April 1953. A good profile of the engine showing how well proportioned they were especially with a bogie tender which normally carried five tons of coal and 5,000 gallons of water. Again a good view of the boiler outline, tapering in that section behind the smokebox. Based at Dover in the 1950s until withdrawal in January 1959, the engine was scrapped at Eastleigh. I believe the turntable shown here has resided in the car park at Ropley station for many years waiting for the Mid Hants Railway to find a suitable site for it. Photograph Frank W. Goudie, www.transporttreasury.co.uk

One of Dover's Arthurs, 30776 SIR GALAGARS at Ashford shed on 22nd March 1956. It would be awaiting repair/parts, for it is on one of the two stabling roads out at the back of the shed (note the vegetation); these roads ran to a headshunt from which a long 'emergency' connection ran back to the running lines. Photograph Peter Groom.

30777 SIR LAMIEL

NBL works no.23223
To traffic as E777 6/1925
Renumbered 30777 8/5/48

Works

12/1927	Smoke deflectors fitted
6/1932	E prefix removed
2/7/35-3/8/35**B**	55,374 Stays: 150 copper riveted over; Plates: Lead plugs; Patches and seams re-caulked; Extension of mileage 10,000
12/5/36-13/6/36**A**	83,274 May 1936 No.777 arrived at Eastleigh Works minus smoke deflectors though with a pair of large square pattern deflectors in its tender
25/5/37-9/6/37**C[EXJ]**	48,042
8/2/38-9/3/38**A**	83,925
23/9/39-18/10/39**A**	85,363 Olive Green livery
29/1/41-7/3/41**C[NE]**	[No mileage recorded]
25/8/41-22/10/41**B**	69,086 Extension of mileage 10,000
27/5/42-5/8/42**B**	88,788 Extension of mileage 20,000
11/8/43-20/8/43**C[NE]**	140,675
30/5/44-15/7/44**A**	175,492 Wartime Black livery
27/3/45-18/5/45**C[NE]**	44,092
29/9/45-16/10/45**C[NE]**	63,906
27/3/46-4/5/46**C**	80,441 Extension of mileage 5,000; T1852 Ashpan down draught closed 10/5/47
31/12/46-25/1/47**A**	101,412 Malachite Green livery from Black; T2070 Wear resistance of Cast Iron
30/10/47-8/11/47**C**	49,872
15/12/47-20/12/47**D**	37,129
29/4/48-8/5/48**C**	51,235 Renumbered 30777
27/9/48-23/10/48**A**	65,827 Snifting valves removed
12/6/50-14/7/50**LC**	49,267
22/11/51-21/12/51**HI**	103,824 BR Green livery
20/3/52-28/3/52**LC**	110,115
8/9/53-17/9/53**NC[AFD]**	148,130
29/1/54-27/2/54**GO**	157,388
8/9/55-8/10/55**GO**	47,832 Stays: Copper renewed, all; Longitudinal renewed, all; Roof renewed, all; 180 holes bushed; Plates: New copper firebox; Steel tube, levelled; Casing covering 2 x three quarters sides; New reinforcing plate; Tubes: Set, new "Universal"; Set, new Superheater tubes
18/9/57-12/10/57**LI-HI**	67,181 Stays: 520 copper renewed; Plates: Rivets replaced by studs and seams caulked; 2 fusible plugs; Tubes: 167, new "Phoenix"; 24 new Superheater tubes; Boiler removed from frame for repair of short stay leads in fire area
27/11/59-2/1/60**GO**	128,924 Stays: Copper renewed, all; Longitudinal renewed, all; Roof renewed, all; Plates: New copper firebox; 2 fusible plugs; Casing covering, three quarters sides; Tubes: 167, new "Stewart and Lloyds"; 24 new Superheater tubes

Tender

No.894 from new

Sheds

Nine Elms 6/1925
Stewarts Lane 5/1934
Nine Elms 7/1937
Stewarts Lane 27/2/40
Nine Elms 1/7/40
Eastleigh 7/1947
Stewarts Lane 1/1949
Nine Elms 5/2/51
Stewarts Lane 27/6/51
Dover 8/10/51
Feltham 14/6/59
Basingstoke 5/10/60

Withdrawn 21/10/61; only preserved Arthur, part of the National Collection
Total 1,257,638 miles

Boilers

No.805 as of 3/8/35
No.737 13/6/36
No.771 9/3/38
No.787 18/10/39
No.1057 5/8/42
No.838 15/7/44
No.785 25/1/47
No.1408 23/10/48
No.450 27/2/54
No.456 8/10/55
No.454 2/1/60

Lovely Southern Region shed scene with the 30777 SIR LAMIEL at Ramsgate on 6 April 1953. BR Green livery had been applied at the end of 1951; the second engine is 30930 RADLEY, in BR Black. Photograph R.C. Riley, www.transporttreasury.co.uk

The only survivor, 777 SIR LAMIEL, the name said to originate from – Cardiff. Here it is at Nine Elms in the period between the end of 1927 when the smoke deflectors were fitted and June 1932, when the 'E' prefix was removed. Very few can remember 777 in this running condition. Once again that conical pile of coal.

30778 SIR PELLEAS

NBL works no.23224
To traffic as E778 7/1925
Renumbered 11/49
Record part missing

Boilers
No.781 20/8/29
(record missing)

Works

1/1928	Smoke deflectors fitted
20/8/29	Stays: 526 copper renewed; Roof renewed, all Plates: Copper tube, new; Alteration of crown; New brick arch studs and plugs; Tubes: 169, new "BM", 24 Superheater tubes ferruled, copper ends; Foundation ring, part renewed
28/3/31	Stays: 563 copper renewed; Roof renewed, all; Plates: New angle patch; Alteration of crown; Tubes: 24 Superheater tubes ferruled; Rivets: Firehole, part; Foundation ring renewed
8/1931	E prefix removed
11/1939	Olive Green livery
2/43	Wartime Black livery
10/1948	Malachite Green livery from Black
11/1949	Renumbered 30778; BR Green livery; Snifting valves removed
11/12/53-9/1/54**GO**	113,644 Injector and feed gear modified; Combination lever and valve spindle modified
27/10/54-13/11/54**LC-HC**	42,608
11/10/55-29/10/55**LI**	82,495 T2256 Tyres turned
29/11/56-3/1/57**GO**	114,658 T2256 Tyres turned
17/10/57-26/10/57**LC**	34,012

Tender
No.895 from new

Sheds
Nine Elms 7/1925
Stewarts Lane 5/1934
Nine Elms 7/1937
Stewarts Lane 27/2/40
Eastleigh 12/1942
Stewarts Lane 7/1943
Eastleigh 13/11/50
Nine Elms 5/2/51
Stewarts Lane 27/6/51
Dover 8/10/51
Nine Elms 20/7/53

Withdrawn 23/5/59; stored at Eastleigh Works 5-8/59; cut up at Eastleigh Works w/e 19/9/59
Total 1,174,925 miles

A brooding 30778 **SIR PELLEAS** at its final shed, Nine Elms, on 14th October 1956, after at least ten transfers during its working life. 'Work stained' might be the best description. Above the running number is the BR classification of 5P, the same as the Schools class; the Lord Nelsons carried 7P. Sanding prominent to the leading coupled wheels. Photograph R.J. Buckley, Initial Photographics.

30779 SIR COLGREVANCE

NBL works no.23225
To traffic as E779 7/1925
Renumbered 30779 9/10/48

Boilers
No.456 7/11/36
No.453 17/8/38
No.1047 28/8/40
No.838 22/8/42
No.457 10/6/44
No.834 19/4/47
No.805 9/10/48
No.1053 7/10/49
No.800 14/11/53
No.1406 11/5/57

Works	
4/1927	Smoke deflectors fitted
1/1932	E prefix removed
20/5/33	Stays: 436 copper renewed; Plates: Copper tube, flanges welded, Copper firehole, flanges welded; Lead plugs; Rivets caulked; Tubes: 67, 2nd hand, welded; 7 new Superheater tubes
7/10/36-7/11/36**A**	79,405 Stays: 200 holes bushed; Plates: New copper firebox; Casing covering, three-quarters sides; Tubes: 169, new "Howell"; 24 new Superheater tubes
28/6/38-17/8/38**A**	89,964 Flaman speed recorder fitted
31/7/40-28/8/40**A**	85,730 Stays: 200 monel steel renewed; 460 nuts renewed; Plates: Rivets and seams caulked; Lead plugs; Tubes: 169, new "Chesterfield". Flaman speed recorder removed. Malachite Green livery
30/6/42-22/8/42**A**	78,436 Wartime Black livery
29/4/44-10/6/44**A**	64,959 Stays: 479 copper renewed; 12 holes bushed Plates: Copper firehole, 2 angles; Rivets and seams caulked; Lead plugs; Tubes: 167, new; 24 new Superheater tubes
6/11/44-9/12/44**C**	14,453
7/6/46-29/6/46**C**	65,062 Stays: 12 copper renewed and 400 repaired; 2 direct crown renewed; Plates: Firebox, studs and seams caulked; 2 drop plugs renewed
22/7/46-25/7/46**D**	65,062
14/3/47-19/4/47**A**	91,215 Malachite Green livery from Black
1/7/47**[NE]**	T2080 Left and right-hand gauge glasses fitted, removed 29/7/47
2/9/48-9/10/48**B**	51,892 Stays: 425 copper renewed; Plates: Firebox, studs and rivets renewed; Protection plate fitted; Steel tubeplate; Lead plugs renewed; Tubes: Set, new "Howell"; Superheater tubes expanded; Extension of mileage 10,000; Renumbered 30779; Snifting valves removed
5/9/49-7/10/49**A**	92,881 T2138 Storm sheets fitted; BR Green livery
12/10/50-20/10/50**LC**	38,301
11/6/52-4/7/52**LI**	95,066
14/10/53-14/11/53**GO**	143,911 Stays: 530 copper renewed; Plates: Copper tube, copper welded; 65 holes bushed; Copper firehole [flanges] copper welded; Fusible plugs renewed; 16 brick arch studs renewed; Tubes: Set, new; Set new Superheater tubes; Foundation ring, 25 rivets drilled out
23/6/54-26/6/54**LC**	26,461
17/10/55-5/11/55**LI-HI**	78,945 Stays: 2 copper renewed; 480 copper riveted over; Roof, bolts caulked; Plates: Copper tube, 16 rivets replaced by studs; Copper firehole, rings caulked; 2 fusible plugs renewed; Tubes: Set, new "Stewart and Lloyds"; Set new Superheater tubes; Foundation ring, 2 cracks welded; 30 studs and rivets caulked and repaired
11/4/57-11/5/57**GO**	125,005
28/7/58-6/9/58**LC-HC**	44,181

Tender
No.896 from new

Sheds
Nine Elms 7/1925
Stewarts Lane 27/2/40
Hither Green 1/7/40
Bournemouth 7/1941
Eastleigh 12/1942
Stewarts Lane 2/1944
Nine Elms 7/1946
Eastleigh 4/9/48
Nine Elms 5/2/51
Stewarts Lane 27/6/51
Dover 8/10/51
Nine Elms 20/7/53

Withdrawn 11/7/59; stored at Eastleigh Works 7-8/59; cut up at Eastleigh Works w/e 19/9/59 Total 1,305,864 miles

Below. King Arthur graveyard at Eastleigh, 22nd August 1959. 30779 SIR COLGREVANCE had been withdrawn the previous month and met its fate at the same time as 30778, in September 1959.

30779 SIR COLGREVANCE on a three coach local leaving Andover Junction, Saturday 14th May 1955, heading west. It was at Nine Elms by now and still had a General to come in 1957, before it was withdrawn in 1959. The first of the Arthurs to get the standard arrangement of smoke deflectors, on this one the steam pipes did not project through. Photograph R.C. Riley, www.transporttreasury.co.uk

30780 SIR PERSANT

NBL works no.23226
To traffic E780 7/1925
Renumbered 30780 6/1/50

<table>
<tr><td colspan="2">Works</td></tr>
<tr><td>12/1927</td><td>Smoke deflectors fitted</td></tr>
<tr><td>22/3/29</td><td>Stays: 549 copper renewed; Plates: Copper wrapping, 2 large, flat patches; Seams and rivets caulked; New plugs; Tubes: 169, new "BM"; 24 new Superheater tubes</td></tr>
<tr><td>7/1932</td><td>E prefix removed</td></tr>
<tr><td>4/9/35-5/10/35A</td><td>86,517</td></tr>
<tr><td>17/11/37-11/12/37A</td><td>96,635</td></tr>
<tr><td>5/12/38-23/1/39B</td><td>49,023</td></tr>
<tr><td>18/1/40-28/2/40A</td><td>93,075 Olive Green livery</td></tr>
<tr><td>15/10/42-5/12/42B</td><td>63,180 Extension of mileage; 10,000 Wartime Black livery</td></tr>
<tr><td>3/6/43-3/7/43C[NE]</td><td>86,463</td></tr>
<tr><td>28/12/43-6/2/44B</td><td>100,093 Extension of mileage 5,000</td></tr>
<tr><td>25/9/44-21/10/44A</td><td>110,886</td></tr>
<tr><td>9/7/45-14/7/45C[AFD]</td><td>23,616</td></tr>
<tr><td>22/11/45-19/12/45C[AFD]</td><td>38,697</td></tr>
<tr><td>26/2/47-29/3/47A</td><td>66,634 Malachite Green livery from Black*</td></tr>
<tr><td>19/1/48-3/2/48C[NE]</td><td>18,120</td></tr>
<tr><td>22/11/49-6/1/50A</td><td>68,083 Stays: 460 copper renewed; 3 roof stays renewed; 2 holes bushed; Plates: Firebox, tubeplate flanges welded; 68 new studs; Steel tubes protection patch; Lead plugs renewed; Renumbered 30780; BR Green livery; Snifting valves removed</td></tr>
<tr><td>9/7/51-13/7/51NC</td><td>35,926</td></tr>
<tr><td>27/12/51-2/2/52GO</td><td>53,723 Stays: Copper renewed, all; Roof renewed, all; 195 holes bushed; Plates: New copper firebox, 2 x three-quarter sides; Shoulder patch fitted, right-hand side; Tubes: Set,new; Set, new Superheater tubes</td></tr>
<tr><td>14/2/52-22/2/52Return</td><td></td></tr>
<tr><td>10/9/53-1/10/53HI</td><td>67,100 Stays: 160 copper renewed; 350 steel nuts renewed; 350 monel metal riveted over; Plates: Internal tube and firehole plates; renewed with studs; Tubes: 30 new</td></tr>
<tr><td>17/3/55-16/4/55GO</td><td>131,482 T2256 Apexior paint, wheels reconditioned</td></tr>
<tr><td>5/1/56-13/1/56LC[BTN]</td><td>34,227 V and P only</td></tr>
<tr><td>28/5/56-30/6/56LC[BTN]</td><td>49,225</td></tr>
<tr><td>31/1/57-16/2/57LI</td><td>67,079 T2256 Tyres turned</td></tr>
<tr><td>4/9/57-7/9/57LC</td><td>91,851 T2256 Tyres turned [U]</td></tr>
</table>

*As with 738 about the same time, 780 was turned out in a very light version of Malachite Greeen 3/47.

Boilers
No.782 22/3/29
No.787 5/10/35
No.789 11/12/37
No.796 28/2/40
No.776 21/10/44
No.789 29/3/47
No.805 6/1/50
No.839 2/2/52
No.1054 16/4/55

Tender
No.897 from new

Sheds
Nine Elms 7/1925
Stewarts Lane after 1/1933
Nine Elms 20/6/36
Bournemouth 11/7/38
Nine Elms 30/1/39
Stewarts Lane 27/2/40
Nine Elms 22/11/42
Stewarts Lane 2/1944
Eastleigh 8/12/50
Nine Elms 12/5/51
Basingstoke 29/1/56
Bournemouth 5/6/56

Withdrawn 11/7/59; stored at Eastleigh Works 7-8/59; cut up at Eastleigh Works w/e 26/9/59 Total 1,112,973 miles

From 'British Railways Illustrated Annual' No.13: The Farnborough Flyer flew under an arrangement made by Mr Alan Pegler, well-known for the 'Northern Rubber Specials' of the period and the subsequent preservation of FLYING SCOTSMAN. He it was who organised The Flyer, on Sunday 12 September 1954 (for his fellow members of the Royal Observer Corps) to view the Farnborough Air Show. The Great Northern Atlantic No.251 was used, assisted by Director 4-4-0 62663 PRINCE ALBERT, an engine unfortunately 'slated for early condemnation' as the *Trains Illustrated* report put it. A B1 worked the train from Leeds to Doncaster where a 'Flying Scotsman' buffet lounge and one of the 'Coronation' beaver tail observation cars were added. 251 and 62663 duly took over, running to Basingstoke via Retford, Mansfield, Leicester, Banbury, Oxford, Didcot and Reading. From there an SR Mogul took the train on to the Show at Farnborough while the engines and observation car were serviced at Basingstoke shed. To get the same order of vehicles for the return, the rest of the train was taken by a pair of SR 2-6-0s on a circuit to Virginia Water, Ascot and Camberley while the passengers enjoyed the show. The Director and the GN Atlantic were re-attached at Basingstoke and: *ended the day with a rollicking 75mph down the hill, running the 23.4 miles from Leicester to Nottingham, a severe slack near Wilford Road included, in under 28 minutes*. The visitors are serviced at Basingstoke along with King Arthurs 30780 SIR PERSANT and 30745 TINTAGEL. Photograph R.C. Riley, www.transporttreasury.co.uk

Another Arthur at Eastleigh, 30780 SIR PERSANT on 3rd August 1955; it would have worked down from London and its home shed, Nine Elms. Its days were ended at Eastleigh in September 1959. Photograph B.K.B. Green, Initial Photographics.

Withdrawal blues for the Blue Knight, as the old boy languishes at Eastleigh in August 1959, a few weeks after withdrawal; plates still in place in those innocent times.

30781 SIR AGLOVALE

NBL works no.23227
To traffic as E781 8/1925
Renumbered 30781 25/3/49

Boilers
No.781 12/1925
No.771 4/4/36
No.799 4/12/37
No.786 29/11/39
No.1001 3/2/43
No.795 25/10/47
No.779 21/2/53
No.1407 30/11/57

Works

2/9/26	Stays: 348 copper riveted over; Tubes: Set, small
28/7/27	Stays: 251 copper renewed; 200 copper riveted over; Tubes: 78, new, 91 expanded
12/1927	Smoke deflectors fitted
1/1933	E prefix removed
4/3/36-4/4/36**A**	81,083
9/11/37-4/12/37**A**	77,846 Stays: 496 copper renewed; Plates: Copper tube, flanges welded and studded; Copper firehole, flanges welded and studded; Rivets and seams caulked; Lead plugs; Tubes: 169, new "Howell"; 24 2nd hand Superheater tubes
17/10/39-29/11/39**A**	71,032 Olive Green livery
21/11/40-30/11/40**D**	31,652
21/6/41-12/8/41**B**	49,001
2/2/42-4/3/42**B**	67,108 Extension of mileage 10,000
12/12/42-3/2/43**A**	101,103 Wartime Black livery
6/12/45-17/1/46**C[BA]**	90,101 Extension of mileage 15,000
10/7/46-17/8/46**C**	101,667
2/10/47-25/10/47**A**	122,315 Malachite Green livery from Black; Snifting valves removed
20/11/47-29/11/47**D**	[No mileage recorded]
28/2/49-25/3/49**HC**	32,475 Renumbered 30781
10/2/50-3/3/50**LC**	60,884
12/4/51-11/5/51**HI**	105,168 BR Green livery
30/1/53-21/2/53**GO**	182,030
3/5/55-21/5/55**LI**	77,521
23/4/56-10/5/56**LC**	107,967
7/11/57-30/11/57**GO**	133,892 Live steam injector and feed gear right hand side

Tender
No.898 from new

Sheds
Nine Elms 8/1925
Stewarts Lane after 1/1933
Nine Elms 20/6/36
Stewarts Lane 7/1937
Nine Elms 1/7/40
Bournemouth 7/1941
Stewarts Lane 2/1944
Dover 4/9/48
Eastleigh 5/2/51
Nine Elms 14/3/51
Eastleigh 11/4/51
Nine Elms 27/6/51
Basingstoke 29/1/56
Bournemouth 5/6/56

Withdrawn 12/5/62; stored at Eastleigh Works 5/62; cut up at Eastleigh Works w/e 26/5/62
Total 1,184,126 miles

Here we have one of the sons of 30738, 30781 SIR AGLOVALE, the youngest, on 28th August 1954 passing Basingstoke shed and coal stage. Its home shed at the time was Nine Elms and with just four coaches in tow, hardly a challenge.

Not quite another sad scene at Eastleigh; it is 14th May 1960 and 30781 SIR AGLOVALE is on a visit from its home shed Bournemouth. It looks like the smokebox is receiving attention. This loco actually survived until May, 1962 and then it met its demise at Eastleigh.

An Arthur at Exmouth Junction shed on 25th June 1960 wasn't a common sight by this time for the shed had lost the last of them a few years before. It is in fact even more unusual to get one here from Bournemouth shed. Salisbury was a much more likely prospect. S15 4-6-0 30842 in the background was an Exmouth Junction loco until October 1963.

Looking doomed, 30781 SIR AGLOVALE on the Eastleigh store/dump on 25th March 1961 nevertheless saw further use and it would be a year before official withdrawal; it is not clear to what extent it worked again after this though it certainly enjoyed the odd foray, as the next view proves. Moreover, pictures on the same 'stored' roads a year later show it coaled up and stabled next to an Ivatt 2-6-2T; additionally it had '12A' chalked where the shed plate should be and though the smokebox plate remained fixed in place the name plate was gone. Instead, YOGI BEAR was chalked on the front...

SIR AGLOVALE during one of its workings off the Eastleigh 'field', at the shed on 14th May 1961. Official records have this engine being broken up week ending 26th May 1962.

30782 SIR BRIAN

NBL works no.23228
To traffic as E782 7/1925
Renumbered 30782 29/5/48

August 1962 at Eastleigh. Photograph John Scrace.

Works

20/8/25	Fitters
5/9/25	Fitters
14/5/27	Stays: 375 copper renewed; 100 copper riveted over; Tubes: 41, new, 126 expanded
10/1927	Smoke deflectors fitted Flaman speed recorder fitted
12/1930	Flaman speed recorder removed
7/1931	E prefix removed
29/1/36-7/3/36**B**	67,259 Extension of mileage 5,000
28/4/36-7/3/36**D**	67,890
11/11/36-12/12/36**A**	99,372
30/12/38-1/2/39**A**	78,477 Maunsell Green livery
1/12/40**[NE]**	Extension of mileage 5,000
15/9/41-22/10/41**A**	84,826 Malachite Green livery
28/3/43-21/5/43**C[NE]**	67,980
14/6/44-5/8/44**A**	99,681 Wartime Black livery
11/3/46-6/4/46**B**	60,367
7/3/47-12/4/47**A**	96,166 190 holes bushed; Plates: New firebox; New three-quarter sides, throat plate and crown plate; Tubes: Set, new "Tubes Ltd"; Set new Superheater tubes; Black livery with green driving wheels
3/5/48-29/5/48**C**	42,852 Renumbered 30782
27/9/49-28/10/49**A**	93,279 BR Green livery; Snifting valves removed; T2138 Fitted with storm sheets
24/1/50-3/2/50**HC**	4,049
5/3/52-28/3/52**LI**	75,592
8/12/53-2/1/54**GO**	139,012
20/9/55-8/10/55**LI**	68,761
27/9/57-12/10/57**LI**	118,042
22/4/60-14/5/60**GO**	161,852
20/11/61-25/11/61**LC**	20,631

Boilers

No.782 20/8/25
No.792 as of 7/3/36
No.931 12/12/36
No.773 1/2/39
No.778 22/10/41
No.830 5/8/44
No.825 12/4/47
No.840 28/10/49
No.450 3/2/50
No.455 2/1/54
No.796 14/5/60

Tender

No.899 from new

Sheds

Nine Elms 7/1925
Stewarts Lane after 1/1933
Nine Elms 1/7/40
Stewarts Lane 7/1943
Nine Elms 8/1947
Eastleigh 5/2/51
Bournemouth 27/6/51

Withdrawn 15/9/62; stored at Eastleigh Works 9/62; cut up at Eastleigh Works w/e 29/9/62
Total 1,197,719 miles

30782 SIR BRIAN at Eastleigh, 14 May 1961, very much in 'BR grey'; 34040 CREWKERNE behind.

30782 SIR BRIAN, looking sprightly, flush in BR green, at Ashford shed on 25th February 1962. Still a Bournemouth engine, it has been dolled up at this late stage for a special working that day, the LCGB 'Kentish Venturer'.

Super side-on, revealing the subtle lines of an Arthur, a certain delicacy attached to brute power. 30782 SIR BRIAN is filling in on empty stock work out of Waterloo, as many main line engines did. Here it is sitting in the approach roads of the Clapham Junction carriage shed on 16th July 1960, awaiting the next job or a return to Nine Elms. Photograph Frank Hornby.

30783 SIR GILLEMERE

NBL works no.23279
To traffic as E783 8/1925
Renumbered 30783 22/5/48

Works

26/3/27	Stays: 116 copper renewed; 300 copper riveted over
3/1927-12/1927	Shovel shaped device in front of chimney
12/1927	Smoke deflectors fitted
2/1932	E prefix removed
28/6/35	Stays: 300 copper renewed; Plates: Copper tube, angle patches; Copper wrapping, flat patches on one-half sides; Lead plugs; Tubes: 60 2nd hand welded
6/1/36**D**	[No mileage recorded]
1/10/36-31/10/36**A**	84,393
15/3/37-18/3/37**D**	20,459
5/1/38-2/2/38**A**	63,916 Stays: 508 copper renewed; Plates: Copper tube, 2 angle patches; Copper firehole, 2 angle patches; Lead plugs; Brick arch studs; Tubes: 169, 2nd hand, welded; 24, 2nd hand Superheater tubes, expanded, copper ends
5/1/39-1/3/39**B**	33,821 Stays: 6 copper renewed; 350 copper riveted over; Plates: Lead plugs; Tubes: All expanded; 169 rebeaded
21/8/40-13/11/40**A**	88,547 Malachite Green livery; three small diameter stovepipe chimneys
20/12/1940	Two larger diameter stovepipe chimneys
5/2/41-11/2/41**D**	Plates fitted between smoke deflectors; Returned to work with a standard chimney
10/4/43-12/5/43**A**	86,595 Wartime Black livery
5/10/44-18/11/44**C**	51,643
19/10/45-12/11/45**C[BA]**	85,243
18/1/46-31/1/46**C[AFD]**	91,425
25/6/46-26/7/46**A**	99,260 Malachite Green livery from Black; New left-hand cylinder
12/6/47**[SL]**	T2080 Left and right-hand gauge glasses fitted
28/11/47-20/12/47**C**	55,207
17/4/48-22/5/48**B**	65,251 Renumbered 30783; Snifting valves removed
13/6/49-29/7/49**A**	125,345 BR Green livery with orange lining and black edging, first of class in this livery; T2070 Special piston heads and rings, of cast iron
24/4/50-12/5/50**LC**	42,803
9/5/51-13/6/51**GO**	79,116
10/10/52-25/10/52**LC**	43,524
31/7/53-22/8/53**LI**	71,899
7/3/55-28/5/55**GO**	130,891 Stays: 129 copper renewed; 149 monel metal renewed; 149 nuts renewed; Plates: 41 rivets replaced by studs; 2 fusible plugs renewed; Tubes: Set, new "Howell"; Set, new Superheater tubes
27/6/57-13/7/57**LI**	66,747 Stays: 272 monel metal renewed; 120 copper riveted over; 272 nuts renewed; Plates: Copper tube, 6 studs renewed; Copper firehole, 40 studs repaired; 2 fusible plugs renewed; Tubes: 30, new "Stewart and Lloyds"; 3 new Superheater tubes
30/10/59-7/11/59**LC**	94,354

Tender
No.900 from new

Sheds
Bournemouth 8/1925
Nine Elms 7/1937
Hither Green 1/7/40
Nine Elms 22/11/42
Stewarts Lane 7/1943
Nine Elms 8/1947
Eastleigh 7/1/50
Nine Elms 8/12/50
Eastleigh 5/2/51
Bournemouth 27/6/51
Salisbury 24/11/60

Withdrawn 4/3/61; stored at Eastleigh Works 2-5/61; cut up at Eastleigh Works w/e 1/7/61
Total 1,221,647 miles

Boilers
No.783 8/1925
No.806 28/6/35
No.788 31/10/36
No.782 2/2/38
No.765 13/11/40
No.837 12/5/43
No.790 26/7/46
No.450 22/5/48
No.491 29/7/49
No.798 13/6/51
No.839 28/5/55

To the keen observer there is no doubt that this is Basingstoke station and it seems it was only the SR that put the large enamel signs on the ends of the station canopies. So here we are in Hampshire with 30783 SIR GILLEMERE on a passenger train, 28th August 1954. It was at Bournemouth through much of the 1950s, from June 1951 to November 1960 when it went to Salisbury where it only survived a few months.

30783 SIR GILLEMERE at Eastleigh on 14 May 1960, retaining the small first tender emblem. Multi-plug boiler 839.

30784 SIR NEROVENS

NBL works no.23280
To traffic as E784 8/1925
Renumbered 30784 30/5/48

Boilers
No.782 29/3/30
No.928 9/11/35
No.775 22/4/37
No.836 14/12/38
No.779 8/1/41
No.764 16/6/43
No.774 15/5/48
No.781 10/11/50
No.764 22/11/52
No.786 25/8/56

Works

1/1928	Smoke deflectors fitted
29/3/30	Stays: 50 roof renewed; Plates: Copper tube, new; Copper wrapping, 2 flanges, one-half sides; New brick arch studs and plugs; Tubes: 169, new "BM"; 24 new Superheater tubes; Foundation ring part renewed
10/12/31	Stays: 434 copper renewed; Plates: 2 copper angle patches; Lead plugs; Brick arch studs; Rivets and seams caulked; Tubes: 62, 2nd hand, electrically welded. E prefix removed
15/10/35-9/11/35A	130,424 Stays: 120 holes bushed; Plates: New copper firebox; Casing covering, three-quarter sides
17/2/36-21/2/36D	12,239
18/3/37-22/4/37A	76,496
18/11/38-14/12/38A	94,824 Maunsell Green livery
26/11/40-8/1/41A	79,827 Malachite Green livery
6/5/43-16/6/43A	85,065 Wartime Black livery
24/9/45-2/11/45A	106,603
1/7/46-20/7/46C	43,730
4/2/47-22/2/47C	64,423
17/4/47-9/5/47D	68,141
30/5/47-4/6/47D	68,141 6/1947 Large diameter pre-fabricated chimney; T2052 Spark arrester fitted
23/6/47	70,606 Weighing only
20/8/47-13/9/47C	73,686
14/4/48-15/5/48A	90,625 Above chimney etc. removed; Malachite Green livery from Black. Renumbered 30784
9/6/48-17/6/48D	[No mileage recorded]
14/1/49-12/2/49C	26,244 Large diameter chimney of 6/47 modified and refitted; Snifting valves removed
2/10/50-10/11/50A	86,250 Stays: 715 copper renewed; 467 holes bushed; Plates: Copper tube, new; 2 new one-half sides; Fusible plugs renewed; Tubes: Set, new; Set, new Superheater tubes; BR Green livery. T2189 Standardisation of white metals; T1891 Thomas "patent" piston rod packing
24/10/52-22/11/52GO	76,078
8/4/54-10/4/54LC	55,622
29/9/54-23/10/54LI	70,697 Large diameter chimney etc. removed; T2214 Exhaust injector cones [U]; T2258 Boiler barrel patch plate [U]
20/7/56-25/8/56GO	128,170 T2256 Tyres turned
7/11/57-16/11/57LC	37,046 T2256 Tyres turned [U]

Tender
No.901 from new

Sheds
Bournemouth 8/1925
Stewarts Lane 27/2/40
Hither Green 1/7/40
Nine Elms 22/11/42
Bournemouth 3/1944
Salisbury 6/1945
Eastleigh 4/1946
Nine Elms 8/12/50
Eastleigh 5/2/51

Withdrawn 17/10/59; stored at Eastleigh Works 10/59; cut up at Eastleigh Works w/e 7/11/59
Total 1,369,983 miles

784 SIR NEROVENS in Bulleid wartime Black livery.

30784 SIR NEROVENS at Eastleigh, then its home shed, on 14th May 1949, awaiting its next turn of duty. Its previous visit to the adjacent works (14/1/49-12/2/49) had seen the refitting of pre-fabricated chimney and spark arrester. Renumbered in May 1948, it carries the early BRITISH RAILWAYS lettering, in the SR 'sunshine' style, as is the number. In the background is one of Bulleid's distinctive Q1 0-6-0s which were always good looking, to my eyes at least. Loco still in Malachite Green from a visit ending 15th May 1948; it wasn't repainted in BR Green until April 1949. The odd looking chimney is a large diameter pre-fabricated assembly fitted in June 1947, removed in May 1948, refitted in modified form early in 1949 and eventually removed in October 1954. Photograph J.H. Aston.

30785 SIR MADOR DE LA PORTE

NBL works no.23281
To traffic as E785 9/1925
Renumbered 30785 14/8/48

Works

2/1928	Smoke deflectors fitted
2/1932	E prefix removed
16/9/35-19/10/35**A**	95,438
4/6/36-2/7/36**B**	36,356
26/2/37-27/3/37**A**	76,755
29/11/38-21/12/38**A**	100,891 Stays: 564 copper renewed; Plates: Copper tube, 2 angle patches; Casing firehole, 2 angle patches; Lead plugs; Throat, seam welded; Barrel, safety valve seating welded; Tubes: 169, new "Talbot Stead"; 24 2nd hand Superheater tubes [copper ends]; Maunsell Green livery
10/6/40-10/7/40**B**	56,094 Malachite Green livery
27/12/41-11/2/42**A**	88,628
6/8/43-11/10/43**C**	62,629 Extension of mileage 5,000; Wartime Black livery
23/10/44-25/11/44**A**	104,813
22/9/45-26/10/45**B**	30,835 New left-hand side cylinder
4/3/46-15/3/46**C[SAL]**	50,389
17/5/46-15/6/46**B**	55,854
25/7/46-26/7/46**D**	55,854
2/6/47-28/6/47**A**	97,677 Malachite Green livery from Black
9/3/48-20/3/48**C**	35,075
12/8/48-14/8/48**C**	48,325 Renumbered 30785
14/1/49-5/2/49**HC**	66,878 Snifting valves removed
17/3/49-24/3/49	Not officially recorded as a repair
1/12/49-23/12/49**LI**	100,936
10/5/51-21/6/51**GO**	149,720 BR Green livery
14/8/51-21/8/51**LC**	2,887
23/1/52-28/1/52**NC[BTN]**	14,976
11/2/53-7/3/53**LI**	51,780
15/2/54-26/2/54**LC[BTN]**	89,750
26/4/54-1/5/54**LC**	93,860
16/12/54-20/1/55**GO**	110,220 Stays: 814 monel metal renewed; 830 nuts renewed; 6 longitudinal renewed; Roof renewed, all; 10 crown bars fitted; Plates: Copper tube, new; Copper firehole, 2 flanges, one-half sides; Copper wrapping, 2 flanges, one-half sides; 2 new fusible plugs; Casing covering, 140 holes bushed; Tubes: Set, new "Howell"; Set, new Superheater tubes; Rivets: 56 studs renewed in copper backplate
20/6/55-25/6/55**LC**	16,659
4/4/57-27/4/57**LI-HI**	79,502 Stays: 502 copper riveted over; Plates: Seams and 110 studs repaired; 2 fusible plugs renewed; Tubes: 167, new "Stewart and Lloyds"; 3 new Superheater tubes; Rivets: Foundation ring, 40 rivets repaired

Tenders

No.902 from new
No.854 from 30746 on 27/4/57
No.908 at running shed on 7/11/59 from 30791

Sheds

Bournemouth 9/1925
Stewarts Lane 27/2/40
Nine Elms 22/11/42
Bournemouth 3/1944
Salisbury 6/1945
Eastleigh 4/1946
Nine Elms 8/12/50
Eastleigh 5/2/51

Withdrawn 17/10/59; stored at Eastleigh Works 10/59; cut up at Eastleigh Works w/e 14/11/59
Total 1,314,287 miles

Boilers

No.841 19/10/35
No.823 2/7/36
No.791 27/3/37
No.825 21/12/38
No.449 11/2/42
No.835 25/11/44
No.830 28/6/47
No.804 5/2/49
No.765 21/6/51
No.1409 20/1/55

Eastleigh Works and despite appearances (this is 22nd August 1959) 30785 SIR MADOR DE LA PORTE is not yet withdrawn, though its 71A Eastleigh shed plate has been taken off. It seems strange to us now that the infinitely more valuable name plate was left on, for it would not be needed again, while Eastleigh kept the shed plate for further use on another engine.

A week later on 29th August 1959 and 30785 SIR MADOR DE LA PORTE has definitely been shunted around for it now faces a sister loco in place of the wooden bodied wagon with a BR standard 2-6-0 76018 behind. Engines were not by definition due for scrapping once on these sidings, as the BR mogul proves; in fact they awaited a decision as to whether they would see another repair or be condemned. For SIR MADOR this came two months later. This loco was the first of the class to be fitted with connecting rods with plain bushed big ends, first noted 11/5/45. Others later fitted were 30454, 30770, 30786 and 30797.

30786 SIR LIONEL

NBL works no.23282
To traffic as E786 9/1925
Renumbered 30786 2/10/48

Boilers

No.789 14/12/35
No.796 20/11/37
No.833 6/12/39
No.928 9/10/42
No.931 27/1/45
No.773 4/10/47
No.801 1/7/49
No.803 24/12/52
No.774 27/8/55
No.931 14/12/57

Works

Probably late 1927	Smoke deflectors fitted
4/1932	E prefix removed
16/11/35-14/12/35A	109,473
1/4/37-27/4/37B	67,919 Extension of mileage 5,000
27/10/37-20/11/37A	94,259 Fitted with Lord Nelson pattern chimney
7/11/39-6/12/39A	97,251 Stays: 120 holes bushed; Plates: New copper firebox; Casing covering, new; Throat, seams welded; Barrel, safety valve seating welded; Tubes: 167, new "Chesterfield"; 24 new Superheater tubes; Olive Green livery
7/3/40-10/4/40C	3,647
27/2/41-10/3/41C[EXJ]	[No mileage recorded]
7/9/42-9/10/42A	102,436 Stays: 385 copper renewed; Plates: Rivets and seams caulked; Leadplugs; Tubes: 167, 2nd hand, welded; Wartime Black livery
25/11/44-27/1/45A	94,521
15/9/47-4/10/47A	104,434 T2025 Spring links fitted with copper plated threads; T2189 Standardisation of white metals; Malachite Green livery from Black; Snifting valves removed
28/8/48-2/10/48C	47,983 Renumbered 30786
27/5/49-1/7/49A	82,934 Malachite Green livery
19/10/50-10/11/50HC	30,191
31/7/51-3/8/51NC	42,000
22/8/51-31/8/51NC	43,584
1/12/52-24/12/52GO	89,701 BR Green livery
12/3/54-6/4/54LC[BTN]	47,574
27/5/54-5/6/54LC	49,438
8/8/55-27/8/55GO	86,506
20/11/57-14/12/57GO	66,163 Right hand side live steam injector and feed gear
9/9/58-25/9/58NC	28,947

Tender

No.903 from new

Sheds

Bournemouth 9/1925
Exmouth Junction 7/1937
Nine Elms 8/2/46
Stewarts Lane 26/9/49
Nine Elms 8/12/50
Eastleigh 5/2/51
Nine Elms 14/3/51
Eastleigh 11/4/51

Withdrawn 29/8/59; stored at Eastleigh Works 8-9/59; cut up at Eastleigh Works w/e 31/10/59 Total 1,389,822 miles

30786 SIR LIONEL (nephew of 30455) at Eastleigh, 22nd August 1959; what might have been its final fire freshly heaved off the footplate – see next.

30786 SIR LIONEL ex-works in July 1949 at Eastleigh. This was the last repaint of a King Arthur in Malachite Green. Tender is blank and deflector and wheels are black. Photograph R.K. Blencowe.

An inter-regional working with 30786 SIR LIONEL (brother of 30797) arriving at Basingstoke on Saturday 25th July 1959. An Eastleigh engine, this must have been one of its last workings. In the background is Basingstoke running shed which at the time had Arthurs 30765, 30770 and 30794 on its allocation. Photograph B.W.L. Brooksbank, Initial Photographics.

30787 SIR MENADEUKE

NBL works no.23283
To traffic as E787 9/1925
Renumbered 30787 1/4/49

Boilers
No.785 as of 17/7/36
No.792 19/12/36
No.779 22/2/39
No.1055 20/11/40
No.1048 31/8/43
No.1055 9/2/46
No.1403 6/3/48
No.1052 10/7/54

Works

11/1927	Smoke deflectors fitted
8/1931	E prefix removed
27/5/36-17/7/36B	73,757
19/11/36-19/12/36A	94,811
22/2/38-6/4/38B	61,589 Extension of mileage 5,000
11/7/38-13/7/38C[EXJ]	[No mileage recorded]
28/1/39-22/2/39A	96,526 Maunsell Green livery
19/10/40-20/11/40A	85,137 Malachite Green livery
29/6/42-20/7/42C[EXJ]	Extension of mileage 10,000
9/12/42-1/2/43C	80,257
7/7/43-31/8/43A	99,112 Wartime Black livery
8/3/44-5/4/44C[EXJ]	25,393
18/4/45-27/4/45C[EXJ]	80,692
8/1/46-9/2/46A	114,248
14/10/46-26/10/46C	30,733
12/2/48-6/3/48A	86,385 Snifting valves removed; renumbered S787. Malachite Green livery from Black
20/3/48-24/3/48D	[No mileage recorded]
3/3/49-1/4/49LI	45,325 Stays: 9 repaired and 350 monel metal repaired; Plates: Seams caulked; Fusible plugs renewed; Tubes: 18 ferrules renewed; Renumbered 30787
24/8/49-20/9/49LC	59,983
5/9/50-10/11/50LI	105,499 Stays: 350 monel metal riveted over; 350 nuts renewed; Plates: Rivets and seams repaired; Fusible plugs renewed; Tubes: Set renewed; 2 Superheater tubes renewed; BR Green livery
30/6/52-8/8/52HI	163,245 Stays: 3 monel metal new and 427 repaired; 427 new nuts; Plates: Rivets renewed with studs; Fusible plugs renewed; Tubes: Set, new; 3 new Superheater tubes
2/7/53-4/7/53LC	195,233
16/6/54-10/7/54GO	229,753
13/9/56-22/9/56HI	72,585
26/3/57-30/3/57LC	83,168

Tender
No.904 from new

Sheds
Bournemouth 9/1925
Exmouth Junction 7/1937
Bournemouth 11/1946
Eastleigh 3/5/49
Nine Elms 26/9/49
Salisbury 9/10/50
Eastleigh 13/11/50
Nine Elms 8/12/50
Eastleigh 5/2/51

Withdrawn 28/2/59; stored at Eastleigh Works 2-4/59; cut up at Eastleigh Works w/e 30/5/59
Total 1,304,180 miles

30787 SIR MENADEUKE, with steam escaping from the injector by the look of it, though in reasonably good nick otherwise, awaiting departure from Basingstoke on an up train on 14th May 1955. The fireman is using the 'pep' pipe to dampen down the coal dust in the tender to give a more comfortable ride; coal not up to much, though still in the traditional cone form. Photograph Frank Hornby.

30787 SIR MENADEUKE on Saturday 30th August 1958 at Dorchester South station and what a performance will now ensue. The train will draw forward, reverse into the up platform, await station duties to be completed and then leave under the protection of the signal at the right of the picture. The headcode shows duty 401 which covered an early morning Bournemouth train to Weymouth, up to Southampton Terminus and back to Bournemouth. The loco is carrying Maunsell boiler no.1052 and the shot illustrates the neat line of rivets around the smokebox edge as well as those on the front buffer beam. Usual joins in the outer casing and a barely visible line along the boiler top. Steam dome and safety valves just add to the symmetry of what was one of the most handsome steam passenger classes to work in these islands. Photograph R.C. Riley, www.transporttreasury.co.uk

30788 SIR URRE OF THE MOUNT

NBL works no.23284
[Originally to be named SIR BEUMAINS]
To traffic as E788 9/1925
Renumbered 30788 16/10/48

Works

12/1927	Smoke deflectors fitted
1/1932	E prefix removed
21/3/35	Stays: 150 holes bushed; Plates: New copper firebox; Casing covering, three-quarters sides; Tubes: 169, new "Talbot Stead"; 24 new Superheater tubes, copper ends
12/8/35-31/8/35**B**	64,825 Extension of mileage 5,000
20/11/35-11/12/35**C**	79,452
24/4/36-6/6/36**A**	10,856 Stays: 338 copper renewed; Plates: Rivets and seams caulked; Lead plugs
12/11/37-11/12/37**A**	88,957
25/8/39-20/9/39**A**	75,777 Olive Green livery
23/10/40-30/10/40**C**	32,805
31/10/41-3/12/41**A**	73,246 Stays: 648 copper renewed; 400 holes bushed Plates: Copper tube, new; Steel tube, electrically welded at rivet holes; Lead plugs; Tubes: 167, new; 24 new Superheater tubes; Malachite Green livery
16/11/42-20/1/43**B**	39,983 Wartime Black livery
10/2/44-11/3/44**A**	88,881
16/9/46-12/10/46**A**	96,876 Malachite Green livery from Black
13/6/47	T2080 Left and right-hand gauge glasses fitted at Nine Elms; removed 8/7/47
25/9/47-11/10/47**C**	46,209
22/9/48-16/10/48**A**	79,652 Snifting valves removed; T2070 Wear resistance of Cast Iron piston rings
28/12/49-6/1/50**NC**	43,011 Mark 3 version of large diameter pre-fabricated chimney and spark arrester
1/6/51-27/6/51**LC**	97,633 Stays: 370 steel repaired; Plates: Copper tube, seams repaired; Copper wrapping, studs renewed; Fusible plugs; Tubes: Set, renewed; 2 new Superheater tubes; Mark 3 chimney etc. removed; BR Green livery
22/5/53-20/6/53**GO**	168,368 Stays: 580 copper renewed; Girder bars taken off and replaced; Plates: Copper tube, new; Copper firehole, 2 angle patches; Fusible plugs renewed; Tubes: Set, new; Set, new Superheater tubes; Foundation ring, new
10/12/54-1/1/55**LI-HI**	57,090 Stays: 530 copper renewed; Plates: Seams and studs repaired; 2 new plugs; Tubes: Set, new "Stewart and Lloyds"; Set, new Superheater tubes
22/4/55-30/4/55**LC**	69,537
21/9/56-13/10/56**GO**	113,460 Stays: Copper renewed, all; Longitudinal renewed, all; Roof renewed, all; 152 holes bushed; Plates: New copper firebox; 2 fusible plugs; Casing covering, three-quarters casing steel sides fitted; Tubes: 167, new "Stewart and Lloyds"; 24 new Superheater tubes; Modified injector and feed gear refitted
15/4/58-26/4/58**LC**	50,399 Stays: 545 copper riveted over; Plates: Seams repaired; 2 fusible plugs renewed; Tubes: 167, new "Stewart and Lloyds"; 24 new Superheater tubes; Foundation ring, 40 corners repaired; Regulator repaired
1/12/58-20/12/58**LI**	68,644 Stays: 530 copper riveted over; Plates: Seams repaired; 2 fusible plugs renewed; Tubes: 30 2nd hand welded; 3 Superheater tubes renewed; Foundation ring, 40 corners repaired
17/2/60-12/3/60**GO**	100,956 Stays: Copper renewed, all; Nuts renewed, all; Roof renewed, all; 160 holes bushed; Plates: New firebox; Steel tube, protection patch fitted; Casing covering, casing sides welded; Tubes: 167, new "Stewart and Lloyds"; 24 Superheater tubes welded

Tenders

No.905 from new
No.3233 on 11/3/44

Sheds

Bournemouth 9/1925
Exmouth Junction 7/1937
Nine Elms 9/1943
Stewarts Lane 26/4/45
Nine Elms 9/1946
Stewarts Lane 12/1948
Eastleigh 3/5/49
Nine Elms 8/12/50
Eastleigh 5/2/51

Withdrawn 10/2/62; stored at Ashford Works 1/62; cut up at Ashford Works w/e 17/2/62
Total 1,423,378 miles

Boilers

No.457 21/3/35
No.784 11/12/37
No.449 20/9/39
No.457 3/12/41
No.804 11/3/44
No.1407 16/10/48
No.826 20/6/53
No.805 13/10/56
No.457 12/3/60

30788 SIR URRE OF THE MOUNT at Basingstoke station; no.23 looks like one of the semi-fasts between Waterloo and Basingstoke on which I saw several Arthurs, including this one. Originally allotted the name Sir Beumains, this was the only 'Scotchman' to be scrapped at Ashford Works. Photograph J. Davenport, Initial Photographics.

And now the other side. 30788 with that romantic name SIR URRE OF THE MOUNT; evidently a Hungarian Knight. During its final period at Eastleigh shed it is running into the station with an empty coach. Photograph J. Davenport, Initial Photographics.

30789 SIR GUY

NBL works no.23285
To traffic as E789 9/1925
Renumbered 30789 4/9/48

Works

8/1928	Smoke deflectors
1/1932	E prefix removed
28/10/35-28/11/35**A**	98,159
10/2/37-6/3/37**A**	71,860
14/3/38-16/4/38**C[EXJ]**	57,007
8/2/39-8/3/39**A**	94,749 Malachite Green livery
28/11/40-8/1/41**A**	90,048 Stays: 850 copper renewed; 50 roof renewed; Plates: Copper tube, new; Copper wrapping, flanges, one-half sides; Tubes: 167 2nd hand, welded; 24 2nd hand Superheater tubes, copper ends. Malachite Green livery
27/7/42-28/9/42**B**	62,060 Stays: 458 copper renewed; Plates: Rivets and seams caulked; Copper wrapping, 2 angles; Lead plugs; Tubes: 167, 2nd hand, welded; 24 2nd hand Superheater tubes, copper ends; Extension of mileage 20,000
21/4/43-26/5/43**A**	80,395 Wartime Black livery
27/10/43-3/11/43**C[EXJ]**	66,897; Main frame welded over right leading spring hanger bracket; Replacing leading and bogie wheels C33/5125
28/11/44-2/2/45**C**	67,379
26/4/45-5/5/45**C**	74,921 Extension of mileage 5,000
15/1/46-9/3/46**A**	98,525 Malachite Green livery from Black
29/4/47-31/5/47**C**	45,465
23/7/47-26/7/47**D**	48,276
21/8/47-28/8/47**D**	49,591
16/9/47-20/9/47**D**	49,980
6/8/48-4/9/48**A**	85,572 Renumbered 30789; Snifting valves removed
15/9/48-20/9/48**D**	[No mileage recorded]
24/9/48-2/10/48**D**	[No mileage recorded]
12/7/49-12/8/49**LC**	23,709
21/8/50-29/9/50**LI**	62,688
1/8/51-3/8/51**NC**	92,823
19/9/51-28/9/51**LC**	95,891
29/4/52-23/5/52**GO**	114,967 Stays: 991 copper renewed; 10 roof bar; 30 roof renewed; 393 holes bushed; Plates: Copper tube, new; 2 flanges, one-half sides; Rivets renewed; Barrel, seams caulked; Tubes: Set, new; Set, new Superheater tubes; Foundation ring renewed BR Green livery
7/5/54-5/6/54**GO**	60,898 T2222 Regulator valve BR alloy new test
6/10/55-15/10/55**NC-LC**	50,843 T2222 [U]
20/2/56-25/2/56**LC**	55,024 T2222 [U]
2/1/58-18/1/58**LI**	108,890
20/6/58-28/6/58**LC**	119,119

Boilers

No.791	as of 28/11/35
No.770	6/3/37
No.791	8/3/39
No.782	8/1/41
No.765	26/5/43
No.794	9/3/46
No.775	4/9/48
No.825	23/5/52
No.804	5/6/54

Tender
No.906 from new

Sheds
Bournemouth 9/1925
Exmouth Junction 7/1937
Bournemouth 11/1946
Stewarts Lane 12/1948
Eastleigh 3/5/49
Basingstoke 8/12/50
Eastleigh 5/2/51

Withdrawn 26/12/59; stored at Eastleigh Works 12/59; cut up at Eastleigh Works w/e 3/1/60 Total 1,383,297 miles

30789 SIR GUY in Malachite Green with Gill sans lettering on the turntable at Bournemouth in April 1951. Photograph C. Caddy.

30789 with one of the shortest Maunsell Arthur nameplate, SIR GUY at Basingstoke shed at an unknown date. SIR GUY was only based here, 70D, for two months, seeing out its days at Eastleigh shed before withdrawal in February 1962. Photograph J. Davenport, Initial Photographics.

30790 SIR VILLIARS

NBL works no.23286
To traffic as E790 9/1925
Renumbered 30790 18/9/48

Works	
2/1928	Smoke deflectors fitted
1/1932	E prefix removed
19/9/35-26/10/35**A**	113,632
9/7/36-11/7/36**D**	39,702
26/1/37-20/2/37**A**	79,244
9/2/38-5/4/38**B**	47,314
27/3/39-19/4/39**A**	89,691 Stays: 505 copper renewed; 300 copper riveted over; Plates: Studs in flanges; Lead plugs; Brick arch studs; Tubes: 169, new "Howell" Olive Green livery
26/6/39**D**	[No mileage recorded]
17/2/41-26/3/41**A**	88,531 Stays: 713 copper renewed; 300 holes bushed; Plates: Copper wrapping, flange one-half sides; Lead plugs; Tubes: 167 2nd hand, welded; 24 new Superheater tubes, [copper ends]; Malachite Green livery
31/12/42-24/2/43**B**	67,510 Extension of mileage 5,000; Wartime Black livery
25/1/44-23/2/44**A**	112,715
31/7/45-4/10/45**B**	56,274 Extension of mileage 5,000
20/8/46-14/9/46**A**	100,015 Stays: 130 holes bushed; Plates: New copper firebox; Casing covering, new; Throat, three-quarters sides and crown plate; Tubes: 169, new "Howell"; 24 new Superheater tubes; Malachite Green livery from Black
26/8/48-18/9/48**A**	86,810 Renumbered 30790; Snifting valves removed
20/6/50-4/8/50**HI**	59,040
1/9/52-2/10/52**GO**	124,726 BR Green livery
23/3/55-16/4/55**LI-HI**	71,981
7/9/55-16/9/55**LC**	83,364
14/2/56-18/2/56**NC**	98,284
29/4/57-25/5/57**GO**	129,528 Stays: Copper renewed, all; Longitudinal, all; Roof renewed, all; 147 holes bushed; Plates: New copper firebox; Casing covering 2 x three quarters sides; Tubes: Set, new "Stewart and Lloyds"; Set, new Superheater tubes; Modified live steam in place of exhaust injector
5/2/59-21/2/59**LI-HI**	49,909 Stays: 525 copper riveted over; Plates: Copper tube, 11 studs renewed; Copper firehole, seams and studs repaired; 2 fusible plugs; Tubes: 167, new "New Phoenix"; 3 new Superheater tubes; Foundation ring renewed, 40 rivets repaired
13/10/60-26/11/60**HC**	94,233 Stays: 526 copper renewed; Plates: Copper tube, 84 studs renewed; Copper firehole, 82 studs renewed; 2 fusible plugs renewed; Tubes: 167, new "Tube products"; 24 new Superheater tubes; Foundation ring repaired, 36 rivets repaired

Above. Topping up the tender axle boxes on Eastleigh's 30789 SIR GUY in the servicing line at Nine Elms, 27th June 1953 along with resident 30780 SIR PERSANT. Both have been turned and coaled so will soon exit stage left for Waterloo and the next job west. Photograph B.K.B. Green, Initial Photographics.

Boilers
No.832 26/10/35
No.826 19/4/39
No.806 26/3/41
No.455 23/2/44
No.805 14/9/46
No.794 18/9/48
No.792 2/10/52
No.782 25/5/57

Tender
No.907 from new

Sheds
Bournemouth 9/1925
Exmouth Junction 7/1937
Bournemouth 11/1946
Stewarts Lane 12/1948
Eastleigh 3/5/49
Basingstoke 8/12/50
Eastleigh 5/2/51

Withdrawn 4/11/61; stored at Eastleigh Works 10-12/61; cut up at Eastleigh Works w/e 13/1/62 Total 1,404,162 miles

No date for this picture but it's Upwey on the Weymouth line, by now thoroughly absorbed into the Southern Region. 30790 SIR VILLARS was another Eastleigh engine; a good number of the later Arthurs finished their days there and no less than nineteen were withdrawn from the shed. All were cut up at Eastleigh save 30788 and 30804. No steam heating on the front, screw coupling in correct position with the distant signal on the left more evidence of the SR takeover, an upper quadrant.

30790 SIR VILLIARS at home on Eastleigh shed on 5th October 1952; it had gone there in February 1951, remaining until withdrawal. 30790 is ex-works, a General having only finished three days before, so the new BR Green is barely dry! Photograph B.K.B. Green, Initial Photographics.

30791 SIR UWAINE

NBL works no.23287
To traffic as E791 9/1925
Renumbered 30791 10/12/48

Works

1/1928	Smoke deflectors fitted
3/1930	Tender tank gauge fitted
3/1931	Tender tank gauge removed
12/1931	E prefix removed
23/7/35-3/8/35C	53,686
15/1/36-30/1/36C	74,732
6/5/36-27/6/36A	88,343
5/2/38-9/3/38A	90,472
20/7/39-13/9/39B	63,621 Extension of mileage 10,000
16/7/40-14/8/40A	104,351 Stays: 740 copper renewed; 40 roof renewed; 400 holes bushed; Plates: Copper tube, new; Copper wrapping, flanges one-half sides; Lead plugs; Brick arch studs; Safety valve seating welded; Tubes: 167, 2nd hand, welded; 24 new Superheater tubes, copper ends; Malachite Green livery
4/9/41-3/10/41C[EXJ]	[No mileage recorded]
30/5/42C[AFD]	[No mileage recorded]
2/9/42-30/9/42A	73,493 Wartime Black livery
26/8/43-9/9/43C[EXJ]	41,781
2/10/44-4/11/44A	90,743
4/3/46-22/3/46C	58,987
3/3/47-5/4/47A	98,103
28/4/47-3/5/47D	[No mileage recorded] Black livery with Green driving wheels
12/6/47[NE]	T2080 Left and right-hand gauge glasses fitted; left-hand removed 10/7/47
29/10/48-10/12/48A	68,324 Malachite Green livery from Black; Snifting valves removed; Renumbered 30791
10/3/49-17/3/49D[NE]	4,466
14/9/49-22/9/49D	22,344
18/4/51-24/5/51GO	81,443 Stays: 499 copper renewed; 4 roof renewed; Plates: Copper tube, new with studs; New fusible plugs; Tubes: Set, new; Set, new Superheater tubes Throat plate, 79 new rivets; BR Green livery; New right-hand cylinder
25/8/52-6/9/52LC	54,864
20/8/53-16/9/53GO	77,922
6/1954	Live steam injector
6/10/55-29/10/55LI-HI	69,127
24/5/56-13/6/56LC-HC	84,623
22/1/57-16/2/57GO	104,403
18/8/58-13/9/58LI-HI	50,201

Boilers
No.776 as of 3/8/35
No.788 9/3/38
No.928 14/8/40
No.1051 30/9/42
No.769 4/11/44
No.838 5/4/47
No.786 10/12/48
No.928 24/5/51
No.1411 16/9/53
No.827 16/2/57

Tenders
No.908 from new
No.854 on running shed on 7/11/59 from 30785

Sheds
Bournemouth 9/1925
Exmouth Junction 7/1937
Nine Elms 11/1946
Stewarts Lane 26/9/49
Nine Elms 12/12/49
Stewarts Lane 13/11/50
Nine Elms 5/2/51
Stewarts Lane 12/5/51
Eastleigh 16/9/55

Withdrawn 21/5/60; stored at Eastleigh Works 5-6/60; cut up at Eastleigh Works w/e 30/7/60
Total 1,353,546 miles

Eastleigh with 30791 SIR UWAINE (son of 30750) in a rather sorry state some time in 1960.
Photograph
R.S. Carpenter photos.

30791 SIR UWAINE's at Petts Wood with a boat train via Tonbridge. This is during one of the engine's three periods at Stewarts Lane during BR days. Although the safety valves are doing the job the front washout plug has decided to spoil the show. Photograph Ted's Dad.

This must be during 30791 SIR UWAINE's last days as the location is Eastleigh, its last shed. Despite this it looks very fine. In the Arthurian legend this Knight was the son of Morgan le Fay and therefore King Arthur's nephew. This loco arrived at Eastleigh shed in September 1955 and survived there until May 1960. Photo J. Davenport, Initial Photographics.

SIR UWAINE at Eastleigh on 8th May 1960 a short period before it was withdrawn, on 21st May 1960. Photo Peter Groom.

30792 SIR HERVIS DE REVEL

NBL works no.23288
To traffic as E792 9/1925
Renumbered 30792 3/3/50

Boilers
No.777 as of 12/6/36
No.825 21/11/36
No.1055 16/11/38
No.801 25/9/40
No.453 6/1/43
No.796 17/3/45
No.769 3/5/47
No.780 3/3/50
No.788 29/3/52
No.450 8/9/56

Works

4/1928	Smoke deflectors fitted
3/1930	Tender tank gauge fitted
3/1931	Tender tank gauge removed
1/1932	E prefix removed
4/6/36-12/6/36C	60,687
26/10/36-21/11/36A	86,335 Stays: 431 copper renewed; Plates: Rivets and seams caulked; Lead plugs; Tubes: 40 2nd hand, welded; 24 2nd hand Superheater tubes [copper ends]
3/1/38-19/1/38C[EXJ]	Extension of mileage 5,000
19/10/38-16/11/38A	104,199
6/8/40-25/9/40A	88,458 Malachite Green livery; Multiple jet blast pipes; Large diameter chimney
20/11/42-6/1/43A	87,578 Wartime Black livery
14/2/45-17/3/45A	84,721
24/12/45-8/1/46C[EXJ]	38,753
31/3/47-3/5/47A	90,024 Malachite Green livery from Black
23/11/48-17/12/48C[NE]	61,610
25/2/49D[NE]	65,183
3/2/50-3/3/50A	98,393 Renumbered 30792; BR Green livery; Snifting valves removed
29/2/52-29/3/52GO	64,068 Standard King Arthur chimney
17/8/56-8/9/56GO	80,950 Modified injector and feed gear, right-hand side
1/2/58-15/2/58LC	39,256

Tender
No.909 from new

Sheds
Bournemouth 9/1925
Exmouth Junction 7/1937
Nine Elms 11/1946
Stewarts Lane 13/11/50
Nine Elms 5/2/51
Stewarts Lane 12/5/51
Eastleigh 12/6/57

Withdrawn 14/2/59; stored at Eastleigh Works 2/59; cut up at Eastleigh Works w/e 21/3/59
Total 1,351,319 miles

792 SIR HERVIS DE REVEL in a line at Eastleigh on 15th October 1938, four days before it entered works for an 'A' class major overhaul when its boiler, no.825, was exchanged for no.1055. The recorded mileage since its previous major in the autumn of 1936 was 104,199 miles. Most of this would have been on the far end of the Western Section as it was an Exmouth Junction engine. Photograph H.C. Casserley, courtesy R.M. Casserley.

At a time when the Arthurs were still usful players on the Southern, 792 SIR HERVIS DE REVEL with large diameter chimney fitted in September 1940 is working a special boat train through Clapham Junction. This would be the period after May 1947 (around sixty Bulleid Pacifics had elbowed them off much of the best work by now) when black gave way to Malachite Green but before March 1950 when BR numbers appeared. Photograph Ted's Dad.

An out of the ordinary photograph at Eastleigh Works shows 30792 SIR HERVIS DE REVEL outside the main offices, being stripped. It demonstrates a curious feature, that these Maunsell Arthurs did not so much have a cab roof as a detachable top half. The cab 'roof' is actually lying in the coal space in the tender; chimney and safety valves removed, hand rail and feed pipe dismantled with the chimney petticoat on the front running plate. Even some motion parts have been unbolted. SIR HERVIS may be awaiting a boiler lift, and often preliminary work (in spring and summer at least) was done outside to save space in the erecting shop. On the other hand it never ran with a six wheel tender so we may be looking at a piece of boiler salvage prior to the locomotive going for scrap. Photograph Paul Chancellor Collection.

30793 SIR ONTZLAKE

Works order no.E121
To traffic as E793 3/1926
Renumbered 30793 30/10/48

Boilers
No.770 19/3/36
No.777 4/12/36
No.831 21/6/39
No.1052 9/12/42
No.786 27/4/46
No.1409 30/10/48
No.767 14/8/54
No.448 17/8/57

Works

4/1929	Smoke deflectors fitted
12/1932	E prefix removed
3-7/1933	Fitted with rail washing equipment for this period
18/2/36-19/3/36B	60,481
3/11/36-4/12/36A	83,727
7/10/37-4/12/37B	34,678
19/10/38-14/12/38B	67,534 Extension of mileage 5,000
17/5/39-21/6/39A	83,678 Flaman speed recorder fitted; Olive Green livery
12/11/42-9/12/42A	76,306 Wartime Black livery; Flaman speed recorder removed
16/3/46-27/4/46A	96,834 Malachite Green livery from Black
30/9/48-30/10/48A	83,274 Renumbered 30793; Snifting valves removed; T2070 Special piston heads and rings
5/4/51-3/5/51HI	69,275 Stays: 450 monel metal stays and nuts repaired; Plates: Copper tube, seams repaired; Copper firehole, seams repaired; Fusible plugs, renewed. BR Green livery
10/10/52-1/11/52LI	112,264 Stays: 470 monel metal repaired and 470 nuts; Plates: Seams chipped and caulked; Fusible plugs renewed; Tubes: 30 new; Set, new Superheater tubes
2/7/54-14/8/54GO	159,161 Combination lever and valve spindle modified
29/7/57-17/8/57GO	49,316 Live steam injector fitted
16/9/59-23/9/59NC	41,751
21/4/60-7/5/60LI-HI	56,467
8/9/61-23/9/61LC	87,799

Tenders
No.910 from new
No.893 from 30776 on 23/9/59

Sheds
Stewarts Lane 4/1926
Brighton 7/1926
Stewarts Lane 1/1933
Eastleigh 4/1943
Stewarts Lane 7/1943
Ashford 12/12/49
Stewarts Lane 17/6/50
Feltham 14/6/59
Basingstoke 17/1/61

Withdrawn 1/9/62; stored at Eastleigh Works 8/62; cut up at Eastleigh Works w/e 15/9/62
Total 979,964 miles

30794 SIR ECTOR DE MARIS

Works order no.E121
To traffic as E794 3/1926
Renumbered 30794 15/1/49

Works	
5/1928	Smoke deflectors fitted
7/1932	E prefix removed
14/4/33	Stays: 147 copper renewed; 48 holes bushed; Plates: Copper tube, flanges welded: Copper firehole, new three-quarters; Lead plugs and studs in flanges; Tubes: 169, new "Howell"; 16 2nd hand Superheater tubes, copper ends
3-7/1933	Fitted with rail-washing equipment for this period
6/1/34	Stays: 350 copper riveted over; Plates: Copper tube, flanges welded; New studs in patches and flanges; Rivets and seams caulked; Tubes: Superheater tubes expanded
10/11/34	Stays: 300 copper riveted over; Plates: Copper tube, 2 angle patches; Copper firehole, flanges welded; Tubes: All expanded; 24 Superheater tubes ferruled and expanded
20/8/35-27/8/35**D**	2,037
14/10/35**D[AFD]**	[No mileage recorded]
15/1/36-1/2/36**D**	17,306
27/2/37-27/3/37**B**	53,027
15/12/37-19/1/38**A**	80,963 Stays: 475 copper renewed; Plates: Copper tube, flanges welded; Copper firehole, flanges welded; Lead plugs; Tubes: 169, new, "Chesterfield"; 24 new Superheater tubes, copper ends
16/9/39-18/10/39**B**	60,054 Extension of mileage 10,000; Stays; 6 copper renewed; Plates: Rivets and seams caulked; Lead plugs; Tubes: 169, new "Chesterfield"
5/8/41-17/9/41**A**	97,415 Malachite Green livery
25/4/44-27/5/44**A**	70,070 Wartime Black livery
31/3/47-6/5/47**B[SL]**	82,342
18/8/47-6/9/47**A**	87,864 Malachite Green livery from Black; Snifting valves removed; T2025 Spring links with copper plated threads fitted
6/12/48-15/1/49**C**	29,947 Renumbered 30794; New cylinders
6/7/49-25/7/49**LC[BA]**	46,977
1/5/50-2/6/50**A**	72,986 Stays: 460 monel metal stays repaired and new nuts; Plates: Internal tube and firehole plates - seams repaired; Fusible plugs renewed; Tubes: Set, new; Set, new Superheater tubes; BR Green livery
28/8/52-19/9/52**LI**	64,170 Stays: 500 monel metal stays repaired and 500 new nuts; 1 roof bolt renewed; Plates: Rivets renewed with studs; 2 fusible plugs renewed; Tubes: Set, new; Re-expanded Superheater tubes
16/8/54-4/9/54**LC**	119,413
29/3/55-23/4/55**GO**	126,967
15/8/58-6/9/58**LI-HI**	68,610

Boilers
No.781 14/4/33
No.827 as of 27/8/35
No.823 27/3/37
No.457 19/1/38
No.452 17/9/41
No.779 27/5/44
No.832 6/9/47
No.1404 2/6/50
No.836 23/4/55

Tenders
No.911 from new
No.917 on 6/9/58 from 30795

Sheds
Stewarts Lane 4/1926
Brighton 7/1926
Stewarts Lane 1/1933
Hither Green 27/2/40
Eastleigh 22/11/42
Stewarts Lane 7/1943
Bricklayers Arms 7/1/50
Dover 8/12/50
Stewarts Lane 5/2/51
Bricklayers Arms 22/6/54
Stewarts Lane 20/8/54
Basingstoke 12/1/59

Withdrawn 20/8/60; stored at Eastleigh Works 8/60; cut up at Eastleigh Works w/e 7/9/60 Total 903,663 miles

30795 SIR DINADAN

Above. **Eastleigh on 22nd August 1959 with 30794 SIR ECTOR DE MARIS (father of 30450).**

Works order no.E121
To traffic as E795 4/1926
Renumbered 30795 25/3/49

Works	
1/1930	Smoke deflectors fitted
9/1/32	Stays: 698 copper renewed; 300 holes bushed; Plates: Copper tube, new; Copper wrapping, flange one-half sides; New reinforcing plate; E prefix removed
15/9/32	Stays: 300 copper riveted over; Plates: Studs, seams and rivets caulked; casing caulked
3-7/1933	Fitted with rail washing equipment for this period.
11/4/33	Stays: 143 copper renewed; Plates: Lead plugs renewed; Rivets and seams caulked
7/10/33	Stays: 235 copper renewed; Plates: Copper tube, flanges welded; Copper firehole, flanges welded; Copper wrapping, top seams of one-half sides welded; New studs in flanges; Rivets and seams caulked; Tubes: 48, new; 3 new Superheater tubes, copper ends
8/1/35	Stays: 361 copper renewed; Plates: Copper tube, 2 angle patches; Copper firehole, 2 angle patches; Lead plugs; Tubes: 169, new "Howell"; 24 2nd hand Superheater tubes copper ends
30/9/35-26/10/35**A**	81,021
17/1/38-16/2/38**A**	83,959
25/11/39-27/12/39**A**	77,348 Olive Green livery
8/1/42-20/1/42**D[BTN]**	44,682
27/9/43-10/11/43**A**	87,781 Stays: 573 copper renewed; 30 roof renewed Plates: Copper tube, new; Copper firehole, 2 angles; Lead plugs; Tubes: 169, new "Howell"; 24 2nd hand Superheater tubes; Wartime Black livery
25/6/45-21/7/45**C[AFD]**	56,608
18/4/46-1/6/46**A**	77,736 Stays: 110 holes bushed; Plates: New firebox; Casing covering, three-quarters sides; Throat, new; Tubes: 167, new "Howell"; 24 new Superheater tubes; T2074 Copper stays fitted; T2256 Tyres turned; Malachite Green livery from Black
22/10/46-25/10/46**D**	11,878
23/6/47**[SL]**	T2080 Left and right-hand gauge glasses fitted
25/2/49-25/3/49**A**	83,529 Stays: 30 holes bushed; Plates: New firebox; New three-quarter sides and throat plate; Tubes: Set, "Talbot Stead"; Set new Superheater tubes; Renumbered 30795; Snifting valves removed
18/8/52-12/9/52**GO**	91,845 BR Green livery
9/9/55-1/10/55**LI-HI**	63,735
27/3/58-26/4/58**GO**	115,114
22/6/60-6/8/60**GO**	44,995 T2256 Tyres turned

Boilers
No.457 9/1/32
No.839 8/1/35
No.781 26/10/35
No.823 16/2/38
No.803 27/12/39
No.829 10/11/43
No.782 1/6/46
No.824 25/3/49
No.766 12/9/52
No.779 26/4/58
No.802 6/8/60

Tenders
No.912 from new
No.917 at SL from 30800 on 22/12/53
No.852 from 30738 on 26/4/58

Sheds
Stewarts Lane 4/1926
Brighton 7/1926
Stewarts Lane 1/1933
Ramsgate 7/1937
Stewarts Lane 27/2/40
Eastleigh 22/11/42
Stewarts Lane 4/1943
Bricklayers Arms 14/3/50
Dover 8/12/50
Stewarts Lane 5/2/51
Hither Green 22/6/54
Stewarts Lane 20/8/54
Eastleigh 30/9/55
Stewarts Lane 5/6/56
Feltham 14/6/59
Basingstoke 5/10/60

Withdrawn 4/8/62; stored at Eastleigh Works 7/62; cut up at Eastleigh Works w/e 3/8/62
Total 963,712 miles

Eastleigh shed on 18th September 1960 and the giant water tank forms a fine backdrop for 30795 SIR DINADAN (killed off in Malory's tome). It had only obtained the double bogie tender from withdrawn 30738 KING PELLINORE in April 1958. This loco was in good condition; it had only undergone its final General in the summer of 1960 but, such were the times, was withdrawn in August 1962. Clearly shows the difference in frame level between engine (high) and tender (low) when a Urie tender was attached to an Arthur in the 30793-30806 series. This involved an adjustment to drawgear level before coupling could be achieved.

30795 SIR DINADAN at Eastleigh on 29th September 1961, after 'a few wipes' rather than 'a clean'. By now a Basingstoke engine, it was withdrawn in August 1962. Photograph Gavin Morrison.

30796 SIR DODINAS LE SAVAGE

Works order no.E121
To traffic as E796 4/1926
Renumbered 30796 3/2/50

Boilers
No.825 21/7/34
No.450 18/7/35
No.766 31/1/36
No.455 17/8/38
No.769 12/3/41
No.768 5/5/44
No.770 7/12/46
No.776 3/2/50
No.1057 10/7/53
No.830 2/11/57

Works

2/1931	Smoke deflectors fitted
7/1931	E prefix removed
3-7/1933	Fitted with rail-washing equipment for this period
21/7/34	Stays: 408 copper renewed; Plates: Copper tube, 2 angle patches; Copper firehole, 2 angle patches; Lead plugs; Brick arch studs; Tubes: 169 2nd hand, welded; 24 2nd hand Superheater tubes [copper ends]
9/7/35-18/7/35C	71,276
31/12/35-31/1/36A	89,494
6/7/36-15/7/36C	4,429
6/12/37-2/2/38B	61,512
7/7/38-17/8/38A	77,940
3/2/41-12/3/41A	78,983 Malachite Green livery
31/12/42-1/4/43C[BTN]	47,665
1/4/44-5/5/44A	76,222 Wartime Black livery
7/11/46-7/12/46A	94,261 Malachite Green livery from Black
4/1/50-3/2/50A	99,727 Renumbered 30796; Snifting valves removed; BR Green livery
16/6/53-10/7/53GO	78,573
7/7/55-6/8/55LI-HI	67,110
5/10/57-2/11/57GO	116,637 Right-hand side live steam injector and feed gear
16/4/59-28/5/59NC	At Redhill shed
9/12/60-7/1/61LI	94,886

Tenders
No.913 from new
No.905 from 30766 on 7/1/61

Sheds
Brighton Summer 1926
Stewarts Lane 1/1933
Ramsgate 5/1936
Hither Green 27/2/40
Stewarts Lane 22/11/42
Bricklayers Arms 7/1/50
Dover 8/12/50
Stewarts Lane 5/2/51
Dover 27/6/51
Ramsgate 27/3/53
Hither Green 12/6/57
Salisbury 14/6/59

Withdrawn 3/3/62; stored at Eastleigh Works 2-3/62; cut up at Eastleigh Works w/e 24/3/62
Total 1,061,295 miles

30796 SIR DODINAS LE SAVAGE at Hither Green (it was there for a while in the late 1950s) on 3rd March 1958. The shed had a reputation of looking after its Arthurs, deservedly so, as this photograph demonstrates. At the same time 30806 SIR GALLERON was on the allocation and the pair shared the one passenger turn that Hither Green worked. See the text for details of this working. Photograph Peter Groom.

30797 SIR BLAMOR DE GANIS

Works order no.E121
To traffic as E797 6/1926
Renumbered 30797 22/1/49

Boilers
No.800 18/12/31
No.797 21/12/35
No.772 26/10/38
No.929 30/4/41
No.797 15/9/45
No.831 22/1/49
No.787 19/10/51
No.778 29/9/56

Works

1/1929	Smoke deflectors fitted
18/12/31	Stays: 638 copper renewed; 30 holes bushed; Plates: Copper tube, new one-half; Copper firehole, flanges, one-half sides; Lead plugs; Brick arch studs; Tubes: 36, 2nd hand, electrically welded
7/1932	E prefix removed
3-7/1933	Fitted with rail-washing equipment for this period
21/11/35-21/12/35**A**	82,470
22/2/37-24/3/37**B**	43,768
24/11/37-10/1/38	66,962 Extension of mileage 5,000
27/9/38-26/10/38**A**	89,969
7/3/41-30/4/41**A**	80,540 Malachite Green livery
19/7/43-22/9/43**C[SL]**	61,358 Extension of mileage 10,000
17/5/44-22/6/44**C**	79,529
2/8/45-15/9/45**A**	107,961 Wartime Black livery
23/6/47**[SL]**	T2080 Left and right-hand gauge glasses fitted
30/9/47-18/10/47**B**	64,554 Extension of mileage 5,000; Malachite Green livery from Black; Snifting valves removed
28/12/48-22/1/49**A**	97,404 Renumbered 30797; T2149 Ferguson and Timpsons jointing compound
24/9/51-19/10/51**GO**	71,912 BR Green livery
2/11/54-27/11/54**LI-HI**	79,669
11/9/56-29/9/56**GO**	129,019 Modified injector and feed gear right-hand side

Tender
No.914 from new

Sheds
Brighton Summer 1926
Ramsgate 1/1933
Hither Green 1/7/40
Stewarts Lane 2/11/42
Ashford 2/1944
Stewarts Lane 3/1944
Ashford 14/3/50
Hither Green 9/10/50
Bricklayers Arms 5/2/51
Stewarts Lane 12/5/51
Dover 27/6/51
Ashford 27/3/53
Dover 20/7/53
Salisbury 14/6/59

Withdrawn 30/5/59; stored at Eastleigh Works 6/59; cut up at Eastleigh Works w/e 20/6/59
Total 953,718 miles

E797 SIR BLAMOR DE GANIS as built, in typically, almost impossibly, spotless condition, at Victoria (Brighton side). Southern cleaning in the late twenties and thirties was second to none.

30797 SIR BLAMOR DE GANIS (nephew of 30455) at the head of the 2.35pm from Ashford, near Pluckley on route for Tonbridge on 11th July 1951. Remnant Southern running number on buffer beam. Photograph R.E. Vincent, www.transporttreasury.co.uk

30798 SIR HECTIMERE

Works order no.E121
To traffic as E798 6/1926
Renumbered 30798 11/11/49

Boilers
No.806 29/7/33
No.841 as of 18/7/36
No.790 13/8/37
No.798 21/8/40
No.781 14/4/45
No.742 1/11/47
No.1054 11/11/49
No.1047 9/10/54
No.832 15/9/56
No.1001 22/10/60

Works

11/1927	Smoke deflectors fitted
2/1933	E prefix removed
29/7/33	Lead plugs renewed
1/11/33	Studs and seams caulked
28/4/34	Lead plugs; Studs and seams caulked
8/6/36-18/7/36**B**	43,601 Extension of mileage 5,000
9/7/37-13/8/37**A**	85,573
18/11/38-21/12/38**B**	42,618
17/11/39-10/1/40**C[BTN]**	72,442
24/7/40-21/8/40**A**	89,606 Malachite Green livery
9/8/43-13/9/43**C[SL]**	71,007 Extension of mileage 10,000
17/3/45-14/4/45**A**	105,382 Wartime Black livery
8/10/47-1/11/47**A**	94,643 Malchite Green livery from Black; Snifting valves removed; T2025 Spring links fitted with copper plated threads
8/4/49-29/4/49**C[BA]**	54,583
6/10/49-11/11/49**A**	69,983 Renumbered 30798; BR Green livery
9/10/52-1/11/52**HI**	91,449
20/11/53-4/12/53**LC**	128,047
10/9/54-9/10/54**GO**	149,139
30/8/56-15/9/56**GO**	48,475 Modified injector and feed gear, right-hand side
2/12/57-5/12/57**LC[AFD]**	36,872
29/9/58-1/11/58**LI-HI**	65,142
21/9/60-22/10/60**GO**	130,055

Tenders
No.915 from new
No.851 from no.30450 on 22/10/60

Sheds
Brighton summer 1926
Ramsgate 1/33
Stewarts Lane 7/37
Ramsgate 27/2/40
Hither Green 1/7/40
Stewarts Lane 22/11/42
Ashford 7/1943
Stewarts Lane 3/1944
Bricklayers Arms 23/4/45
Stewarts Lane 7/45
Bricklayers Arms 7/47
Stewarts Lane 12/5/51
Dover 27/6/51
Salisbury 14/6/59

Withdrawn 16/6/62, stored at Eastleigh Works 6/62; cut up at Eastleigh Works w/e 28/7/62
Total 1,093,868 miles

Trackwork and ballast is new as the Kent Coast electrification moved remorselessly on. The 13th of June 1959 was the last Saturday of steam in North Kent and 30798 SIR HECTIMERE of Dover shed is at Petts Wood Junction on a Victoria-Folkestone line train. 30798 moved on to Salisbury shed that June, losing its six wheel tender in October 1960; it turned up a few times in my Surrey stamping ground. Photograph Peter Groom.

Eastleigh on 18th September 1960; three days later 30798 SIR HECTIMERE went in the works for its last and one of the final Arthur Generals. It got boiler no.1001 and tender no.851 from 30450 SIR KAY.

May 1953 finds 30798 SIR HECTIMERE at Ashford; with six wheel tender and larger BR totem, looking odd the way it's applied across that join.

The phrase 'battered but unbowed' comes to mind. 30798 SIR HECTIMERE (BR Green, second tender emblem, now with bogie tender) is, sadly, already condemned at Eastleigh, on Sunday 10th June 1962; it was cut up by the 16th. Quite likely, this is the last photograph of 30798 but those were the days when plates could be left on till the end. It would soon change! Some sort of work has been carried out, with a certain amount of dismantling having taken place at the firebox, including removal of the steam pipe to the injector and a section of hand rail; the cladding section is now secured by ropes. Perhaps what was uncovered prompted the engine's withdrawal. Photograph Gavin Morrison.

30799 SIR IRONSIDE

Works order no.E121
To traffic as E799 7/1926
Renumbered 30799 15/5/48

Boilers
No.799 15/7/26
No.474 3/8/35 (Urie)
No.829 11/9/37
No.799 20/12/39
No.834 13/10/43
No.763 4/1/47
No.828 4/3/49
No.1051 29/6/50
No.1412 12/11/55

Works

7/10/27	Stays: 8 roof renewed
7/1930	Smoke deflectors fitted
5/1932	E prefix removed
3/7/35-3/8/35A	88,118 Urie boiler, the only Maunsell Arthur to get one
23/12/35-28/12/35D	13,709
23/10/36D[AFD]	[No mileage recorded]
6/8/37-11/9/37A	73,414 Rivets and seams caulked
4/10/37-12/11/37D	1,132
12/11/38-2/12/38C[SL]	[No mileage recorded]
23/11/39-20/12/39A	81,674 Lead plugs, Olive Green livery
27/11/41-11/2/42C[BTN]	48,793
7/9/43-13/10/43A	95,645 Wartime Black livery
9/2/46-26/3/46C[AFD]	86,255 Extension of mileage 15,000
10/12/46-4/1/47A	107,123 Malachite Green livery from Black; T2070 Wear resitance of Cast Iron; T1891 Thomas "patent piston rod packing"
22/4/48-15/5/48HC	48,668 Renumbered 30799
17/2/49-4/3/49B	78,249 Snifting valves removed
7/2/50-8/2/50D[BA]	107,318
18/5/50-29/6/50A	114,652 BR Green livery
16/2/53-7/3/53LI	64,743
8/10/54-2/11/54LI[BA]	106,521
14/10/55-12/11/55GO	129,388 2 Fusible plugs renewed
29/8/57-7/9/57LC	48,879 2 Fusible plugs renewed
8/10/58-25/10/58LI	68,580 Seams and studs repaired; Blowdown valve gear and silencer HO 10026

Tender
No.916 from new

Sheds
Brighton 7/1926
Ramsgate 1/1933
Stewarts Lane 7/1937
Ramsgate 27/2/40
Stewarts Lane 1/7/40
Ashford 7/1943
Bricklayers Arms 23/4/45
Stewarts Lane 7/1945
Bricklayers Arms 7/1947
Salisbury 14/6/59

Withdrawn 25/2/61; stored at Eastleigh Works 2-3/61, cut up at Eastleigh Works w/e 18/3/61 Total 1,001,005 miles

Below. **799 SIR IRONSIDE at Ramsgate with Urie boiler No.474 (note safety valves) which it carried from August 1935 til August 1937. This was the only known case of a Urie boiler on a Maunsell Arthur. Photograph R.K. Blencowe.**

30799 SIR IRONSIDE, the Red Knight. It is in its final year, at Nine Elms shed and a Western Section loco since moving to Salisbury in June 1959 upon the end of steam in North Kent. Still coupled to its six wheel tender with 5P over the running number, water treatment disc underneath and first BR totem. Photograph Peter Groom.

There is no mistaking the location – this is Stewarts Lane of course with the prominent repairs to the giant Depository marking the damage from the German rocket. It was one of those sheds which offered only a fleeting and frustrating glimpse as you passed on a local electric. A South Eastern section loco for the vast majority of its working life, on 5th August 1955 30799 SIR IRONSIDE was visiting from nearby Bricklayers Arms. Eventually transferred to the Western Section in June 1959, to Salisbury, the loco survived until February 1961. Photograph B.K.B. Green, Initial Photographics.

30800 SIR MELEAUS DE LILE

Works order no.E121
To traffic as E800 9/1926
Renumbered 30800 4/11/49

Boilers
No.800 15/9/26
No.838 as of 14/11/35
No.828 22/5/37
No.792 3/7/39
No.928 3/2/45
No.802 29/3/47
No.1001 4/11/49
No.457 13/2/54
No.803 10/1/59

Works

29/10/26	Water test-filled up
19/11/27	Steam test to 200 lbs psi; Smoke deflectors fitted
23/3/29	Rivets and seams caulked; New brick arch studs and plugs
11/1932	E prefix removed
11/11/35-14/11/35**D**	30,331
9/4/37-22/5/37**A**	79,107
6/6/39-3/7/39**A**	74,916 Olive Green livery
17/12/42-16/1/43**C**	5,932
21/6/44**[AFD]**	[No mileage recorded]
30/12/44-3/2/45**A**	60,286 Rivets and seams caulked; Wartime Black livery
20/3/45-24/3/45**C**	60,286 Seams and studs recaulked
28/5/46-4/6/46**C[NE]**	48,819
25/2/47-29/3/47**A**	61,561 Black livery, green driving wheels
29/9/49-4/11/49**A**	78,760 Renumbered 30800; BR Green livery; Snifting valves removed
12/1/50-3/2/50**LC**	3,192
1/7/52-8/8/52**LI**	52,877
11/1/54-13/2/54**GO**	82,233 Combination lever and valve spindle pin modified; T2081 Regulator valve special material valve no.8. New test
4/6/56-30/6/56**HI**	62,503
9/12/58-10/1/59**GO**	124,449 Briquette container fitted; right hand side injector and feed gear modified; Blowdown valve and operating gear fitted; Silencer fitted
29/6/60-9/7/60**LC**	37,395
10/5/61-11/5/61**NC**	58,954

Tenders
No.917 from new
No.912 at Stewarts Lane from 30795 on 22/12/53
No.918 at Bricklayers Arms from 30801 on 2/12/58
No.868 from 30454 on 10/1/59

Sheds
Brighton 9/1926
Ramsgate 1/1933
Stewarts Lane 22/11/42
Ashford 7/1943
Hither Green 6/1947
Bricklayers Arms 14/3/50
Hither Green 17/6/50
Bricklayers Arms 8/12/50
Ashford 5/2/51
Bricklayers Arms 12/5/51
Eastleigh 14/6/59

Withdrawn 2/9/61; stored at Eastleigh Works, 8/61, cut up at Eastleigh Works, w/e 16/9/61
Total 960,510 miles

30800 SIR MELEAUS DE LILLE (son of the King of Denmark) at Nine Elms on 19th May 1959. It was another of those Arthurs that spent most of its time on the Eastern Section and did not officially 'come west' until period ending 14/6/59. I suspect that here, a month earlier, we see it already on its way. It got the double bogie tender as late as its final General (9/12/58-10/1/59).

30800 SIR MELEAUS DE LILE, from Bricklayers Arms, at Ashford shed about May 1955. No cylinder panel, cover plate where snifting valve used to be. It was another Arthur that only worked on the Western Section in its last days.

Final days for 30800 SIR MELEAUS DE LILE back at its birthplace, Eastleigh Works after 36 years and dumped on the scrap line on 15th August 1961, though it was not officially withdrawn until 2nd September. Cutting up took place in the week ending 16th September 1961. Behind is one of the push-pull fitted M7s. There's no real reason why one should be surprised of course but nevertheless it still seems slightly unreal the way SR engines in these times were taken out of service; they came in off a job, had the fire dropped and that was it: 'get him over to the scrap road'. Photograph Gavin Morrison.

30801 SIR MELIOT DE LOGRES

Works order no.E121
To traffic as E801 10/1926
Renumbered 30801 1/7/49

Tenders
No.918 from new
No.912 at Bricklayers Arms
from 30800 on 2/12/58

Sheds
Brighton 10/1926
Ramsgate 1/1933
Hither Green 27/2/40
Stewarts Lane 1/7/40
Hither Green 22/11/42
Stewarts Lane 12/1942
Ashford 7/1943
Stewarts Lane 6/1946
Ashford 4/1947
Bricklayers Arms 12/5/51

Withdrawn 8/4/59, stored
at Eastleigh Works 4-5/59,
cut up at Eastleigh Works
w/e 13/6/59
Total 939,617 miles

Works	
2/1928	Smoke deflectors fitted
22/5/31[BTN]	Roof bars and recuring stays
8/10/32	New lead plugs; E prefix rmemoved
10/1/33[BTN]	Flanges caulked
1/4/33	Lead plugs; Rivets and seams caulked
9/9/35-5/10/35A	86,618
27/5/37-30/6/37B	49,189
15/2/38-16/3/38A	73,488 Rivets and seams caulked; studs in flanges; Lead plugs
14/6/39-8/7/39B	55,663 Rivets and seams caulked; Lead plugs
24/5/40-19/6/40A	71,745 Malachite Green livery, black and yellow lining, black cylinders, half lined smoke deflectors; Lead plugs; Brick arch studs
18/9/43-3/11/43A	83,971 Wartime Black livery
10/9/46-5/10/46A	91,473 Malachite Green livery from Black
10/11/47-24/11/47C[AFD]	36,713
23/5/49-1/7/49A	80,224 Renumbered 30801; T2070 Wear resistance of Cast Iron; T1891 Thomas "Patent piston rod packing"
13/2/51-8/3/51LI	60,397 BR Green livery
20/1/54-13/3/54GO[AFD]	135,007 W/E 27/2/54 heavy frame repairs
29/3/54-5/4/54Defect	28
21/8/56-15/9/56HI	61,101

Boilers
No.805 22/5/31
No.764 5/10/35
No.781 16/3/38
No.829 19/6/40
No.803 3/11/43
No.491 5/10/46
No.1049 1/7/49
No.768 13/3/54

A rather sad 30801 SIR MELIOT DE LOGRES at Eastleigh on 11th April 1959, three days after its official withdrawal. An Eastern Section loco, its only visits to the Western Section were for attention at Eastleigh, though its last General had been at Ashford in February 1954. No doubt it had come to Eastleigh for assessment and it was decided to withdraw it rather than repair it for they were still rebuilding the light Pacifics at Eastleigh; the operating people wouldn't miss another Arthur, what with the surplus due to the Kent Coast electrification.

Ramsgate's fine clean 801 SIR MELIOT DE LOGRES, passing the Casserley back garden at Bromley on 24th July 1938. It was the BR number plate at the front of course, that so radically altered the look of these Arthurs, for that unusual conical look of a Dan Dare rocket was entirely lost. Photograph H.C. Casserley, courtesy R.M. Casserley.

30801 SIR MELIOT DE LOGRES at Ramsgate shed on 2nd February 1952, with Britain's most south-easterly coaling plant – an obscure claim to fame I admit. This is another of 'the Brick's' Arthurs, having worked in on duty no.102. This involved an afternoon working from Charing Cross returning from Ramsgate at 9.10pm, not reaching Charing Cross until after midnight. It's interesting to observe that the smokebox door straps carry a row of bolts; many others, usually earlier on, are flush. And that, surely, can't be anything other than a window wiper – see the other two pictures of 30801 here too! Photograph R.C. Riley, www.transporttreasury.co.uk

30802 SIR DURNORE

Works order no.E121
To traffic as E802 10/1926
Renumbered 30802 10/7/48

Boilers
No.800 5/5/30
No.451 as of 10/1/36
No.826 5/2/37
No.770 22/3/39
No.835 4/11/41
No.1057 9/12/44
No.790 10/7/48
No.778 27/1/51
No.781 24/4/53
No.1053 7/6/58

Works

9/1928	Smoke deflectors fitted
5/5/30	New brick arch studs and plugs
15/10/30	Rivets and seams caulked
10/1931	E prefix removed
30/11/35-10/1/36C	51,485
28/8/36-18/9/36C	70,399
8/1/37-5/2/37A	84,753 New Copper firebox
29/4/38-22/6/38B	49,080 Lead plugs
1/3/39-22/3/39A	74,483 Maunsell Green livery
11/9/41-4/11/41A	83,503 Malachite Green livery
21/6/44[AFD]	[No mileage recorded]
31/10/44-9/12/44A	86,547 Wartime Black livery
10/1/46-26/1/46D[AFD]	46,905
28/11/46-14/12/46B	70,868 Malachite Green livery from Black
8/2/47-22/2/47C	71,009
9/6/48-10/7/48A	100,934 Renumbered 30802; Snifting valves removed
10/12/48-8/1/49C	16,133
2/1/51-27/1/51A	74,420 BR Green livery; New left hand cylinder
7/7/52-11/7/52LC	53,030
25/3/53-24/4/53GO	77,360
26/11/53-12/12/53LC	29,366
31/1/55-19/2/55LI-HI	73,598
12/6/56-30/6/56LI	128,903
22/3/57-30/3/57LC	167,592 Left-hand cylinder, special material supplied by Incandescent Heat Co.,ltd [U]
6/5/58-7/6/58GO	195,409 Right-hand side injector and feed gear modified
24/6/60-29/6/60LC	40,068 AWS gear

Tenders
No.919 from new
No.923 from 30806 on 19/2/55
No.864 from 30750 on 7/6/58

Sheds
Brighton 10/1926
Ramsgate 1/1933
Hither Green 22/11/42
Ashford 3/1944
Stewarts Lane 6/1946
Ashford 4/1947
Stewarts Lane 6/6/58
Eastleigh 14/6/59

Withdrawn 8/7/61, stored at Eastleigh Works 7/61, cut up at Eastleigh Works w/e 5/8/61
Total 1,096,024 miles

This really is a weary looking Arthur, at Eastleigh on 15th April 1960; it is not quite a year since 30802 SIR DURNORE arrived on the books at Eastleigh shed, from Stewarts Lane.

A late spring day at Stewarts Lane, a wonderfully rambling place with all those running lines and bridges and buildings in the background. 30802 SIR DURNORE is coaled up and ready to work a special on Monday 30th March 1959. Well it is 'SPL 37' but where was it going? 30802 eventually moved to Nine Elms in the June and even underwent a Light Casual at the Works in the following June. Photograph R.C. Riley, www.transporttreasury.co.uk.

30803 SIR HARRY LE FISE LAKE

Works order no.E121
To traffic as E803 11/1926
Renumbered 30803 24/7/48

Works

3/1928	Smoke deflectors fitted
6/1932	E prefix removed
3/3/34	Stays: 416 copper renewed; 30 holes bushed; Plates: Copper tube, 2 angle patches; Copperfirehole, new three-quarters; Lead plugs; Brick arch studs; Tubes: 24 2nd hand Superheater tubes,copper ends
28/9/34[BTN]	Stays: 540 copper riveted over; 2 roof nuts renewed; Plates: Flanges, seams and collar bolts caulked; Lead plugs; Tubes: 6 new, 36 expanded and rebeading; 1 Superheater tube expanded; Foundation ring, corners part expanded
14/12/34[BTN]	Stays: Roof, 4 direct, 2 fulcrum; Plates: 2 fulcrum stay holes bushed
8/7/35-10/8/35A	82,820
29/11/35-30/11/35D	10,690
2/2/37-27/2/37A	64,354 Stays: 401 copper renewed; 1 roof renewed Plates: Copper tube, angle patches; Copper firehole, angle patches; Lead plugs; Tubes: 169out, 84 welded
13/5/38-22/6/38B	52,650 Stays: 400 copper riveted over; 6 roof renewed; Plates: Rivets and seams caulked; Lead plugs; Tubes: 3 out, 84 welded; 10 new Superheater tubes
19/12/38-25/2/39B	67,941
30/9/39-25/10/39A	91,422 Olive Green livery
9/42	Wartime Black livery
26/3/45-28/4/45A	62,670
24/7/46-24/8/46C	47,654
15/1/47-1/2/47B	57,758
14/4/47-10/5/47B	63,741 New right-hand cylinder
19/8/47D[AFD]	72,587
14/2/48D[AFD]	85,570
26/6/48-24/7/48A	93,873 Malachite Green livery from Black; Renumbered 30803; Snifting valves removed
15/11/48-11/12/48D	11,876
25/11/49-16/12/49LI	43,210 T1891 Thomas "Patent piston rod packing" [Railway Observer]
19/5/50-16/6/50HC	59,123
28/11/51-22/12/51LI	108,908 BR Green livery
29/9/52-11/10/52LC	137,723
31/3/53-2/5/53GO	156,388
7/7/54-6/8/54LC	55,734
23/3/55-2/4/55LI-HI	79,482
25/7/56-25/8/56GO	137,341 Modified injector and feed gear fitted
18/12/56-4/1/57LC[BTN]	13,847
16/4/57-9/5/57LC[BTN]	27,556
27/10/59-7/11/59LI	64,802

Tenders
No.920 from new
No.909 on 7/11/59 from 30792

Sheds
Brighton 11/1926
Ramsgate 1/1933
Hither Green 22/11/42
Ashford 3/1944
Stewarts Lane 6/6/58
Eastleigh 14/6/59

Withdrawn 2/9/61; stored at Eastleigh Works 8/61; cut up at Eastleigh Works w/e 23/9/61
Total 989,396 miles

Boilers
No.805 3/3/34
No.455 10/8/35
No.451 27/2/37
No.491 25/2/39
No.774 25/10/39
No.777 28/4/45
No.455 1/2/47
No.1057 24/7/48
No.777 16/6/50
No.778 2/5/53
No.930 25/8/56

803 SIR HARRY LE FISE LAKE (how could you hack someone to death with a name like that?) at Ashford shed on 7th June 1947; six wheel tender, Malachite Green. The 'sunshine' lettering certainly suited the class but come 1948 and BR everything was to change of course. Ashford remained its home shed until 1957. Crosshead bracket for one-time vacuum pump. Photograph H.C. Casserley, courtesy R.M. Casserley.

Ashford's 30803 SIR HARRY LE FISE LAKE on the 2.32pm Margate to Charing Cross on 11th May 1952. The box is Kearsney Loop and the line to Kearsney runs to the left; SIR HARRY is taking the curve to Dover. The bridge carries Old Park Hill and the blackened brickwork on the down side is testament to the tough gradient up to Guston tunnel after the sharp curve off the Dover-Canterbury line. Set 467 was a four car 'Restriction 1' low window set, its carriages remaining together until 1963. Photograph J.J. Smith.

30803 SIR HARRY LE FISE LAKE arriving at Ashford station on 23rd March 1957 and below, after coming to a stand. Although at Ashford until June 1957, it paid two visits to Brighton Works in 1957 for Light Casuals; perhaps Ashford had a full load and Brighton needed the work.

30804 SIR CADOR OF CORNWALL

Works order no.E121
To traffic as E804 12/1926
Renumbered 30804 13/11/48

Works	
10/1928	Smoke deflectors fitted
31/10/30	Stays: 737 copper renewed; Plates: Copper wrapping, 2 flanges, one-half sides; New brick arch studs and plugs; Tubes: 169, new; 24 Superheater tubes expanded
12/12/31[BTN]	Stays: 725 copper riveted over; Plates: 2 lead plugs and 20 iron collar bolts at flanges; Seams and old collar bolts caulked; Tubes: Foundation ring renewed
3/6/1932	Stays: 397 copper renewed; Plates: Copper tube, new one-half; Lead plugs; Rivets, studs and seams caulked; Tubes: 61 2nd hand, welded; Superheater tubes expanded; E prefix removed
16/9/32	Stays: 200 copper riveted over; Plates: Studs and patches, chipped and caulked
16/6/36-18/7/36A	80,963
18/6/37-16/7/37B	36,852
17/10/38-16/11/38A	94,242
27/2/39-6/3/39D	5,762
23/5/39-6/6/39C	9,986
27/3/40-30/4/40B	40,234
7/1/42-18/2/42A	82,637 Malachite Green livery
23/2/44-4/3/44D[AFD]	81,991
3/5/45-7/7/45A	85,505 Wartime Black livery
14/2/46-20/3/46D[AFD]	30,368
26/4/47-24/5/47A	68,717 Malachite Green livery from Black; Snifting valves removed
21/10/48-13/11/48C	51,333 Renumbered 30804
29/11/48-4/12/48C	51,831
10/1/50-3/2/50GO	84,622 Stays: 164 new and 500 repaired; 36 new crown bolts; Plates: Firebox, seams and rivets caulked; New lead plugs; BR Green livery
10/1/50-3/2/50GO	84,622
12/5/52-13/5/52NC[AFD]	[No mileage recorded]
3/2/53-6/3/53GO	86,887
19/8/54-23/9/54NC-LC	49,806
25/2/55-26/3/55LI	70,363
22/3/57-13/4/57GO	151,895 Stays: Copper renewed, all; Longitudinal renewed, all; Roof renewed, all; 180 holes bushed; Plates: New copper firebox; Casing covering, 2 x three-quarter sides, fitted and welded; Tubes: 167, new "Stewart and Lloyds"; 24 new Superheater tubes; Live steam injector and feed gear
12/3/58-29/3/58LC[AFD]	36,334
16/2/59-7/3/59LI	71,412 Stays: 2 copper renewed; 510 copper riveted over; Plates: Copper tube, seams repaired; Copper firehole, seams repaired; 2 fusible plugs; Tubes: 30, new "Tube products"; 3 new Superheater tubes; Foundation ring, 40 rivets repaired
15/2/61-25/2/61LC	113,391 Stays: 11 copper renewed; 570 copper riveted over; Plates: Studs and seams repaired; 2 fusible plugs renewed; Tubes: 167, new "Phoenix"; 3 new Superheater tubes; Foundation ring, 40 rivets repaired; Tubes and tender bearing

Boilers
No.781 31/10/30
No.794 18/7/36
No.742 16/11/38
No.772 18/2/42
No.841 7/7/45
No.826 3/2/50
No.448 6/3/53
No.826 13/4/57

Tender
No.921 from new

Sheds
Brighton 12/1926
Ramsgate 1/1933
Hither Green 22/11/42
Ashford 3/1944
Dover 12/6/57
Eastleigh 14/6/59

Withdrawn 17/2/62; stored at Ashford Works 2/62; cut up at Ashford Works w/e 24/3/62 Total 1,115,634 miles

Once again something stirs at the bottom of the Casserley garden in Bromley, 11th May 1935. A lovely look at Ramsgate's 804 SIR CADOR OF CORNWALL (a good English Knight for once, and father to 30805) at work, a good year before its next 'A' overhaul at Eastleigh. Photograph H.C. Casserley, courtesy R.M. Casserley.

30804 SIR CADOR OF CORNWALL at the Ashford coaling stage on 12th August 1953; this was its home shed, then coded 74A and it looks like coaling is complete on the six wheeled tender, which 30804 kept until 1958. SIR CADOR transferred to Dover in the middle of 1957. Photograph J.H. Aston.

30805 SIR CONSTANTINE

Works order no.E121
To traffic as E805 1/1927
Renumbered 30805 2/10/48

Works	
13/12/28	Stays: 364 copper renewed; Plates: Seams and rivets caulked; New brick arch studs and plugs; Tubes: 73, new "BM"; Smoke deflectors fitted
1/4/30	Stays: 559 copper renewed; Plates: Rivets and seams caulked; New brick arch studs and plugs; Tubes: 4, new "BM", 60 2nd hand
9/9/30**[BTN]**	No boiler work
11/4/31	Stays: 828 copper renewed; 36 roof renewed; 220 holes bushed; Plates: Copper tube, new; Copper wrapping, flanges, one-half sides; Alteration to crown; Tubes: 169, new "Chesterfield"; 21 Superheater tubes ferruled, copper ends
10/6/32**[BTN]**	Stays: 631 copper riveted over; Plates: Lead plugs; Seams and flanges caulked
3/2/33	Stays: 554 copper renewed; Plates: Tube plate flanges welded; New lead plugs; Rivets and seams caulked; Tubes: 58, new "Chesterfield"; 24 new Superheater tubes [copper ends]; E prefix removed
12/12/35-18/12/35**D**	35,092
11/5/36-6/6/36**B**	52,316
19/2/37-20/3/37**A**	75,194
10/8/38-21/9/38**B**	64,532 Extension of mileage 5,000
24/6/39-19/7/39**A**	96,772 Olive Green livery
9/2/42-25/3/42**A**	69,547 20 copper renewed; 400 copper riveted over; Plates: Lead plugs; Electrically welded right side at shoulder; Tubes: 167, new "Talbot Stead". Malachite Green livery "...last light green fully lined engine to leave Eastleigh Works"
30/8/44-14/10/44**A**	69,470 Wartime Black livery
19/11/45-26/1/46**C[AFD]**	43,293
27/3/47-3/5/47**C**	63,824
8/9/48-2/10/48**A**	95,412 Malachite Green livery from Black; Renumbered 30805; Snifting valves removed
29/1/49-5/2/49**C**	6,829
19/11/51-8/12/51**HI**	96,685 BR Green livery
11/6/53-10/7/53**GO**	155,845 Stays: 130 holes bushed; Plates: New copper firebox; New steel wrapper plate; Tubes: Set, new; Set, new Superheater tubes
22/6/54-26/6/54**LC**	40,469 T2256 Apexior paint on wheel and tyre mating surfaces [U]
4/4/55-30/4/55**LI**	60,699 Stays: 400 copper riveted over; Plates: Seams caulked; 2 plugs renewed; Tubes: 30 renewed, 2nd hand; 3 new Superheater tubes; T2256 Apexior paint tyres returned
29/2/56-10/3/56**LC**	90,235 T2256 Tyres turned [U]
26/4/56-17/5/56**LC**	95,112 T2256 [U]
9/5/57-1/6/57**GO**	134,285 Stays: Monel metal renewed, all; Nuts renewed, all; Roof renewed, all; 131 holes bushed; Plates: New copper firebox; Casing covering, 2 x three-quarter sides; Tubes: 167, new "Stewart and Lloyds"; 24 new Superheater tubes; T2256 [O]; Modified live steam injector right-hand side and feed gear
3/7/58-9/8/58**LC[AFD]**	38,537
8/12/58-20/12/58**LC[AFD]**	48,981

Boilers
No.805 1/1927
No.456 11/4/31
No.837 18/12/35
N0.828 19/7/39
No.781 25/3/42
No.801 14/10/44
No.1406 2/10/48
No.829 10/7/53
No.1401 1/6/57

Tender
No.922 from new

Sheds
Brighton 1/1927
Ramsgate 1/1933
Hither Green 22/11/42
Ashford 3/1944
Dover 26/9/49
Hither Green 7/1/50
Ashford 17/6/50
Dover 12/6/57
Eastleigh 14/6/59

Withdrawn 28/11/59; stored at Eastleigh Works 11/59; cut up at Eastleigh Works w/e 19/12/59
Total 1,019,198 miles

30805 SIR CONSTANTINE, coaled and being readied at Ramsgate shed on 6 April 1953; coal irons in and against the cab suggest the fire will be done next. 30772 SIR PERCIVALE had been transferred here a week or two before, in March. Photograph R.C. Riley, www.transporttreasury.co.uk

30805 SIR CONSTANTINE at Tonbridge shed, some time during its sojourn as an Ashford loco, from June 1950 to June 1957. Photograph J. Davenport, Initial Photographics.

30806 SIR GALLERON

Works order no.E121
To traffic as E806 1/1927
Renumbered 30806 30/9/48

Works

17/4/28	Stays: 70 copper renewed; 250 steel riveted over; Plates: Box and casing caulked; New plugs; Smoke deflectors fitted
31/8/29	Stays: 560 copper renewed; Plates: Rivets and seams caulked; New studs in flanges; New brick arch studs and plugs; Tubes: 61, new "BM"
25/4/31	Stays: 928 copper renewed; Roof renewed, all; Plates: New alteration of crown; New brick arch studs and plugs; Tubes: 169, new "BM"; 24 Superheater tubes ferruled, copper ends; Firehole, rivets, part: Foundation ring,rivets, part
25/2/33	Stays: 203 copper renewed; Plates: Copper firehole, backplate flanges welded; New studs in flanges; Lead plugs; Rivets and seams caulked; Tubes: 169, new "Chesterfield"; 6 Superheater tubes, copper ends. E prefix removed
3/2/34	Stays: 46 copper renewed; Plates: Copper tube, 2 angle patches; Copper firehole, 2 angle patches; Lead plugs; Tubes: Set expanded; 18 Superheater tubes, copper ends
11/10/34[BTN]	Stays: 416 copper riveted over; [3 direct stays and nuts and 1 fulcrum stay and nut]; Plates: Lead plugs; Flanges and patches welded
10/2/36-14/3/36B	26,172
9/6/37-10/7/37A	82,261
22/11/38-24/1/39B	59,976 Stays: 535 copper renewed; Plates: Copper tube, new; Lead plugs; Throat welded; Barrel SV seating welded; Tubes: 169, new "Talbot Stead"; 24 new Superheater tubes; Extension of mileage 10,000
24/4/40-22/5/40A	99,757 Stays: 403 copper renewed; Plates: Copper tube, 2 angles; Copper firehole; 2 angles; Lead plugs; Brick arch studs; Tubes: 169 2nd hand welded; Olive Green livery
21/10/42C[AFD]	Extension of mileage 5,000
11/9/43-3/11/43A	88,033 Wartime Black livery
7/6/44D[AFD]	[No mileage recorded]
p/e 23/9/44	Flying bomb damage, Railway Observer 1944-1945 page 117 (details at end of entry)*
16/10/44-13/1/45A	98,546
22/11/45-29/12/45D[AFD]	38,647
22/4/47-24/5/47A	72,804 Stays: 140 holes bushed; Plates: New copper firebox; Steel tube, new; New throat plate and crown plate; Tubes: Set, new "Howell"; 24 new Superheater tubes; Malachite Green livery from Black
7/7/48-30/9/48B[BTN]	46,912; Renumbered 30806; Snifting valves removed
28/3/50D[AFD]	95,035
20/10/50-17/11/50A	115,948 BR Green livery
26/1/53-21/2/53GO	66,001 Stays: 1,171 copper renewed; Longitudinal renewed, all; Roof renewed, all; 200 holes bushed. Plates: New copper firebox; Steel tube, new; Tubes: 167, new "Stewart and Lloyds"; 24 new Superheater tubes
9/2/55-5/3/55LI-HI	65,803 Stays: 485 copper renewed; Plates: Copper tube, 12 studs; Copper firehole, seams caulked; Lead plugs; Tubes: 167, new "Howell";3 new Superheater tubes; Internal examination extended from 2/58-10/58. Ref 1163 17/12/56
4/12/56-22/12/56HI	113,719 Stays: Copper renewed, 6; 490 copper riveted over; Roof renewed, 1 [crown]; Plates: Renewed with studs, seams repaired; 2 fusible plugs; Tubes: 167, new "Stewart and Lloyds"; 3 new Superheater tubes
14/8/58-30/8/58GO	150,980 Stays: All monel metal renewed; Nuts renewed, all; Roof renewed, all; Plates: New copper firebox, Casing covering, 2 x three-quarter sides; Tubes: 167, new "Tube products"; 24 new Superheater tubes; right-hand side injector and feed gear modified
24/8/59-5/9/59LC	31,687 Plates: 2 fusible plugs renewed; Tubes: 167, new "Stewart and Lloyds"; 3 new Superheater tubes, 21 repaired
4/10/60-15/10/60LC	57,382

*The incident occurred at a small bridge over a road (at Newington, Kent) which had been hit by a flying bomb. 806 was derailed and pieces of 'Sir Galleron'were brought to Eastleigh on four wagons whilst the engine was on its own wheels although minus one deflector, the cab, connecting rods, dome and other fittings. One wagon carried the buckled frames of the tender and the tender tank rested on a well wagon. 'Sir Galleron' rests on the shop road-a very battered knight!

Boilers

No.806 1/1927
No.928 25/4/31
No.790 14/3/36
No.779 10/7/37
No.805 24/1/39
No.454 22/5/40
No.795 3/11/43
No.832 13/1/45
No.928 24/5/47
No.1057 17/11/50
No.454 21/2/53
No.1056 30/8/58

Tenders

No.923 from new
No.3208 from N15X 32331 on 30/8/58

Sheds

Brighton 1/1927
Ramsgate 1/1933
Hither Green 27/2/40
Stewarts Lane 1/7/40
Hither Green 22/11/42
Ashford 3/1944
Dover 31/5/49
Hither Green 5/2/51
Eastleigh 14/6/59

Withdrawn 29/4/61; 4-5/61 stored at Eastleigh Works; cut up at Eastleigh Works w/e 17/6/61 Total 1,127,096 miles

The highest numbered Arthur, 30806 SIR GALLERON at Hither Green shed on 4th October 1958. It was a favoured son, kept pristine for the only passenger turn, no.182, 5.47pm Cannon Street-Dover Priory, which also included a freight job. It duly made the trek west in June 1959, taking with it tender no.3208 off withdrawn N15X 32331 BEATTIE, which it had acquired in August 1958. Photograph Peter Groom.

30806 SIR GALLERON in its last days at St. Mary Cray, in Kent, on 9th May 1959. This was once the 'pet' of Hither Green, for its duty no.182 which included the only passenger turn from that shed, the 5.47pm Cannon Street to Dover Priory. 30806 was soon on its way to Nine Elms for its final days. Poor old SIR GALLERON can't help but look out of place in this very modern station. Photograph R.C. Riley, www.transporttreasury.co.uk